Hey, Sport! It's Me, Your Dad.

Random "DADvice" for Random Sons

Who Need Random Advice from a Random Dad

By The Quick and The Dead:

Jamin Edward Bassette, PhD.;

Jeffrey L. Bassette, LTC (Ret.);

Trevor Johnson;

Trevvor Clark;

& Seth Heinle

Edited by Jeffrey Bassette

Cover photo by Janette Bassette

Hey, Sport. It's Me, Your Dad.

20th Anniversary

Dedications

From Jamin: "To Seogyun, who inspired most of the book's content with our guys' night movie marathons and cookouts. Regardless of what job you may have or wherever you may live, if you are a great husband and father, then I passed with flying colors. I love you, Gyuns Gyuns.

To Jay, whose artistic inclinations are something I hope grows every day. I pray that I get to share these pieces of advice with you directly through our own guys' nights together with your cousin. Just in case anything happens to me before then, I am writing it all down now. I love you, bud.

To Jeffrey Bassette, thank you for showing me at least half of these pieces of advice first hand. I love you, young man."

From Jeffrey: "I delight in dedicating my contributions of this work to my wife, Janette. Her unwavering support, gentle persuasions, and godly counsel have inspired me to be a better man. Which in turn has inspired her six sons to aspire to be better men. Thanks for saying, "Yes, I'll marry you!" nearly five decades ago."

From TJ: "To Cara for being a Godly and guiding person in my life. I find you more and more interesting and inspiring every day and feel so grateful to have you in my life."

From Trevvor: "To my sons Charles, Frederik, William, and Edmund: Love, Papa."

From Seth: "To Adina Daniela, the love of my life, my best friend, my rock, and my favorite. Our life has been a wild ride of ups and downs, with failed plans and unexpected successes. Through it all I have treasured your love and support, and cannot wait to see where God takes us next."

Table of Contents:

Forward

I consider myself, above most things, as a husband. I am a father, of course, but I became a husband first, so I have a little more practice at it. Well, just barely. While it is true that my son, Jay, was not born until three days after my third wedding anniversary, I had actually been a semi-dad for over a year. My nephew, Seogyun, had a situation where he needed a male role model in his life, and I was the closest thing for him within a 60-mile radius. At the time, he was a little spoiled (only child and the first-born child of that generation), and didn't see much need for anyone other than his mother. I'll admit, I was not great at first, fearing over stepping whatever invisible lines exist for... not step-parent, but... live-in-uncle semi-father role-model?

I spent most of the early months just trying to get him to say "please," "thank you," and "I'm sorry" more. You know, trying to humble the little emperor in the way a mother never would. Then I noticed that he started acting differently around his younger male cousins. This became even more evident once my son was born. Seogyun wanted to be seen as their "big brother" and took a level of care and responsibility for them that I never explicitly taught him. My realization was that he was learning through watching me and his other uncles, while I was learning dad stuff by watching him. Before I was biologically a father, the learning was already well underway.

For some of you reading this, that revelation is quite comforting. You had lots of father figures who have already primed you to become the great dad, husband, or just the man that you need to be. However, I know some of you are in the opposite camp. You were thinking about some of the men in your life and how they may have done as much harm as good for you. Maybe that makes you a little afraid about when you will have to hold a human life in your own two hands. Don't worry, I wasn't sure I was ready either, or that I had properly prepared Seogyun. In the memo app on my phone I started writing random thoughts I had about being a man: values, lessons, hardships, loves, loss, and everything in between. In ten or so memo chunks at a time, we started going over them together, just the two of us, with some pizza and chicken wings before watching a nice war movie together to round out our "guys' nights." As of writing, we still do these.

I guess that is the dual role of this book. I have lost too many friends and family to know that I may not be able to share everything I want with my son and my nephew before I'm gone. Additionally, I want to give some of that advice, as meager as it may be, to any son who is on that path to future husband and then to future father. If any of these thoughts help even one guy on this journey, then it was worth it. I never got to have too many of these talks with my dad when I was younger. He was very busy and had a lot of kids to deal with, but as adults we have had many great talks that made me realize how much his actions spoke to me. Even still, I wish I could have had some of these conversations just a little bit sooner. Teenage me was a punk and needed to be punched in the face just a few more times than he did.

Keep in mind, I am not going to put in the "but not all" caveat most of the time. When I say something like "Women like to feel secure" or "Men like to feel appreciated," a personal anecdote about someone's aunt who never worries or their grandpa that has never wanted a compliment is not going to suddenly change the normal distributions on anyone's charts. There are exceptions for almost everything, so pointing them out is pedantic, unnecessary, and just a distraction from something generally true for most people. I like to think you are among the "most people," too.

As I write this, my son in elementary school and nephew getting ready for high school, I still feel like a husband first and father second. But I will be with my wife for the rest of my life and, if I did everything right, these two boys should be out of the house sooner rather than later, becoming husbands and fathers themselves. Such is the way of men since time immemorial. Real bros, help out other homies. Pass it on.

Chapter Zero: Everyone Has an Opinion

No one likes unsolicited advice. In fact, the act of offering good advice to someone who did not ask for it actually makes them more likely to not do the right thing just out of spite. Kind of makes sense why teenagers are always getting into trouble, right? So, in this book, we have to proceed with a little mutual understanding.

First, I must pretend that you want to hear some of this advice. Maybe not all of it, of course, but I have to assume in good faith that you are someone who wants to get this random advice in the first place. Otherwise, you would not be reading this book. Unless a parent bought it for you and is making you read it. In which case, you have my sympathies.

Second, I must acknowledge that some of this advice will not be useful to you in particular. Most adults give their recommendations based on either it being something that worked for them in the past (that may or may not work in the present), or something they wished they had done (that could play out differently now). Regardless, no one is trying to trick you with their advice. I, like all adults, am just telling you what we learned either too late or just in time in our own lives.

They say opinions are like buttholes: everyone has one and they all stink. But I think it may be more accurate to say that opinions are like trying to share test advice to someone at a different school twenty years later: I have a lot of answers I now know were right for my problems, and I can only hope they fit some of your questions.

Hey, Sport. It's Me, Your Dad.

Chapter 1: Surviving Your School Years

"Whenever people talk glibly of a need to achieve educational 'excellence,' I think of what an improvement it would be if our public schools could just achieve mediocrity."

-Thomas Sowell, American Economist

"In the first place, God made idiots. That was for practice. Then he made school boards."

-Mark Twain (Samuel Clemens), American Author

"Education is what remains after one has forgotten what one has learned in school."

-Albert Einstein, German Physicist

Hey, Sport. It's Me, Your Dad.

Seek friends who are better than you

They say that you are the sum of your five closest friends. I'm not entirely sure the math works out, but it is true that being friends with people that are going nowhere in life will quickly take you with them. If they skip school, drink, slack off, and don't work hard, you will be dragged down to their level eventually. Likewise, if you surround yourself with good, hard-working kids that are trying to make their lives better, you will benefit just from being around them. There is a strong instinct in young men to be loyal to their friend group. After all, 3000 years ago, these would be the people helping you hunt, keeping you alive, and making sure you had the meat and fur to survive the upcoming winter. However, that loyalty can be abused by bad, low-quality friends who will keep you from maturing and becoming a proper man.

I was lucky enough to have friends that not only wanted to play video games and watch movies, but read books and talk about theology and philosophy as well. I was the 'bad friend' of my group, wanting to be lazy and slack off when I could. But my group forced me to take breaks from the PlayStation and Xbox every now and then and try soccer, music concerts, and read classic British literature. Good friends will drag you up to their level and make you a better man for it. Find friends that make you better just by being with them. You cannot choose your family, but you can choose your friends, so pick ones that will push you into being a better version of yourself.

Men will have more family than friends

You will most likely make some close friends by the time you leave school. Some may seem like lifelong "battle buddies" that you will be with forever. But realistically, you will lose most, if not all, of your friends once you get older. You only have so much time between work, family, and everything else you need to get done, and the same is true for all of them as well. Most men have only one or two close friends by the time they reach middle age. For a majority of men over the age of 40, they say that their wife is their best friend. Explains why divorce hits men so hard: despite whatever issues may be going on in the relationship, she might literally be his only friend.

What does this mean for you? Two things: one, enjoy your time with your friends while you have it. Don't take it, or them, for granted. Sure, be a little rough, make some scars to go along with the memories, and just 'hang' when you need to. But don't forget that this too shall pass. Two, don't try so hard to impress them, or take it too personally if they move on from your relationship first. Learn from them, grow with them, and then be ready to move on. Your family is often there for life, so they should be your priority. As tragic as it may seem, the goal of having good friends is to help you through the hard times and make you into a better man to start a great family. This was always the plan, my man. That being said, try to maintain at least one or two of these relationships with someone who is going to help give you perspective on how your family life is going. If you have a good, optimistic friend who challenges you to be a better man, try to keep that friendship going, if possible.

Hey, Sport. It's Me, Your Dad.

You do not always need a girlfriend

Whether it is just you falling in love, or peer pressure from all of your friends coupling up, you will likely feel really left out if you do not have a girlfriend at some point. While this is natural, and very useful as motivation for self-improvement, you don't need a girlfriend right away. I had two semi-serious girlfriends from middle to high school, but because I was overweight and had no ambitions nor future prospects, both broke it off when their families didn't like me. I was not good "son-in-law" potential, so they did the right thing and got me out of the picture. At the time, it hurt. To be honest, it hurt my ego just as much as my heart. However, family as the gatekeepers in relationships, especially early on, is how all social animals behave and for good reason. It forces you to square yourself away and be "son-in-law" material first.

You know how many dates I had in the military? Zero for the first four years. I spent that time ranking up, getting paid, doing classes, and getting jacked. By the time I started dating again, everything that their families might object to were long since gone. I had not only become "good enough," I became someone that fathers and brothers were jazzed about their family dating. It's not just about the potential, it's about how much of it you can achieve. If you need to focus on being a better boyfriend prospect first, then take a break from dating and become that better guy. Think about what you offer to a relationship as a partner and make sure your "dating resume" matches the kind of woman you are looking for. Once you are squared away, there will be plenty of great women waiting for you on the other side.

Schools are mostly designed by women for girls

Hundreds of years ago, schools were mainly created by men for boys. Many of the early education institutions were either for the military or clergy: both male focused organizations. Once the idea of education being something that every person needed really became mainstream, women moved into many of these educational roles. Makes sense, as the average woman tended to have both the interest and temperament for a job like becoming a school teacher. However, boys and girls mature differently, with most adolescent girls about two years ahead of their male peers. Girls learn to speak faster, they start puberty sooner, and they socialize earlier and in more complex ways across every culture in the world. This likely helped them survive in a world that was much harsher and even more unequal thousands of years before. This is actually one of the reasons why girls like slightly older guys.

What that means for you is that finding schoolwork hard is normal. It was designed by a woman for what she remembers being age appropriate when she was in school as a little girl. That being said, don't get discouraged and do not use this as an excuse to do poorly. Keep learning as much as you can, as those foundations will really help you when you catch back up with your female peers developmentally. This normally happens in your mid-20's, or right after university. You know, when you don't need school anymore. However, don't use this as an excuse to not care about school. Don't stress about being top of the class, but do work hard and learn as much as you can. Your future self will thank you.

Do homework during the "dead time"

I got a part time job when I was back in college after leaving the army. While the GI bill took care of my school tuition, I still needed money for basic living stuff. My then fiancé, now wife, got me a tutoring job near her work. Super sweet of her, but one problem: it was a three-hour round bus trip for only two hours' worth of work. The pay per hour was generous, but that commute was killer and I almost turned it down. However, I remembered that I had homework to do every single week, that most of it was reading and note taking, and I now had a three-hour bus trip twice a week. What was once a reason to turn the job down, was now something that I could use to force myself to study.

If you find yourself getting home from school and not wanting to start on your homework, I understand. You are tired, have been studying all day, and just want to relax. However, the homework is not going to get any easier. If anything, thinking about it in the back of your mind is going to make relaxing harder and less effective. How about this: get it (or most of it) done before you even get home. Do you have time on the bus? Start your homework. Do you have dead time between lunch and classes? Get work done. Do you have to wait at school for an hour before mom picks you up? Put down the phone and get your school work done. If you do this, you can return home and have some actual relaxation waiting for you. Even now as I write this, I have a three-hour round trip to work every single day. It is not fun. However, I get some of my best work done here with books read, outlines typed out, and research started long before I make it back home. Because of this, I rarely ever have to do any work once I step through my front door. Get into this habit of maximizing your dead time and then get that well-earned rest.

Be careful of scammers

You may think that your personality determines what kind of job you have. This is partially true. There are more extroverted teachers and introverted programmers, for instance. However, sometimes opposite personalities can be found in the same job. Research on personalities and different jobs routinely finds that people who are very charitable and selfless are more likely to become pastors, but that very Machiavellian people are also more likely to do so. Why? Because the job has access to a lot of people who need help. Good people see that and want to help. Bad people see that and see an opportunity to exploit.

This is by no means exclusive to churches. Far from it. Teachers, politicians, cops, and journalists are actually more likely to find people who love kids and want to help them, and psychos who love kids in all of the wrong ways. There are eight billion people on this planet, so just by sheer numbers, there are a lot of bad people who will take a job that makes them look good, solely for the opportunity to harm others.

This is most true on the internet, where people lie and cheat all of the time due to being anonymous while having access to children. Likewise, this can be found in school where bullies want to maintain their authority. Mean girls lie and gossip to keep their rivals in check, while boys lie to gain unearned praise. Did your friend really get a PS6 from his uncle in Japan? No. Did he really see some super rare lost episode of SpongeBob on an old website? Nope. Did he really make it to second base with Stacy? Not on your life. With anyone important to your success, like your pastor, teacher, or friend, you need to verify just as often as you trust. Real trust should be earned through verification.

Your teachers are not gods

You may have a great teacher, but you may also have a lot of bad ones. Considering how important the job is, you think it would have a better screening process. In the past, teachers tended to be among the most, or even only, educated members of a community. Many teachers during the early days of compulsory education (requiring children legally to go to school) actually were moved into poorer and less educated areas as their best was not even good enough for the role. Modern teachers are certified after attending university, so that sounds like a lot of qualifications too. However, the minimum standards for attending and graduating university has dropped consistently for the past few decades, with the average graduate being no more intelligent than the population in general (102 vs 100 IQ). Additionally, the certification organizations are a bureaucracy who care far more about maintaining their power and status than they do about children's education. This is just the natural process for any large organization, especially one that is unaccountable to market forces (you can stop buying a bad product, but most people cannot quit a bad school).

What all of this means is that your teacher is just a regular person. Maybe even less than average, depending on the case. If they are more interested in their political causes, social status, or working up the union ladder, then don't take their word for gospel. Some will be well meaning, but wrong. Others won't care either way and just collect a paycheck. Just do not use this as an excuse to leave the classroom empty headed. Educate yourself, if you have to. After all, "trust but verify" is the first step of replicating anything within the scientific method. As long as you learn to separate the good from the bad, even poor teachers can teach you something. As venture capitalist, Naval Ravikant, once said "The smartest people are self-taught; even if they went to school."

J. E. Bassette

Nor are your teachers devils

Remember how we talked about scammers and how the opposite temperaments can be drawn to the same profession? Well, it's true in the case of teachers as well. Many teachers are people who have an inflated sense of narcissism and think they must indoctrinate all children with their special truth that only they happen to know in order to save the world. Or, some such self-important political nonsense. However, the exact opposite personality type, selfless folks who truly wish to pursue truth, are also drawn to the profession. You know, people who just generally like school and the idea of teaching.

That being said, even they are ultimately humans. Teaching is one of those rare jobs where virtually no one can be perfect at it. That's because it is not one skill set, but several: researching the field, making class materials, teaching the subject, interacting with students, testing the material, grading and evaluating, and finally counseling. Most teachers are good if they do two of those well and great if they can manage just three. How do I know? I have been a professor for more than a decade at this point. I love researching and writing classes, even brand-new topics, but still dread walking up to the front of the room every single class. Don't get me started on how much I hate making tests and trying to get that perfect 75-80% class average every single time. It's always stressful, and rarely fun. For me. I have plenty of colleagues who are the opposite and love teaching and quizzing, but hate doing any research or writing of their own, and prefer to just teach from packets every semester (gross!). I say all that to say this: be realistic with your expectations of your teacher. They're only human after all.

Be humble, as you know almost nothing

So, remember me telling you to question and vet authority, as many of the occupations that tend to have good people also attract some very bad characters? You might take that to mean that you are the one who can tell these two groups of actors apart and that you are the best judge of such things. I hate to break it to you, but you know almost nothing, and "future you" will cringe every time he thinks about how little he used to know. Being curious and cautious is the opposite of knowing it all. Blindly following could get you into trouble with bad actors. Blindly questioning will just keep you ignorant forever. Be humble and realistic about what you do and do not know.

Two Psychology professors once wanted to understand why their freshmen tended to be the most certain and boastful about their knowledge, while their seniors were more cautious about what they definitely understood. What was going on? Well, the freshmen knew so little about the real world and their actual field that they did not even realize how little they knew. Quick! How many different kinds of bugs are there? How many can you name? Regardless of your answer, think about how many of the 900,000 known species you could actually learn about in just a four-year degree. Now, imagine that once you graduate, you learn that there may be as much as 30 million more species left undiscovered. Suddenly, you feel like you don't know a lot, right? Feeling a little more humble, maybe? This is the process for all scholars, regardless of field. The previously mentioned Professors were named Dunning and Kruger and now the effect that shares their names is a reminder to stay humble, stay curious, and always be learning (even if its effect is slightly exaggerated on the internet). The truth is, the more you know, the more context you gain for what you still have yet to learn.

Getting angry is easy, but helps no one

You may have noticed that you cry, or get emotional in general, less than some of your female peers. You may be told at some point that this is a purely cultural phenomenon and that men are taught to hold in their feelings because of toxic masculinity, or some such societal reason. This is simply not true. Hormones literally affect how your brain processes and shows different emotions. The truth is, you may cry less, because your brain is prioritizing other emotions. Yeah, they never told you about that, right? Guys do feel emotions just as much as girls, but they are different emotions. Girls often report feeling sad, lonely, or afraid during puberty. Boys reported feeling... well you already know: horny or angry. Sometimes both.

Contrary to the academic excuse, boys are often told to moderate their emotions by their mothers, not fathers, because moms see how either of those two emotions could get their sons into a lot of trouble or cause others a lot of pain. Historically, these two emotions were really useful for boys. One made them interested in trying to be kind and friendly, at least to pretty girls, while the other made them more likely to survive a bear or tiger attack. I hope you already know which helped in each of those respective scenarios.

Regardless, you are not weird for not crying as much as some of your peers, nor are you repressed. You have emotions, but you are being told to moderate them because they are less useful, and more dangerous, than they were in the past. If you do cry, feel sad, or get lonely sometimes, that's also normal. You are capable of every emotion, but some will just come more frequently than others. This is especially true as you get older and your hormones guide you to what was more useful 3000 years ago. Go easy on yourself, but do not give into the easy feelings that are just going to make a situation worse.

We are not disappointed you cannot do something; we are disappointed that you did not even try

Out of all the emotions that your parents can feel, disappointment may seem like the worst. Abandonment of injured, sickly, or underperforming children was sadly more common in the past when food was scarcer. Because of this, you have an understandable built-in fear of disappointing your parents. In fact, children that never feel this way, that disregard their parents' feelings or even actively try to cross them, tend to do worse at school, in the job market, and in their romantic relationships. Your fear of disappointing them actually helps shape you into a better person.

That being said, don't beat yourself up or get discouraged for thinking you disappointed them when you really didn't. You may think, especially from the example above, that parents are disappointed when you fail at something. Lose the soccer match, fail the math test, or mess up the table you were building and they are going to be upset. But in reality, disappointment often comes from feeling like you are not trying to get better, not that you are not perfect now. Think of it this way: did you practice before the soccer game? Did you do all of your math homework before the test? Did you measure everything twice before constructing the table? Did you try to succeed before you failed? A child who is trying, but failing, is a work in progress: a future success. A child who fails with little effort is, well, a failure. Which would you be more disappointed in? Always try your best, and fail forward where you can.

Your parents blame themselves for your failures

This is one that may not be true, depending on where you live, but for many children of parents from Confucius or religious backgrounds, your parents are under a lot of pressure to see you succeed. In Confucianism, children are seen as the direct results of the type of parenting they received. "Score cards" for your ability to perform your duties as a parent, as it were. If the child is successful, that is because you are a good parent. If they are a failure then, well…

The same is true, if a little different, for most of the world's religions, but especially so for Abrahamic ones: Christianity, Judaism, and Islam. God specifically tells parents that they must instruct their children on how to live, and that these children, in turn, will bless their parents. Children are a blessing from God himself, so if your kid turns out to be trash, well, what does that say about how God must feel about you, right?

Ultimately, it's more complicated than that. Some kids get good instruction, but are little punks. Others, their parents are dirt bags, but the kids still square themselves away and become great people. Life is complicated. However, when you do well on a test, realize that your folks see this as their positive report card as well. Likewise, when you fail, well, they are going to take that a little personal too. Always try your best, for both or your sakes.

School bullying, sadly, comes from nature

I know you don't want to hear it, but bullying is not some invention of sadistic Hollywood writers or the patriarchy or something. Bullies exist in most species as a way for people to try and outstrip influence or authority from their peers. For girls, it is often not the prettiest girl that is the bully, as she is often a target instead. Girls that are pretty, but not the prettiest, may target those they see as a threat (the actual prettiest), or those beneath them that they see as future threats (the late bloomer who is starting to come into her own after joining the soccer team, for instance).

Sound familiar? Boys do the same thing, but targeting physical threats. The actual strongest guy is very rarely in charge, as those a little weaker, but still fairly dominant, will gang up to put him in his place. No, the real school bully is the guy smart enough to make friends, create alliances, and punish those that step out of line. In movies, it is often kids who are lonely, abused, or have family problems that are the bullies. I am sad to report that this is rarely true. They are often kids with something to offer their "followers," in exchange for loyalty, like influence of their own. That means, most of these bullies do not get their "comeuppance" in the end. Truthfully, most of them go on to be successful in fields that require a lot of two-face-ness or back stabbing: actors and politicians, most likely.

What this means for you is that if you are a bully, know that those who fail to properly keep this difficult balance are usurped by those who can. Even in chimpanzees and lions, it is common for the top bully to eventually die by the hands of the next top bully. It's a dangerous game. Best to never play it. If you are getting bullied, get allies of your own, create a stalemate with the bullies, and then get back to your studies. They aren't worth your time and will be long forgotten once everyone leaves school and becomes real adults.

Why your friends are always "joshing" you

What may appear as bullying initially, but is very different, is "joshing," or the "poking fun" and "ball busting" that virtually all males across the world do. This universality means it is very likely not cultural, but built into our species. What benefit could humans have for calling each other "gay" and nut checking you when your hands are full with books? Yeah, it's survival again. It's always survival.

Historically, a weak link could cause the downfall of an entire hunting party. If just one member is too soft, unsure of himself, too quick to anger, or is unwitty and incapable of joshing back with his peers, he could be a liability. It is in the group's best interest to identify those weak links and get rid of them. It is a test of trustworthiness, character, and potential comradery. Hence, joshing around.

Try to take it in stride, as they very likely do not hate you, no matter how personal some of their barbs come across. It is instinctual for them to poke and test you, like a velociraptor testing an electric fence for weaknesses. Show you can take a joke, keep your cool, and josh them back. This shows that you are not only not a liability, but are actually able to participate and work within the team's framework. Now, there might actually be some real jerks and bullies that are busting your balls because they really do hate you. In that case, joshing back is still the best move, as it will display your sense of humor, wit, and backbone to other groups who may be watching, likely earning their respect instead. Test the fence, try not to take offence, and play offence.

People flexing with Gucci

My wife's cousin wanted a present for his birthday, but after seeing the price tag, he was told he would just get money as a gift and would have to save up the rest of the cost on his own. So, what was it? A PS5? A computer? The complete One Piece Manga collection? Nope. A wallet. He has no money, hence asking his folks for the gift, so what did he want it for? It was a Gucci wallet that he knew the girls at school would think was cool. How much was this bit of flexing going to set him back? 500 dollars. Even with the birthday money, it would take months of saving up for something he would almost never actually use, and even the girls he was trying to impress would rarely get an opportunity to see.

What was his strategy here? Well, women wear expensive clothes to impress other women and seem resourceful and a good friend to have. Men buy expensive clothes to impress... women, again. Male birds actually do this a lot, with the flashiest or prettiest bird getting the girl, because it shows his resourcefulness. Think of it from her perspective: if he has 500 dollars to waste on a wallet, how much more could he waste on me? Now, it's not so cold and calculated. In actuality, it's instinctual. No different than you liking her because she has nice skin and pretty hair. Her attraction is to signs of future safety and stability, and yours are to future healthy children. But the takeaway here is that the wallet is just a symbol. It represents potential. The wallet itself doesn't actually matter. Save your money. Show your stability and resourcefulness in other, smarter ways. Invest it into learning a musical instrument or a useful hobby instead. Show off your potential. Chicks dig potential.

J. E. Bassette

Your school clique does not define you
post-graduation

To make friends and keep safe from bullies, you may find yourself in a school clique. Maybe the computer club, football team, or band. Regardless of who you pick, there is a temptation to turn them into your whole personality. If you join the goths, you just think that you have to be a goth forever now and make them, and whatever they like, the center of your entire identity. You can see this around a lot of cliques that form around some kind of activism or cause. They make it the only personality they now have, so whenever the group decides to be really interested in something, no matter how stupid, the whole group feels like they have to be 100% onboard as well.

In middle and half of high school, I was a theater kid. Mostly Shakespeare. I still love the guy. Theater was classy, had history, pomp and circumstance, and most importantly... it had girls. Nerdy girls, which was the kind I was into. Whatever stupid thing they liked, I pretended to like just to keep in their clique. Their music became my music. Their fashion became my fashion. That is until they made me watch the musical "Rent." It sucked. Like, really was the worst piece of garbage I had ever seen. The "villain" landlord was the only tolerable character at all. I realized at that moment, as the credits rolled, that I had to either pretend to like this monkey-poop-aids-fire of a musical, or risk losing my clique. I dyed my hair black, became emo, and got the heck out of the theater group. No regrets. Except for the black hair. Left the emos one year later, and dyed it again. Once you leave the school, the clique dies too. Don't let them define you.

Buy only what you need, invest the rest

My dad once installed a gravel walkway at a friend's house. The original quote was for thousands of dollars, but my dad (being an engineer) said he could probably do it for less than half the price. With no theater productions to prepare for anymore, I was also roped in with the promise of at least enough money to buy the new RPG video game all of the magazines were raving about. Over the course of a few days, we measured and dug the walkway and then shoveled wheelbarrow after wheelbarrow of rocks to fill it in. About a week or so after we were done, dad asked me how much I thought I deserved for my labor. I told him that the game was 50 dollars, plus tax. He then told me that my cut was actually 300 dollars. Before I could start thinking of five other games I would like to buy, he made me a deal: I get the 50, plus tax, now and the rest of the 300 goes into stock in a local company. Being too tired from wheeling rocks around, I agreed. Over ten years later, my dad reminds me that I hadn't cashed out yet and that he would do so and give me the money at my wedding. The (now) over 700 dollars paid for my wedding photos.

Whenever you get money that you did not expect, be it a gift, on your birthday, or from some job you helped someone with, don't spend all your money. Pick one thing you need or really want as a reward, and then put the rest away in a savings account. I know it sounds cheesy and like something your grandparents would say, but they know because the friends that did that survived the hard times. Set "future you" up for financial success. Buy only one thing you need, and give the rest to future you. This is a habit that will serve you throughout not only your childhood, but for most of your life. Fiscal responsibility is a key factor in both escaping poverty and keeping out of it later in life.

J. E. Bassette

Drugs are (almost) never worth it

There has been a lot of debate around the decriminalization of drugs in the US and western world. When I was a child, great efforts were made to make kids afraid of drugs, but significantly more political will is now being spent to convince adults that they are actually OK. The reality is far messier. Alcohol is a type of drug that most cultures have incorporated into religious and social life, while others have been more stigmatized. What we can see from this example is that, even with the most cultivated and regulated version of a drug, some people do OK with alcohol and others do not. Some groups are more fun when drinking, others more violent and destructive.

In general, many of the people wanting to legalize drugs are doing so either from an absolutist freedom standpoint ("let people be free to make even very bad choices") or because they think that since they can handle it, others can too. Again, the reality is messy. If you can do drugs and not hurt yourself and your family, good for you. However, that does mean you are gambling on other people's families. It should be telling that most places that totally decriminalized, are now trying to recriminalize most drugs. If you do not know until you try it, would you really want to put yourself and your family at that kind of risk? There is already a long since vetted drug option, alcohol, and even that is far from perfect. Ultimately, there are better ways to spend your money and less risky ways to have fun and reduce stress that put zero risk on your loved ones. Drink responsibly and just avoid drugs altogether.

Hate actions, not people

Even those that claim to not believe in God, still must believe in a devil. Human civilization runs on having some evil that we fight against, be it some enemy country, ideology, or group that has it out for us. This tribalism is natural, but quite unhelpful in the modern world. Case in point: China is the most likely serious military threat to both the US and Korea, and they have a Communist government. We have both an enemy state and a proven bad ideology rolled up into one hate-able devil shaped package. So, should you hate Chinese people? Every one that I have personally met have been really nice people. Good food, good sense of humor, even a good appreciation for many of the cultural things I find interesting. It doesn't seem to make sense to hate them, if I end up having more in common with them than some of my fellow countrymen. So, who do we hate?

No one, Lord willing. Instead, hate actions rather than just groups of people. When the Chinese government does something to put Americans, Japanese, or Koreans at risk, I hate it. That being said, the Chinese family running the café next door literally had nothing to do with that action. I should be mad at some general behind a desk, a politician trying to make a name for themselves, or a leader saber rattling with my government. By hating actions, rather than people, it also allows you to point out the bad actors in your own tribe and try to correct them, rather than attempt to justify their poor actions. When you see something you do not like, try to isolate what action is provoking your reaction rather than the individual. This can help you stay more consistent with your beliefs, level headed in your anger, and prevent you from becoming the devil that you hate.

Lean into your strengths, even for looks

There seems to be a mythological creature whom all parents truly believe in. This animal is not only good at every single academic discipline, but is also talented in sports, a musical instrument, social skills, and housework. This perfect "renaissance boy" is what every mom and dad wishes their little Billy and Jimmy to become one day. Preferably on the very first day of school. On the one hand, this makes sense. A perfectly well-rounded child, by nature of those diverse skills, has maximum opportunity to succeed in the future. The logic falls apart when you realize that humans are only human and even if they had given you the perfect genes to even try and be perfect at everything, your own personality and interests were likely to get in the way.

So, what do you do? Find the stuff you are best at. Not things that are fun (although that helps too), but things that you have a genuine knack for that other people would be willing to pay you to do when you are an adult. I was two grades behind in math my final year of high school and one grade behind in science. In contrast, I had finished my English and History requirements two years early and had taken college classes in those subjects instead. I found something I was good at, and eventually found people willing to pay me for that skill set. The same is true for your looks. You want a perfect nose, eyes, chin, biceps, and pecks, but maybe you only have one or two nice features. Lean into them. Girls liked my blue eyes, so I wore clothes and glasses that showed them off. I could build pecs pretty easily due to my frame, so I focused on those. Eventually, I found a girl that liked those two things in particular. So will you. That fact that you are alive at all means that you have the genes to look good to somebody and the skills to attract someone, because your parents did just that. You just need to lean into those things and find that girl.

Dress yourself in the classics, not the trends

Take a look at photos of guys from the last 100 years. There are going to be a lot of different clothing trends, fads, fashions, and even brands that may no longer exist. However, you will likely also see some things that looked good 100 years ago, that still were fashionable 50 years later, and would still get you approval from your mom and a random girl on picture day today. It makes sense that young men care about clothing trends to some degree. After all, young women care about it a lot, so it could be a way of getting their attention and maybe even admiration. However, these trends change quickly, are likely expensive, and will make any photo you take with them instantly dated and cringy when your future children discover them.

Classy looks, in contrast, tend to look good at any time. Clean slacks, nice shirts, maybe a light sweater here or there: these are all men's styles that have stood the test of time and can be found in any color or cut imaginable. Find something that looks good on you, that fits your body type and shape, and in colors that bring out some of your features. Get your mom or a lady you trust to help you out. Don't trust an older person's opinion on current fashion? Well, they are helping you pick out classic fashion, so it doesn't matter. Find something that works for you, that will still look good on you even into the future, and then buy two sets. Always buy two of something priced well that looks good on you. You won't find that every day, you know.

Focus on dental hygiene

Hygiene is important for anyone. Not only does it keep you healthy, but it signals to women two very important things: you can take care of yourself (so she doesn't have to be your second mom) and that you are conscientious and can take some pride in yourself and your appearance. You probably already know this and take showers and change your clothes for this very reason. The key is to remember your dental hygiene. Brush your teeth, floss, and don't drink sugar all the time.

For one, it gets expensive to fix after you lose all of your baby teeth. Braces, fillings, and crowns are painful on top of costing you an arm and a leg. However, there is another important reason to care about keeping your pearly whites shiny: it will help you deal with self-confidence. The mouthwash company Listerine was able to take advantage of the fact that it is hard to smell your own breath to make people self-conscious about it all the time. How do you know that your breath doesn't stink right now! How about when talking to the cute girl in your class? How about your first kiss? How can you be sure? Better buy their product!

In reality, you just need to make healthy habits a part of your daily routine, and brushing at least twice a day is an easy way to start. If you know your breath is good, because you always take care of your dental hygiene, you will find yourself worrying a lot less, and feeling confident a lot more. Maybe you can have some mints as a backup for that first kiss, but otherwise, taking care of your equipment means never having to doubt it.

Humans are inherently selfish

In the film "Second Hand Lions," one of the elderly gentlemen is giving some of his own DADvice to the young male main character. He tells him that because mankind is basically good, it is important to do good things. You know, keeping people's faith in human goodness alive by being good. I remember watching this and thinking, "If mankind was basically good, then doing good would be nothing. It would be both expected and the norm. Doing good things is only special if humans naturally like doing bad things. This movie sucks."

OK, I definitely did not articulate it quite like that, but I certainly had that sentiment. Every person I knew had learned to lie without their parents teaching them how to. Every little boy was a perv sometimes, despite every adult in their life telling them not to be. Every little baby had to be reminded to share and not steal, because both came so naturally to him. People did do good things sometimes, maybe every single day. But it feels good to be treated nicely by a stranger because you know, from your own personal experience, that they have every ability and inclination to not be good. This choice to go against their nature is what makes being good seem special and worth praising.

Everyone is a selfish jerk sometimes. This self-centeredness really helped babies not die at a time when resources, time, and attention from protectors may have been scarce. However, there is a reason that every single one of the world's great religions preach that man is basically bad and needs to change themselves to do good. If it was already in our nature, we wouldn't have needed reminding of it all the time. Selfishness is natural and most common, so it is not special. Be special. Do good.

J. E. Bassette

People online are naturally jerks

Since mankind is naturally selfish and jerks, it would make sense that in places where people cannot see nor identify us, we tend to be at our most "natural." That is to say when we are at our most jerk-like. You have undoubtedly seen people act their most extreme, hatefully, and ignorant when masked by the 1s and 0s of the internet. Online, no one knows you are secretly a dog in a penguin suit. As such, everyone feels freest to not only say things they would never actually say in person offline, but to lie their butts off in the process.

I once saw a former classmate arguing with a random person online (as everyone seems to do now and again) over something stupid (as everyone seems to do now and again). He tried to win the argument by claiming to be an expert on the topic they were fighting about and mentioning learning it as his university. Having been in the exact classes he was talking about, I knew he was definitely not an expert because I was not one. Why lie about something so dumb where people can easily find out you are full of crap? Because they feel anonymous and like nothing they say matters online. They feel free to be jerks because there are no repercussions.

Except there are. If you are putting more anger and garbage out into the world, you are doing the opposite of "good." Just don't engage these people. Do not take the dumb stuff they say seriously, and try your best to never add to the level of jerk already in cyberspace. I remember some YouTuber talking about how it takes 20 positive comments to counteract one negative one he would read on one of his videos. To me, that says I must write at least 20 positive messages before I am allowed to write one mean one. Do that, and at least you will be balancing yourself out.

No man is righteous, no not one

Remember how men are fundamentally flawed and all of us are naturally inclined to be jerks? Well, a lot of people tend to forget this when it comes to their personal heroes or when they are trying to draft political policy. The America Economist, Thomas Sowell, noticed this first hand when he worked for the government. He saw that many policy makers would create programs and policies that assumed that human nature was fully malleable. That, if we try hard enough and just make the perfect conditions for it, human beings can be perfected and actually make a society where everyone, by default, was righteous.

Sowell could not help but notice that, even among the politicians and government employees championing this idea of perfecting mankind, they were pretty flawed people. Cheating on their wives, stealing from taxpayers, ignoring problems if they were from the same political party, downplaying and erasing successes if they were from political rivals, etc. Sowell called this world view the "unconstrained" vision: that humans had no limitations and only bad societies were holding us back. In contrast, every single one of the world's great religions (yes, every single one) all hold the "constrained" vision: humans are all flawed broken creatures that are civilized through the hard work of society building and are destined to work within the constraints of human nature forever, redeemed only through the grace of God(s).

It should be obvious which one I believe, and have witnessed throughout the different countries, cultures, and societies I have experienced. However, even I sometimes forget this. If there is a personal hero I have, a politician who is saying the right things, or a pretty girl I met, I would start to think that maybe someone is perfect. There was one, but everyone else hated him and literally crucified him. Shot and chaser. Lesson learned. All of us are flawed human beings and only charlatans and naïve dreamers tell you otherwise.

To everything there is a season

My younger brother seemed like one of the least lucky people I knew. Every job, every girlfriend, and every college course, his plans always seemed to fall through and keep him in a fairly stagnant position for almost 10 years of his life. To make matters worse, he wasn't starving. If things were actually bad, it would have forced him to move on or try something drastically different. But the fact he was still doing "OK," just "unlucky," meant that he was just kind of stuck in neutral. Except, he wasn't.

All of these half-finished plans finally came together when he decided to move to a new area to chase a girl, a job, and a degree all at the same time. A lot of spinning plates, and any of them could fall at any time, but he decided that as long as one landed, he was making progress. He landed all three. It was only when looking in retrospect that he saw all of his unluckiness as actually preparing him for this future success. If he had been luckier in love, his job, or his classes, then he would have stayed put. He never would have gained the motivation to move on to the place where he found success all those years later.

For everything there is a season. We are used to planting a seed, caring for it, harvesting it, enjoying it, and then starting the process over the next year. Unfortunately, the seasons in life are measured not in days or months, but often in years. It is only when looking back at our lives that we realize everything happened how it was supposed to, just not when we thought it was supposed to. "God helps those who help themselves," as Benjamin Franklin once quipped, but there is wisdom in placing yourself in the best possible path for providence to aid you. Do the work, try your best, and be ready for whenever it is your season.

Have dumb fun hobbies,
but have at least one smart one

I always hated questions about my hobbies whenever I did interviews. I love video games, especially single-player story-based Role-Playing Games. They held a special place in my heart as an un-athletic young man who used them as a way to feel strong and capable. As a much older man, I still love them, but as a way to relax and be entertained with stories and characters I like more than most movies or TV shows. However, women and employers both hate this answer. They see it as childish or a waste of time. If my hobby was something like tennis or taekwondo, they argue, it would at least be healthy and something a little more useful.

However, the point of a hobby is to have fun and relax. Some people can relax with tennis, but I am not one of them. I picked a hobby that I enjoyed and found something worthwhile from it. That being said, I know that, deep down, what they really mean is that at least some of my free time should be spent on something that is more meaningful than just "it's fun." So, my other hobby is reading. A lot of history and international relations books mostly. This is generally less fun than video games about those same topics, but they are both more "useful" as a way to spend my time and more fun for me than tennis. A compromise, if you will. It is OK to have a dumb fun hobby that is just something you do to relax. However, you should also have a second "smart" or "useful" hobby as well. This can be learning a language, a sport, an instrument, or even a life skill like cooking or gardening. The balance between fun and utility will do you some good and make interviews easier. Not to mention help buff out your resume: both the work and dating kind.

No good deed goes unpunished

My father has a real hard time saying "no" to people. Not to us when we asked for allowance or wanted McDonald's after church. Rather, he had a very hard time saying "no" to people asking for his help. This could be someone at work, an old friend, a stranger in a broken-down car, or even just someone he just met at the gas station. He was always ready to say "sure" and volunteer his time to help others. It's what made him a great soldier and an even better pastor. However, it also meant people were able to take advantage of his kindness.

On more than one occasion, dad's willingness to do a good deed ended up costing him, usually financially. Not once, but twice, his trying to provide housing for people in need ended up becoming long-term problems that turned real estate gains into, well, real estate pains. However, this never stopped him from trying to help others. It's a really difficult balance to make as a man. On the one hand, putting yourself or your family in the position where you can be taken advantage of is not going to help them any. On the other hand, isn't the fact that he is a great guy, willing to live his faith and help others, the reason mom liked him in the first place? Isn't he living the example of the kind of man he wants his sons to become?

Try not to be taken advantage of by people who abuse other's niceness. Don't reward crappy people like that and try to stop them from doing it to others in the future when you do "get got." However, also never put yourself in a position where you no longer want to do good deeds for others. Closing yourself off completely from helping those in need will not make you the kind of man you really want to become. It's a balancing act. So, act accordingly.

Failure teaches us more than success

My sister and I are pretty different people in some key ways, despite sharing a sense of humor and many hobbies. She was the ideal student who hated herself if she got "only" 102% on her test after extra credit. I, by contrast, was very lucky to finally finish grade 10 algebra... in my final year of high school. However, there was one time when I finally became the top student who could do no wrong. I knew nothing but success after success... and it almost ruined me.

When I joined the army, it was very apparent that I was good at the entire "vibe," of the place. I lost all my weight very quickly, went from 12 pushups to 73 in just three months, and was motivated enough to teach myself before we even had the classroom instruction. I was exactly the kind of kid the army envisioned when they wrote the lyrics "In all the posters that I read, they say the army needs men. So, they're tearing me down to build me over again." This came to an abrupt stop when I went to Special Forces Assessment and Selection (SFAS) to join the Green Berets. I did every test they asked, performed every mission I was given, and aced everything they threw at me like the top soldier I was. But they didn't pick me to join. They thought I was still young, so could try again later, versus older guys who this was their last chance to join.

While devastated, I learned more that one day than any entire month I spent in the army. I learned that my successes were not always down to me doing my best. I learned that sometimes what you are being evaluated on (like, age) can have nothing to do with the actual job. Some people in important positions will make dumb choices you will have to live with. Finally, I learned that success taught me to never question "why," but failure always made me reflect on it. It is only through failing at something, evaluating how to do better in the future, and executing a plan for self-improvement that you can become better at anything. Do not be afraid to fail. Rather, fail and immediately learn from it.

Problems are a feature of life, not a bug

Along those same lines, problems in life are not always something to get angry at. If everything in your life is going great and you have no problems ever, then your opportunity to grow and get better by reflecting on your situation never comes. In a game, a bug is a mistake, but it gives the developers the opportunity to reflect on the product. In the game "Street Fighter," developers at Capcom noticed that some players were exploiting a mistake where they could "juggle" opponents by linking together moves to stun the computer AI and link together separate actions. These "combinations" of moves ("combos" for short), were not supposed to happen and should have been fixed once the problem was well known.

Capcom did not fix them, however. They noticed that players who found and used the exploits had much more fun with the game then players who played it correctly. After all, there is a reason people remember this series, but never bothered to play the first one. It stunk. For the sequel, Capcom decided to design the entire combat system around these "combos," with each character having different ones at varying speeds, strengths, and reach so that players would have to play for hours to learn them all. After 58 million sales across six games, I would say that this "bug," ended up being an important "feature."

When you get hit with a problem, when life serves up a bug that ruins your plans, think about if this is an opportunity. Maybe you are discovering something that may be a new feature for you. After I failed SFAS, I never went back, even after they offered for me to try again. I instead went to Korea and focused more on finishing my Bachelor's Degree. I was overlooked because of my age, so while I waited on getting older, I decided to buff up my resume even more and prepare for other opportunities. Turns out, the university system wanted me a lot more than Special Forces did and treated me better as a result of it. The bug eventually led to both my wife and my future career.

Hey, Sport. It's Me, Your Dad.

Save all of your work at least twice

My wife thinks I am a paranoid weirdo for always saving my game twice before I turn the PlayStation off. Obviously, she has never put in a five-hour grinding session in an RPG only for the power to go out before you found a save point. It sucks to lose your entire afternoon. I have permanently quit games I absolutely loved over a loss like that. Feels bad to go back to an old save.

I have incorporated this paranoia into my work as well as my play. When I am working on an important project for school, and later my job, I would always hit save twice before closing the program. However, I took it one step further: once a week, I would back up everything I was working on to a thumb drive. One a month, I would back everything up to an external hard drive. Crazy? Maybe. But in those few times I needed it, it was worth every minute of paranoia. I had a file get corrupted, and rather than starting from scratch, I was able to get a backup and only lose an hour or two. Likewise, I have had colleagues quit their doctoral program, as data they had been collecting for four or five years suddenly was lost and they would have to start over.

This also helps build the habit of double checking. Even when you know you saved, you do it again, just to be safe. This eventually evolves into double checking that you turned off the stove. Even when you know you sent out everyone's pay checks, you double check. Locked the front door? Tucked in the kids? Closed the trunk? Paid the light bill? And so on and so on. This should also happen with all important documents, with the originals, physical copies, and digital versions all being maintained just in case. Save "future you" a lot of heartache and just always save twice. And then back up everything twice.

Do the important thing in the morning

The greatest lie we tell ourselves is "I will do it tonight before I go to bed." No, you won't. No one does. If you do not finish it before you start relaxing for the evening, you will never get it done. Be it homework, working out, telling your mom you love her, or whatever. If it is something important, do it first thing in the morning. Waking up early on a day off is hard, but it is significantly harder to switch from "relax" mode to "dialed in" mode at nine o'clock at night. Once you start reclining for the day, it is very difficult to re-motivate yourself.

In contrast, when you first wake up, doing anything, even fun things, is difficult. It is the only time in the entire day where "go to the gym," and "make nachos," are even in the same ballpark of difficulty when it comes to motivation. The difference, of course, is that making those nachos will get easier and more enticing the closer you get to lunch time. The gym? It's only going to get much much harder.

When you wake up, go to the bathroom, do your business, and then immediately do the hardest thing on your to-do list. It can be to work out, read the book for class, fix the door knob, or even just wrap mom's birthday present. It doesn't matter, just get it off of your to-do list. After you do that, not only will you feel better the rest of the day without that task hanging over your shoulder, but you will get less nagging from mom when you do make those nachos and start up the PlayStation. Win-win.

Sacrificing for the future

There are a lot of things that the world's great religions all share, such as the concept of the "golden rule," of doing to others what you would have then do unto you. However, there is another shared concept that they all have that may explain how they became great religions in the first place: sacrifice.

Saving for the winter can be found in some animal species, like squirrels or bears. Yet, it did not really catch on for many primates. When a chimpanzee gets a big kill, he never thinks to save some for later by drying it into jerky or to use salt to cure it into bacon. Most apes have to live in jungles or temperate places that do not have drastic shifts in seasonal weather to compensate for this. Given how many ice ages we have had, it does mean most of them got killed off at various points in the past. Always living in the present, those goofy monkeys.

In contrast, humans seem pretty good at saving for the future. In fact, those that don't, tend to fall behind everyone else in their community, country, or even the world. Counties that have colder winters tend to have more large and successful companies, for instance. Those who learned to sacrifice today to live better tomorrow tended to thrive better. Remember all of the world's great religions? They all teach sacrifice. Sometimes literally, like animal sacrifice, but mostly giving up the worldly pleasures of today for something better tomorrow. Delayed gratification that promises rewards later if we are patient and make little sacrifices today. Let's keep the tradition alive, and sacrifice a little fun today for a better you tomorrow.

Most problems can be fixed by planning

I remember my dad always saying "now is not the time for crying," or "you can cry later," when there was a problem. I always interpreted it to mean "stop crying," but he literally meant "fix the problem first, then cry about it." If you cry first, well, the problem is still there and may be making things worse for you. When you have a problem, solve it first before you do anything else. But how are you supposed to start fixing an issue that you did not learn about until this very second?

Generally, you make a plan for how to fix it. In the army, you were expected to think on your feet and solve complex problems quickly on the fly. Plans should have been made before you even started the fight. However, sometimes that is not possible and you have to make a new play with information that you never even knew until right now. In these situations, you can take a "tactical pause:" briefly stop what you are doing and make sure you understand the problem and what you need to do to fix it.

Likewise, whenever you have an issue, like a failed math test or a girl you like who you just embarrassed yourself in front of, there is no point crying just yet. Take a tactical pause and think of a plan of attack. OK, do I know why I got those questions wrong? Can I teach myself these formulas, or do I need outside help? Do I know someone who could tutor me? Did I embarrass myself because I lack a skill I was trying to show off? Is it something I can work on by myself, or do I need help? Does she have a cute sister who maybe is less judgmental? Whatever the problem, stopping, making a plan, fixing it, and then crying about it (most likely, laughing about it in hindsight), will always be the best course of action.

Avoid "Intellectual Masturbation"

In his 1945 Science Fiction book, "That Hideous Strength," C.S. Lewis wrote about how often it is the very smart and clever among us that end up doing some of the greatest evil. In an exchange between one of the novel's antagonists with the book's still naive hero, there is discussion of the idea that manipulation works best on people who feel well educated. Quote: "But the educated public, the people who read the high-brow weeklies, don't need reconditioning. They're all right already. They'll believe anything." The older I have gotten, the more I have come to understand this sentiment. At school and at work, I began to see how the people who felt themselves the most educated in the ways of the world, tended to believe the stupidest things. They were quick to turn on a dime, and believe the opposite of their own position weeks before. The cause, 100% of the time, was reading and watching the news a lot.

Some time around COVID I stopped being one of them. I thought I was doing it in a more clever way, choosing only the papers with good reputations and reading all of the fact checks. However, I ran into stories and checks that I knew (first hand) to be incorrect, littered among the ones I thought were real. I read about how much Koreans hated black actors, which was why the Little Mermaid underperformed at the box office. Yet, Black Panther over performed, by over double expectations, just a few years before with Korean audiences. Then I started talking to exchange students from the US and the UK, who had almost canceled their year abroad due to reading the news and fearing racism. I suddenly realized that it was high-brow garbage with real world consequences. The same papers writing about Korean racism now once defended Hitler in the 1930s, covered up for Stalin in the 1940s, defended North Korea in the 1960s, and simps for terrorist organizations now. They never made anyone smarter. They just made them feel smarter. "Intellectual Masturbation" that leaves you feeling ashamed when you realize it. Always assume all headlines are an attempted lie, and wait to draw any judgments, as truth always takes some time to come to light. Don't be a dupe.

Always be learning (ABL)

You may think that once school is done, you never have to pick up a book ever again or that all that learning business is behind you. One day, you will meet an old classmate who did exactly this, and went from an average young adult to a seemingly stupid adult. They did not get dumber, they just stayed the same while everyone else, to include you, continued to grow. My dad used to say that "every day you learn something new is a good day." With the overabundance of great books, films, games, and an internet to connect us to the books, films, and games of others, there is no better time to learn something new every day.

Humans love novelty. We even have a bias, the recency bias, that favors new (even incorrect) information over old (even correct) ideas. Remember the awkwardly named "Intellectual Masturbation" and its focus on feeling smart by reading new things, even if they are completely false? This is the biological root of that. But do not despair! You can correct for this bias and learn something actually new and true every day: focus on old things that have been true forever. Read and watch the classics that have stood the test of time. Not only will this give you a good foundation to understand the works of others, chances are if it was good advice or clever storytelling 2000 years ago, it is probably still good today.

Finally, seek out skill sets that you do not currently have. Take up cooking, wood working, plumbing, robotics, programming, photography, etc. Learning something brand new will make it exciting (novelty) while teaching you something that you could use in the future. And even if you never get to use your horticulturist skills in real life, you now have something cool to share on a date. Always Be Learning, so you can always be growing.

Work on your body and your mind

Schools are pretty good about beating things into your head. Some of your classes are actually more important than others, but since you do not even know your skills yet, how is the school supposed to know? It is best to try your hardest to improve your mind in general in many different disciplines until you figure out your strengths. The same is true for your body. You should be trying out different sports, outdoor hobbies, and martial arts to keep your body healthy, but also to get it ready for growth once you find out what you are good at.

Believe it or not, these two different things go hand in hand. While you may have a stereotype of high schoolers either being brainy or jock-like, historically most great men were both. Roman generals were expected to study philosophy and theology, but also farming and what counted as basic science for the time. Albert Einstein was fairly athletic in his youth and would take frequent walks during the day to think and reinvigorate his mind. Buddhist monks literally incorporated martial arts into their daily routines to help focus their minds, as well as to help protect them if attacked by outsiders.

You should always be thinking about both your body and mind. If you already like sports, think about listening to some audio books while you work out and then discussing them with your buddies: a book gym club, as it were. If you are already a pretty great student, try going for a hike to think through your homework and try to free your mind up for creativity when writing your essay. Just make sure to bring a notebook to write down some of these ideas. Your growing body needs both, and the results will also help with the ladies. Win-win.

J. E. Bassette

For a man to be considered good, he must be capable of violence, but refrain from it

I cannot say that I have met too many pacifists in my line of work. However, there is an important mental test I subconsciously make whenever I see someone on TV or in a film talk about pacifism: "Could they take me in a fight?" If someone is half my size, but twice my weight by volume, tries to talk about how anti-war they are and how they think everyone should just stop fighting, my first inclination is to outright reject their opinion on absolutely everything. Not just wars and foreign policy, but even health care, children's education, women, public transportation... everything. Here is a man who cannot fight his own battles and who must now rework his entire world view around this very sad fact.

In contrast, if this guy was built like a brick house, and seemed like he would walk quietly while still beating my butt with a big stick, my first thought would be that he had earned the right to his opinion. Regardless of who was right, the first man was given his opinion and has no real choice in the matter. The second man could believe anything he wanted, selfishly or not, and chose his world view. The first man is a passenger in his philosophy, but the second man is a driver. You are free to believe anything you want, but make sure you have the strength to back it up. If the first man says he's not going to fight me, I laugh and say "yeah, no crap." The second guys? He gets my respect. Pacifism only means something if it is coming from someone capable of doing the opposite. Make sure you are a peaceful man capable of something other than that, if you want others' respect. Heck, you should do it if you want to earn your own self-respect.

Not your trash, but it is your country

I was on a walk with my son to the local Burger King. I have to get in my 10,000 steps every day, and he had a disagreement with his mom so needed to cool off before he said something that turned into a fight with both his mom and I. A quick 60-minute walk in Eastern Seoul seemed to fit the bill for both problems. About 15 minutes into the adventure, we passed by a building under construction, but with all the crew gone for the day. I saw some cigarettes discarded on the ground about twenty meters from a trash can. I almost passed them by. I had to hesitate and think about it for a second. This was not my responsibility, after all. These were grown men, with a trash can readily available, that failed in their basic duty, not me.

However, with my son watching me, I realized that just because they failed in their duty did not give me leave to fail mine. It was not my trash, but it was my country that they were dirtying up. That fact that it was so easy to fix made it even more obvious to me what the right thing to do was: make my son do it. Only half kidding. We cleaned it up together, making a pit stop at the convenience store to clean our hands and get something to drink as a "reward." There was no one to notice us doing the right thing, but that made the action all the more important in the end.

Doing the right thing, doing your duty, even in small things and when no one is looking is what makes a boy into a man. There will always be an excuse you can use to not get something done. The task being someone else's responsibility is probably the most common. However, a real man takes needed action regardless of who was supposed to do it or who will get the praise from it. If you don't clean it up, likely some old lady will have to do it instead. Is she more of a man than you are? Prove it by stepping up and taking action. After all, it may not be your mess, but it is your country you get to fix.

You need a narrative for your life (we carry the fire)

In Cormac McCarthy's novel "The Road," the unnamed man and his son are trying to survive in the post-apocalypse after the death of their wife/mom. Rather than her dying of some illness or getting killed by bandits, it is heavily implied that she took her own life. Having gone blind, she was completely consumed by the anxiety, worry, and neuroticism that would be understandable for any woman in that setting. The father, though, seemed to blame himself a little for his wife giving into despair. He felt like he needed to do something to prevent his son from ever getting to that point. The father told him that they are special. That they "carry the fire," inside and need to keep on living to keep that fire alive. It worked as a deterrent to suicide, but also gave an easy way of explaining good guys from bad guys to the boy: bandits need to die, because they do not carry the fire, for instance.

Believe it or not, you also carry the fire. The fact that you are here today means that you have within you the blood of a fighter, the soul of a survivor, and the drive of a champion. Humanity has had enough war, famine, and disease to kill most of us, yet here you remain. You have that fire in you, but fire can both create and destroy. With fire you can cook the perfect steak, warm the whole family, forge the strongest sword, or even clean drinking water. However, it can also kill, teardown, incinerate, and decimate. You carry the fire, but make sure it is a tool to help others and yourself. You need to believe in something to keep going every single day. For me, my faith has been both a fire to keep me going and a guiding light on how to use that fire in me. It has motivated me to not stop, keep moving forward, and always look for a way out of a bad situation. It led me to our family, and that is a reason worth living for.

Every man has a religion, whether he realizes it or not

For me, and many people who read it, McCarthy's line about "carrying the fire" had an obvious religious implication. The fire of life, the spark of the soul has been a strong deterrent to suicide for most of the western world. As religiosity declined, suicidality increased in places like England, France, Canada, and the US. However, has religion actually decreased? Or, have those who have fallen into despair just found a new, darker religion? If someone worships fame, money, sex, or drugs and then can no long have them, would suicide just be the obvious response to being "rejected" by your "god?"

This can be found in the fact that, throughout all of human history in every culture across humanity, women have been more religious than men. Yet, women now are the most likely to claim no religion in the western world. Have they really changed that much? Or have they just found new religions? One needs only to look at celebrity worship culture, the climate change movement (especially of the protest heavy and eco-terrorist variety), transgenderism (doubly so for the "non-binary" concept), or modern politics to see a lot of very passionate, angry, and depressed young women. Some may even frame their actions and attitudes as being "zealot-like."

The fact is, everyone has a religion, whether they realize it or not. What do you invest yourself into? What gives you meaning? I'm telling you right now, if it is food, games, drugs, or sex, you do not have a "new" religion, but one of the oldest. And, frankly, one of the least useful for creating a version of yourself that will inspire others to "carry the fire" within them. Find your faith, as that will lead you to the fire that can forge a path ahead. Become the pathfinder that you would want your own sons to follow.

You are not that special

I was a fresh-faced 21-year-old Staff Sergeant at Jump School, the US Army's paratrooper training and certification course. More so than heights, which I am not a big fan of, I had a weak constitution which caused me to vomit when moving quickly and violently, like on a roller-coaster... or jumping out of an airplane. Our medic had given me Dramamine, a medication to make me feel less motion sick, but it made me sleepy, causing me to have a very blank expression. My jump master must have thought it was pre-jump jitters as he tapped me on the helmet and said, "You know how many jumps have been done here at Ft. Benning? Over 20 million. Know how many people died on those jumps? Six. That's like winning the lottery twice. You aren't dying today. You aren't that special."

Special has one meaning, but two opposite uses. Since special just means something unusual, or of note, it can mean "good special (unusually talented)," or "bad special (unusually late to class every day)." The fact is, you are probably not that special. In either direction. If you are in one of the top 25 economies in the world, even at the bottom of them, you are already doing better than most of the planet. If you are in the top 51% of your class, you are already one of the lucky ones. We often lose sight of this because access to successful people (or fakes pretending to be successful) are so easy to find nowadays on the internet and through social media. We see so many "special people," and wish we could be among them.

Do not play the "comparison" game, especially with people whom you do not get to see their whole life. You only see the good parts, with all the rough edges edited out. Don't worry about being special, and instead focus on where you are "above average" and work on those: improving your strengths (the good) and patching up your weaknesses (the bad). Don't worry. You aren't dying today. You (probably) aren't that special.

It is OK to hate school, only if you are good at it

Confession time: your old man never liked school as a kid. I liked reading and I loved learning, but school felt like work and very rarely clicked with me. I remember once having a report due on something I was not interested in, but I was allowed to use the interactive encyclopedia CD we had to do research. I spent the entire day, easily over six hours, reading about giant squids and the historical practice of drawing sea monsters on old sailing maps. I even wrote a report on this practice in a future class. The actual report I was supposed to be doing? Cannot remember it for the life of me and likely got a C or less after doing only a few minutes of reading.

School as it is structured in the 20th century is not very well suited for every personality type, and for very few male students on top of that. However, this cannot be an excuse to do poorly. I left high school with middling grades and my first few years of part time university classwork while in the army were equally mid (a 2.6 GPA, if I remember correctly). However, I then realized that I would have to leave the service and that if I wanted to go to graduate school in Korea, I would have to get my grades up. In only 14 months, I switched to full time evening classes and even retook my two lowest scoring courses on my own dime to get my GPA up to a 3.4. Not great, but good enough to squeak by into Korea's Ivy league where I got a 4.28 upon graduation.

Throughout this process did I learn to love school more? Nope. Still hated it. Still hate it to this day. However, I got good at it. Hating school and then doing poorly will just make you sound like a loser. No one will feel sorry for you nor will be willing to throw you a lifeline in such a situation. If you love school, but are bad at it, at least a teacher is likely to help you or take pity on you. Now, if you hate school, but are good at it? It does not matter what anyone else thinks or says. You got the grades to back you up. It's only OK to hate school if you happen to be really good at it. Put in the work to get those grades up to shut the haters up.

Chapter 2: Surviving Puberty

"When I became a man, I put away childish things, including the fear of childishness and the desire to be very grown up."

- C. S. Lewis, English Author

"The age of puberty is a crisis in the age of man worth studying. It is the passage from the unconscious to the conscious; from the sleep of passions to their rage."

- Ralph Waldo Emerson, American Essayist

"No matter when you were born or where, puberty is the same. It's the same for your parents as it is for you - what's happening in your body dictates everything."

- Francine Pascal, American Author

Puberty hits boys later than girls, and in spurts

One of the odder things about our species is the fact that men and women are on different timelines when it comes to development: both physical and mental. A thousand years ago, boys taking a year or two longer to start puberty would not matter too much, as there was no tangible difference between a 20-year-old and a 22-year-old. However, with the invention of compulsory education, and standardized schooling for boys and girls, we suddenly had the concept of "coevals:" people of the same age being roughly the same level of academic, social, and professional development. A modern 20-year-old is a student, while a 22-year-old is likely a bachelor's holder who must now juggle a job, a social life, and car payments.

Nowhere is this more noticeable than in middle school. Not only are girls a year or two ahead of you in terms of academic ability, but now they are physically developing before you. Just as they are getting the physical features that make you more interested in them, they are now liking the physical features in boys who look nothing like you. Kind of sucks. Worse still, this is a process, which both starts and stops at will. Because of this, it is possible for you to catch up with them at 13, but it may be 14. Or 15. For some unlucky guys, at 16. My dad did not need to shave regularly until he was 20. By contrast, his younger brother was bald at 20. Puberty hits every guy differently and at different times. It's OK. Do not pathologize the weirdness and awkwardness of the situation. Every guy who has been a man went through the exact same thing. Whenever it hits, however it hits, there will be women waiting for you on the other side. I promise.

Puberty affecting sleep

The first place that puberty really messes with you is your sleep schedule. Babies need lots of sleep. Children need only a few hours less, but are full of energy and try their best to never sleep. Teenagers need only an hour or two less, but their bodies are constantly tired and getting out of bed some days is like trying to function on a quarter tank of gas. What gives? Some of it is just your body growing exponentially quicker. The bigger you are, the more energy is needed to grow an inch taller. And you will be adding extra inches to your height for a good chunk of time. This is very resource intensive, so keeping you still in bed helps conserve some of that energy. Being a little careless with energy helps keep kids alive when you might have to run and hide from bears or tigers. Saving energy until you actually need it helps teenagers preserve it all for the hunt to keep their families fed and alive.

The other reason is to keep you from getting too excited. A very excited little boy is going to be rambunctious and maybe a little annoying, but he is not likely to kill anybody. An overly excited teenager is likely going to be angry, horny, or both. Either way, a lot more trouble can be had by a 15-year-old than a 10-year-old. One way to deal with this is to just figure out what your body is trying to accomplish. Is this a growing phase (growth spurts, leg pain, etc.) or is it trying to keep you calm and unexcitable (feel lethargic)? Understand what it is trying to help you with and avoid doing activities that are going to exacerbate the issue (i.e., don't go running around during the recovery phase and don't play or watch anything titillating during calming phases). This too will pass. Getting all of your work done first is vital, but getting some rest is important too.

Morning wood and wet dreams

Speaking of puberty and sleep: let's get awkward. Your body is going to do a lot of involuntary things. You have some agency in avoiding stimulation (e.g. "don't look at the girl in the skirt because that will make things worse"), but you have very little control at all about when you get an erection. It is an involuntary reaction to stimuli and, unfortunately, your pubescent brain is actively trying to find as much stimuli as humanly possible. It's hard (pun not intended), but at least you can choose to look away, think about sports, pinch your leg, and hum a tune in your head to slowly get back to normal. While you are asleep? It is much harder (again, sorry) to avoid this situation.

So, what is going on with erections while you sleep? There are actually two different phenomena going on at the same time that is resulting in this issue. The first is basically a "hardware test" by your brain. As your body goes through sleep cycles, one of its tasks is to check and make sure everything is functioning as normal. Your eyes, heart, lungs, etc., are all going through quick little tests to ensure that nothing is damaged and needs to be repaired while you are resting. It is not dissimilar to how your computer acts during a reset. When you turn the PC back on, it takes a minute to "warm up" as it checks the function of all its physical hardware pieces to make sure everything is connected, they all can receive and send signals, and nothing vital to starting up is malfunctioning. In the case of your private parts, it just so happens that this check generally happens at the end of a sleep cycle. This is important because your brain generally wakes up at the end of a cycle. The result? Waking up with a problem.

The other phenomena at work? Well, your brain is trying to problem solve while you are sleeping, putting you into random situations pieced together from things you were thinking about while you were awake. What were you thinking about? At least once or twice (or 40,000 times) a girl you fancied entered your mind. Your dreaming brain assumes she is a problem to solve and... well, you can guess the rest. Both cases are your brain trying to help, but missing the mark slightly.

Puberty affecting how you smell

Of all the ways your body changes during puberty, the most counterproductive one is making you stink. Great, I finally like girls and they kind of like me, and I smell like old cheese, soggy cheerios, and wet dogs. It seems like a cruel twist of fate, but like with a lot of things our bodies do, there is a method to the madness. The first reason why we start to smell is that our bodies need to signal to potential mates that we have, in fact, reached puberty. You would think growing two feet taller, a beard, deeper voice, and body hair would be a give-a-way. However, thinking about it in this way is another case of failing to cross sex mind read. You see, women can tell certain diseases and immunities from men's sweat. It's true. As crazy as it sounds, women are able to tell if you would help produce safer and healthier babies from the way you smell. Wild.

However, this ability requires you to separate from the general funk that you smell like versus when you go without showering. While a little bit of sweat lets her know if you are biologically compatible, too much grosses her out. Which brings us to the other great use of teenager stink: it makes you take personal hygiene seriously. Your mom tells you to shower every day, but it is when you start to smell bad and are worried about missing out on girls that you start to take cleanliness seriously. The fear of grossing them out makes you keep yourself clean. And you know what girls really like in their men? Someone with the discipline to keep themselves neat and tidy. Your body is just trying to help you, bro. Genetics play a big role as well, with some people just smelling worse than others. However, daily showers, deodorant, and always cleaning your feet/shoes will help regardless of your natural inclination to stink.

Shower twice a day, every day

You do not realize how much you stink. Literally. Your brain starts to filter out old information to favor new things, so the longer you stink, the less you realize it. This can be a big problem as you go through puberty, as your body starts to smell more and in new ways, but then starts to help you ignore it. You know who cannot ignore it? Women. Girls are really in tune to smells, as they can help tell them a lot about the potential health of a mate. However, they are also very sensitive to signs that men are mature, dependable, and self-reliant for basic survival skills. You know what screams "I am an immature kid who is unreliable and needs mommy to force me to do basic survival things?" Not showering.

So, how often do you need to do it? Twice a day, every day. I know that sounds like a lot, but it is the only way to be sure that you are clean and not just think you are because your brain stopped telling you that you reek. Once in the morning, once after school. This is flexible, so if you have a sports thing to do or the gym to go to, you can schedule one of your showers for right after that. Also, do not put it off until later that night, as you will just make an excuse not to do it, and now your bed will smell like garbage, making it even more likely that your brain will filter that smell out. Wash twice a day, every day. Put on deodorant after that first shower. If you are blessed with the genes that make you not need deodorant every day, count your lucky stars, but also you should wear it to school, just in case. As puberty develops, you might just suddenly get hit one day with a bad case of the stinky pits, and if you have the good hygiene habits already built up, you will be good to go.

Puberty affecting your hair, voice, and looks

The much more noticeable change with your appearance will be your hair. It will start to grow in basically every single place it has not grown yet: back, arms, legs, face, chest, you name it. Genetics plays some role, with some ethnicities getting more, less, rougher, or smoother hair depending on what our ancestors needed some time about 4000 years ago. This also includes color, so while I am as hairy as the average middle-aged tiger, it is all blonde so hard to notice. For you, it may be darker and stand out more, even if you physically have fewer hairs. Regardless, women seem to not necessarily like nor dislike hair itself. Rather, they like the idea of you being clean and kept. This is going to vary depending on what your situation looks like, but it does mean to not fret if you have way more or way less hair than your buddies. Guys care, but chicks care far less.

Your voice is a much more prominent feature of male puberty that does seem to have some correlation with female approval. Women tend to like men with deeper voices, but it is not necessarily linear. So, "very deep" is not necessarily way better than just "normally deep." Rather, just having a "deeper than a prepubescent boy" level is normally good enough. Again, think about why your body is even doing this: it signals to women that you are physically maturing. Think of it kind of like a peacock tail, but much more subtle. For the bird, its tail is all it has to show off and attract a mate. For you, your voice is just the tip of the iceberg. "Hey ladies. It's been a while. Can you hear? I'm something of a man now myself. How much of a man? Well, wouldn't you like to know." Or something like that. I am sure your aura is somewhere south of that, but you know what I mean. These changes combine to make you look and sound significantly different before and after puberty. For most of us, change in a good way.

Use hot and cold water when shaving

When I joined the army at 17, I shaved maybe once a week. While I was able to grow a full blonde, brown, red, and gray beard if given enough time, I took after my dad with a fairly young face that took its sweet time getting to a "five-day shadow." However, at boot camp it did not matter if you had nothing on your face, you were shaving it. The first thing you are going to need to figure out is how sensitive your skin is or is not to razor burn. I just used the same two blade cheap disposable razor as every other Private at the time. Only years later would I discover that this was actually really bad for my skin and I was constantly breaking out into acne and getting bumps all over my neck. Switching to an eclectic razor helped me, so too did just using a better-quality razor. Figure out what kind of skin you have and what works best for it.

One tip you can use regardless of razor, is to wash your blades with very hot water, but wash your face with ice cold water. After shaving, you will need to rinse off your blade to remove hair, dirt, dead skin, etc. Doing it with cold water may cause the edge to become duller just a little bit quicker, but the bigger issue is that it will eventually start to smell like wet hair. Washing it in very hot water fixes both of these problems. Conversely, you should use very cold water on your face after you have completely finished shaving in order to close up your pores. While shaving, your pores will open up, making it easier to cut hair, but also easier for dirt, bacteria, and dead skin to now cause acne on your face. The cold water closes them up and prevents this. Aftershave, face lotion, or aloe vera does the same thing if kept cold in the refrigerator. Remember, hot for blades, cold for face and you will save your skin a lot of issues.

J. E. Bassette

Do girls even like beards?

You have likely come across the "Giga Chad" meme at least once. It was a photograph of a real person at some point in time, but was digitally altered to make his already very masculine features even more dramatic. Guys saw it as the ultimate "guys' guy" and wished that they could look like that. However, one cross cultural survey of women found that the aggregate score for his picture was a full point and a half lower than what men rated it. Why? Part of the problem was that, being digitally enhanced, women found a slightly "off" feeling to his features. Another, much bigger issue, is that women do not find all masculine features equally attractive. This sounds crazy to men, as virtually all of us find every feminine feature attractive, but women are wired a little differently from us.

Let's take the example of beards. They are very tied to masculinity, as (outside of serious hormonal conditions) they are something only men experience. With not even a word exchanged between you at the distance of several meters away, a man can be very easily spotted by his beard. So, women must love them, right? They kept mating with men who had them, so they must find them attractive. Well, only some times. Some women like them, others hate them, some only like stubble. What gives? Well, what women are actually attracted to are signs that you are disciplined, well put together, healthy, and proactive. You can signal this in many different ways, from clean shaven all the way to having a neatly maintained Viking beard. This is the reason why an unkempt beard (a "neckbeard") is an insult and is generally the only style that does not have any female fans.

The fact is, beards and other very masculine features are cool to us guys because they were useful to pick up mates in another way: fighting. Men with beards suffer 30% less facial injuries. Strong jawline, shoulders, necks, etc., all mark someone as having strong bones and muscle structures. Masculine features are not always a peacock's tail to attract women; they are sometimes warning signs to other men. Keep that in mind when deciding on a look for yourself.

Puberty affecting "monkey butt"

One place where puberty is going to hit you kind of hard, that you have not prepared for, is your butt. Hair is going to grow in all sorts of uncomfortable and seemingly useless places to include your bum. There are two ways this is really going to make being a teenager a pain in the... well, you know. First is that even when wiping with toilet paper, it is possible that some of your business is going to get matted up in your booty fur. When you start to sweat down there, especially in the summertime, this will cause you to literally smell like crap for the rest of the day. Not ideal. The second way this affects you is that when you start to sweat, it causes the skin down there (especially between your butt and your other sensitive area) to get wet and waterlogged before rubbing against the hair and the inside of your underwear as you walk around. The result? The skin literally rubs off and starts chafing that would kill a buffalo. Plus, all of the salty sweat begins dripping onto the raw wound. In the army, we called this "Monkey butt syndrome." It's the worst.

To deal with the first problem, start carrying baby wipes in your school bag. After wiping with toilet paper, finish with the baby wipe to make sure you get the hair cleaned too. Don't throw it into the toilet, as it just clogs up the sewer system. Yes, even the "flushable" ones. For the second problem, we used baby powder in our pants to soak up sweat, smell, and have a soft barrier to prevent chafing. You will smell vaguely of babies, however. Who knows, maybe chicks dig that. Regardless, "smells vaguely of babies" will always be better than "smell vaguely of poo and waddles like a duck" any day of the week. Before you complain that guys have it tough in this department, keep in mind that pubescent girls have their own pants related hygiene issues exclusive to them, and it is a whole lot worse. Just plan ahead, keep clean and dry, and take care of your body. You will do just fine.

Puberty affecting where you look at girls

With puberty affecting the way you look, and the way that you look, it is only fair that it would also affect where you look. You will start to notice a change in your visual activity, almost like a reflex. You will still look at their eyes. After all, women's eyes are simply the best. However, your brain will start to worry. "Are you sure you are still talking to a girl? Yes, she sounds like a girl. Looks like a girl. Smells like a girl. But can you be certain? You better look at her boobs, just in case." When you first see them? Boob check. After about thirty seconds of conversation? Boob check. When she glances down at her phone to check the incoming text message? Boob check. What is going on?

Your brain has a built-in dopamine reward system that makes you want to do things that the brain believes will lead to greater reproductive success. This is actually the same part of your brain that reacts positively to eating chocolate, holding a baby, and landing a sick kick flip in front of your crush. Now, imagine you could get that feeling without the calories of the chocolate, the responsibility of holding the baby, or the risk of landing the kick flip? You guessed it: boobs. You will also notice this for her butt when walking up some stairs, she leaves the room, or has to pick anything up. Your brain says "Let's double check that she's a girl, and I will buy you chocolate if she is." Again, your brain is just trying to help you out. Women who had these bodily features were more likely to survive childbirth. So, your brain is just making sure that you are the kind of man who likes those healthy body features. Just try not to make her feel self-conscious. You know how awkward you feel? It's three times worse for her. While you know that you are doing it reflexivity as a dopamine reward response, she does not know that. Women have an entirely different internal reward system. Be a little mindful of her situation, as you would like her to be for you.

You will never be more self-conscious than right now

I want you to take a second and think of this hypothetical: let's say you are a deer. You know that some humans, even most humans, like to look at deer. They smile, grab their phone, and stare at you longingly. Now, you also know that some humans, not even a lot, just some, like to smile at and take pictures of deer because they plan on shooting them. How confident would you be to know the difference? How much risk are you willing to take on your ability to distinguish between the two? Now, what if you are a very young and inexperienced deer? Can you kind of see where I am going with this?

Girls have their own dopamine reward system, but it is far less visual based than boys. This means that they have no idea why you stare as much as you do. They literally have no personal experience with why your brain is telling you to do that. They do know that some men stare for far less charitable reasons. As the fairer sex, girls have to be afraid of the minority (maybe as few as 2 or 3%) of men who are literal monsters who stare for the worst possible reasons. They do not have the experience or confidence to tell between the two groups, so are very vigilant. This is doubly so if they have any personal experience with that bottom 3% of men. You don't understand what is going through her head in the same way that she does not understand what is going through yours. Meet her half way at the fact that you, maybe for the first time, worry about how you look. Are you cool enough? Handsome enough? Tall enough? Buff enough? This level of self-consciousness will fade when you have more experience, but that experience is very different for boys and girls.

Hating your body is understandable, but a little misguided

I remember even back in the 1990's there was the idea that puberty made girls hate their bodies, but that this didn't affect men. On the female side, body dysmorphia (the phenomenon where you do not accurately perceive your own physical features) is a common issue. Biologically speaking, it makes some sense. Women know that men are very visual creatures, so they put a lot of stock into women's looks. Puberty is both making girls knowledgeable about this fact at the same time their body starts changing in weird and unpredictable ways. Couple that with the natural levels of neuroticism and worry that girls already have, and this creates a recipe for body fears.

However, to think this is only a women's issue is lacking a little empathy or insight. Yes, with their lower levels of neuroticism and higher levels of risk taking, boys are less likely to feel body dysmorphia. But less does not mean never. With an increased importance of material signs of wealth (like nice clothes and hair), along with good gene indicators (like height and jawline), it is very easy to see young men who hate their bodies and are trying to compensate for it. Even I went through a phase where my weight, yellowing coffee teeth, and bald head really bothered me. Still does sometimes. After all, I know how much I love my wife's hair and body, so she has to look at me the same way, right? Well, actually, no. While young girls may put a little more value in appearance, women tend to favor it much lower than other features like kindness, competency, skills, occupation, etc. Men think women care more than they do because we care a lot. In both cases, worrying about your body makes sense, but do not let it consume you. Just be a better version of you, and not try to look like someone else. Everyone can do the former, and very few of us can ever pull off the latter. No one is ever born in the wrong body.

The difficulty not staring at girls and ad companies

You know who intimately knows how much your brain likes to reward looking at woman shaped things? Ad companies. It has been a back-and-forth struggle between ad agencies and broadcast censors since time immemorial. Selling soda? Pretty girl. Selling burgers? Pretty girl. Selling a dating app? Believe it or not, pretty girl. That code was cracked long ago. Just look at old Greek statues, renaissance art, or the pictures that soldiers drew on the sides of their bombers. Girls get guys' gazes.

That does mean you will be inundated with distractions. Everywhere you look on TV, the internet, and even billboards on the side of the road you will find someone trying to draw your attention to something using someone. If you are trying your best to learn not to stare, as not to "spook the deer" or real-life women you meet, these companies are not making your job easy. Likewise, you may trick yourself into thinking that, since these are just pictures of girls and not real ones, that it does not count. But ask your brain if it counts. It offered you dopamine and you took it up on the offer. Now it knows that you will react to that in the future. Thanks, brain.

I know it's hard, pun not intended, but you really have to learn to not stare as much. It will take your entire life, and even then, only becomes manageable, not easy. However, you will one day find a girl who does not mind the stares (although she will likely call them "longing glances"). If you fill up on the junk food of billboard girls, you'll not be able to enjoy the steak of your future deer/wife. Don't let the ad makers win.

Puberty affecting schoolwork

At the time of your life when you need to study the hardest and best prepare yourself for the job market, your puberty idled brain decides that school sucks and that it would rather sleep than do homework. Great. Once again, it thinks it is doing you a favor, rather than sabotaging your success. First of all, school is getting harder and the structure, lessons, level, and style were all literally not made for you. As stated before, it was generally designed by women for girls who are all hitting puberty and maturing faster than you are. Add in the fact that your brain can either respond to this by being angry or being lethargic and you can see why it would make this decision.

The second reason may be even more emblematic of the weird position modernity is putting you in: your brain thinks that sitting around thinking all day is wasteful, because it uses up calories when you "should be" out hunting to replenish those calories. From your perspective, you are getting smarter to make you better prepared for the future. From your brain's perspective, you are draining the gas tank with no obvious indication that you plan to refill it and even have a future to begin with. For what it's worth, you are not alone. You feeling angry, bored, or disinterested is a very common issue for young men going through this. However, it is never an excuse to not do your best. As an adult, you will still have to deal with environments not made for you, boring office stuff, and the itch to go out and do something, but the obligation to sit and think hard. Get in some practice now and understand that your brain is just trying to help you out. I know you can do it and have a great future, whether your brain knows it or not.

You are not cool, but neither is anyone else

At some point during puberty, you will be hit with one of two very real developmental dilemmas: either you will realize that you are not very cool and become overly concerned with being seen as cool, or you will actually think you are cool only to realize years later that you were actually very very very lame. For the latter, you just need to keep some humility about you. You are not the main character of the world and you are not special; the good kind nor the bad kind. For the former problem, it is your brain trying to make sure that you do not miss out on any social benefits that come with being one of the "cool kids."

Humans are social creatures, so being accepted by our peers means that we are more likely to survive. More allies mean more people to help on the hunt, to save you in a fight, or take care of your family should something happen to you. However, more so than even acceptance, your pubescent brain wants something even more socially important: praise. To be valued by your peers means not only access to more allies, but access to women. Girls seek the approval of their friends for their choice in boyfriends precisely because having a mate of high status means greater potential support for their future children. Guys? Your friends only care if your girlfriend is hot or not. For girls? They need their boyfriend to be seen as "cool," as that means greater safety in the future.

Your brain knows this and is very worried about being uncool. The dirty secret? Everyone, even the "cool kids," are constantly paranoid about this, because what is or is not cool changes all the time. The fact is, none of you are actually cool, but are too inexperienced to realize this. Don't stress out about it, as the coolest kids are the ones who always keep their cool.

E-girls are not real relationships

I liked my childhood, for the most part. We never had a lot of money, but were fairly safe, had access to some forms of entertainment, and a halfway decent roster of friends. However, technology was very expensive, and I had to get my own job at 12 in order to even afford the, relatively primitive, games of the time. Nowadays, gaming has become the hobby of the middle and upper-lower class. No longer is a PlayStation the thing that the one rich kid in your friend group has. It has become omnipresent. Just like the internet. It used to be only for the very wealthy and very nerdy. Now? All your friends are online.

For all of the jealousy I could have about your access to technology, there is one thing I am glad did not exist: E-girls. What if we could combine your three favorite things (games, the internet, and girls) into one commodity? That sounds great, right? Well, going by how much money people throw at them, it would seem that many lonely men feel the same way. The reality is, this is just an easier to access version of a stripper who is pretending to like you in order to get your money. The pretty streamer online is not actually that pretty (make-up, filters, and playing into the specific features that young men find attractive) and are optimizing specifically for lonely men who want female attention. In the past, you had to actually go out of your way to head to the dangerous part of town to see a stripper. Now? The internet brings her to you, and can even make it seem like you have a chance with her. You give her money, and she says your name! She smiles, says thank you, and makes it feel like you have a shot. You do not. Just like the stripper never actually liked you, the e-girl only knows you as a screen name. None of this is real. Real girls may not look that pretty without all the filters, but they can actually like you for real.

Spray cologne on your chest

Should you wear cologne? After all, all of the girls at school that you like always smell really nice. Surely, they want a guy who smells nice too, right? Yeah, sure. As long as you are showering every day, you will not smell bad and likely smell like grapefruit or whatever Irish Spring is. Already, you will be ahead of the pack. However, should you spend a little extra money and get some cologne to complete the package?

Two things to keep in mind: first, don't over use it. Remember how your brain filters out familiar smells? After one spray, you only smell nice to yourself for half a second. Because of this, we sometimes put on two, three, four, or even more sprays. You only need one. That's it. It is already premeasured and designed to give you as much as you need. You are not trying to cover up your stink, as you should already be showered after all, and are just adding a little extra spice.

The second thing to remember is to put a majority of the spritz on your chest area. Why? Well, where is her face going to be? Chances are her nose is right above chest level, meaning that should be your destination. That is why girls sometimes rub perfume on the back of their ears: because that is often our nose level. Notice, that also means if you put on too much, she will need to pull away from you, but if you only have on a little, she has to pull in closer to get a sniff. Cleaver, right? To accomplish this, spray a full arm's length away so that the mist hits the whole chest plus a little of your lower neck. Similarly, you can do the spray directly in front of you in the air and then walk into it. In both cases, a little goes a long way.

Intrusive thoughts

Have you ever been holding a knife and, for just the briefest of seconds, thought something really messed up like "what if I just stabbed somebody right now?" Or, maybe you were standing at the end of a cliff and your brain just decides "what would it be like if I just took a running jump off of this thing?" Or, have you ever been handed someone's puppy and your jerk of a brain just decides now would be a great time to think about the consequences for punting it like a field goal? You are the only one who does that. What is wrong with you? Nah, just kidding. Once again, it is your brain thinking that it is helping you out.

Your brain loves to problem solve and run scenarios quickly. Doing this allows you to come up with options for what to do in a new situation in a way that saves calories versus giving lots of concentrated contemplation about a particular issue in great detail. The downside of this process? Sometimes your brain will give you a possible option that sounds like the worst choice in a "choose your own adventure game." Why are they so extreme sometimes?

Well, two reasons: first, you are hormonal and getting physically stronger and bigger by the day. This means that you have some brand-new violent options that you did not have access to before and your brain is testing some of them out in its internal algorithm. Second, just like with dreams, your brain is filtering out most of it. You did not have one messed up thought, you had twenty different thoughts, but the messed up one stood out to you because it was messed up. You only remember it because it was so "unlike you." Don't worry. You are not a psycho if this is happening every now and then. Thoughts are just thoughts and your brain is just spit balling options.

No one looks out for the boys

Working for the governments of both the US and Korea at different points in my life, I was surprised at the number of programs designed specifically to help women and girls. It did not matter the field, the issue, or the seriousness of the problem, there was always an agency somewhere whose purpose it was to help out people in need using taxpayers' money only if they were from the larger 51% of the human population. On the one hand, you will hear about how bad women in the past had it. On the other hand, the person who is telling you this is your very successful boss and she had all sorts of help throughout many different phases of her career. Likewise, you will be told that this is fair because men had it so good in the past. This will likely be from some guy who did have it good, and is going to share none of it with you.

The fact is, we humans (despite everything you may have been told) greatly favor women in most of our decision making. Every large-scale test of human psychology has confirmed that we, regardless of sex, have a built-in "women are wonderful" bias when it comes to wanting to help others. There are a few reasons for this. For one, they can actually have children, making us instinctively protective of them and much more willing to sacrifice our young men. Source: every single war in the history of humanity. Another reason is some men really did have it better in the past. Heck, even at present. The key being "some" men. It has always been a gross minority of men who benefited from these structures. Think about male dominated societies like some in the Middle East: yeah, that dude gets four wives. But doesn't that mean three dudes get none? The fact is, women think collectively about this issue (either all women must be ahead, or none are) and men think about it individually (how can men be ahead if I am not). Truth is, governments only care about one group, so don't look to them for help. Would you even respect yourself if all of your success came from pity? Instead, look out for your buddies, your future sons, your nephews, and any guy who needs someone to have his back. No one else will. And that's OK.

Men are like engineers; you either build or destroy

In the military, different Corps have their own insignia or emblems that are supposed to tell you about their history or mission. In the Infantry, we had crossed rifles, the ones used to win America's independence from the British. For Civil Affairs, we had a globe, torch, sword, and scroll to show the role we played as a bridge between winning hearts and winning wars across the world. My dad, though, was an Engineer. Their insignia was a castle wall. I remember thinking it was kind of lame compared to guns, rockets, or cannons like the other Corps. However, dad told me it had to do with why Engineers were added to military ranks in the first place: to build our defenses and to tear the enemy's down.

Within every young man, there are two Engineers: one who wants to build and one who wants to tear stuff apart. We all love to create a Lego city, and then to pretend to be Godzilla and smash it to pieces. But notice how when you are focused on building things, really in the zone, you are too busy to wreck stuff. Now think about how whenever riots happen, it tends to be people without a job or family most likely to start fires and destroy stuff. Those who are not building something for someone, will seek out something to break.

That's not to say breaking stuff is always bad. Think about how often we need to let off steam with some fireworks, a few rounds of Call of Duty, or when we actually do have to take up arms and bombs to destroy in order to protect the ones we love. Therefore, it's safe to say that both impulses are natural and are part of being a young man. The key is to know what to build and what actually needs tearing down. A good rule of thumb is that everything you build should be for someone, even if that someone is just you. And everything you tear down should be in service of protecting someone else. Just don't let other people hijack your destructive side into becoming a brown shirt or red guard for their loser political cause.

There is evil in all of us, and we must fight

Along with those two Engineers, there are two other forces inside of you and everyone else. There is another commonality between all of the world's great religions: every single one of us is born with the potential to be wickedly evil. Darkness in the spirit of those who only live to destroy is something that every child is born with. Only through constant vigilance, discipline, meditation, prayer, and the grace of God do any of us not become those monsters. There is a reason that we excuse troublesome behavior in children (like biting and hurting animals) that we never tolerate in middle schoolers: we can excuse children for not knowing any better and their dark impulses are just them running on pure baby survival instinct. After all, what damage can baby teeth actually do? For teenagers, however, we are very aware of what damage you could do if you gave into those impulses.

We read about the Mongols, the Nazis, or terrorists and think that we could never be evil in the way that they were evil. We like to think that if we were in their shoes, we would have been different. The reality is that the same darkness that took their hearts is always taking up residence in ours. The Mongols wanted glory and to feel powerful. The Nazis were angry at their incompetent government, depressed about the economy, and jealous of a minority group that was way more successful than they were. Most terrorists think they are "liberators" or "freedom fighters" who just have to kill a few more random people to finally be a hero. They are all humans at the end of the day. That same spirit of hubris, resentment, and bravado is within the human spirit itself. Be always vigilant that someone is not manipulating you into giving into that darkness. Especially not yourself.

Do not linger in dark corners, they always grow

How can we remain vigilant against the darkness in our hearts if it is inherently part of the human experience? The first thing to do is avoid dark corners. Sometimes these places are physical. Think of bad areas where the people who tend to be drawn to that dark part of themselves hang out: the druggies under the bridge, the street corner in the bad part of town, maybe even the café in front of the local university that is always going on about "the system" and how "somebody should do something about it." There are places where darkness likes company and it quickly spreads to those who have nothing to build, so are keen to find something to tear down.

Increasingly, these places are turning up online. It is one thing to avoid going to places where you know trouble will find you. It's another thing to have that trouble served to you through an invisible algorithm. Misery loves company and that darkness is pretty miserable. By having forums, websites, video channels, and even platforms dedicated to people who are perpetually unhappy, it is easier than ever for a dark corner to find you. Like most evil, it is not an explosion like a missile, but rather a poison that slowly grows and infects. What was once edgy and novel becomes boring and routine. Once darkness becomes routine, it becomes shockingly easy to do evil things. Part of being on your guard against the darkness is avoiding the corners where it likes to grow. In much the same way you would leave a neighborhood if you started to feel unsafe, click away from internet places where people seem intent on being unsafe.

Hey, Sport. It's Me, Your Dad.

Fight or flight instinct

Before I joined the army, I hoped that I was the kind of person that would be brave in the face of adversity. In my imagination, I am always the hero and very quick to spring into action and do the right thing. The reality is more complex. In most situations, your brain has to do a quick calculation: Do I stay and fight, or do I run and make a flight to safety? Complicating matters is your pubescent brain. Estrogen means women are far more likely to choose flight, as their safety and survival is often linked to the survival of our offspring. For men, testosterone tricks us into taking on fights that we probably should run from, but we need to give the women and children time to escape. It's not sexism; it's a survival technique that worked often enough in the past that it was bred into our genes.

But what if you don't stay and fight when it really matters? You probably have seen people run from fights they could have won, or not even trying to hold on for others' sake. Just as with heroes being able to pass on their genes, some cowards likely also were able to live long enough to breed some of that into us as well. How do you know you will do the right thing? You don't until you are faced with it.

We were on vacation in Indonesia when a monkey attacked my niece. Without even thinking, I immediately squared up and took on that primate like a champ. Would I have still reacted so quickly if it was a Gorilla? Maybe I will find out one day. Maybe. Until then, I will prepare my mind and my body so that if the fight takes place, I can fight to try and win, or fly fast enough to fight another day. You won't know how you would actually react until it happens, but you can train your mind and body to maximize your chances at success until then. Plus, the increase in confidence alone will make you at least feel like you have more choice and control in those situations.

J. E. Bassette

The utility of guilt and shame

I always hate it when women are mad at me. Be it my mom, my wife, or just co-workers, there is a certain type of personality common in many women where they cannot just be "angry mad," like we can, but are "disappointed and want you to really *really* know that they are disappointed" kind of mad. I have already apologized and thought we were working on fixing the problem, but they insist on still discussing it and refusing to move on. What gives? Part of it is that you are physically stronger than them, or will be pretty soon. The average high school boy has more upper body strength and height than 95% of all women. This is by design, as women kept choosing men bigger than them as mates. However, it means that they need to shame us into changing behavior because they cannot physically make us do something.

It sucks, but think about how useful it has been already in your life: I bet you are cleaner now than as a five-year-old, right? You make sure to put on pants before you answer the door, you remember to feed your pets, you put the toilet seat down, you carry your plate to the sink, you put on deodorant, etc. Why? Because mom would be mad. You do not want to disappoint her. It feels bad to feel bad, but that shame and guilt to do something you have been told to do in the past is very useful in shaping you into someone that another woman would like to live with one day. Feeling ashamed of who you are is not useful, but feeling a little shame or guilt for something you have done (or have not done yet) is a very productive tool for civilizing a young boy into a real man. So, thanks, mom, for the nagging. Kind of.

Short vs long term mating strategy

If I were to ask you whether "cute" and "hot" were different kinds of women, you would almost certainly say yes, but would have some difficulty explaining why. Let me help you out: "cute" is the girl your brain tells you would make beautiful babies and she would look equally great in a cocktail dress or flannel pajamas. Doubly so if it is just your oversized flannel pajama top. "Hot," by contrast, is something more primal, where your brain tells you both that she would make cute babies, and that your window of opportunity is very short to even try. The cute girl would be a great mate, but will take some work to woo her. The hot girl looks like she is already wooed and you better get while the getting is good.

We find women more attractive more often than they do for us. Makes sense, as they have far more risk involved with reproduction than we do, especially in terms of time, calories, and physical danger. Therefore, any time our brain thinks that a pretty girl is actually coming on to us, that she is as interested in something now as we are, your brain tries to get you to take advantage of the opportunity. The short term easy "hot" girl versus the harder long term "cute" girl.

Here's the problem: the clues our brain uses to determine this are all out of whack because of make-up, provocative clothing, and the internet screwing up our expectations about women. Why do you like girls who wear that pink blush makeup? Because women become flush when sexually aroused, and that make up is tricking your brain into thinking that she likes you in that way. Oops. Your brain makes the calculation, but gets it wrong more often than not. More tragic, is that the long-term cute girl will almost always be your better option, but your brain does not realize that in the moment because it thinks it is helping you with a limited time opportunity. "Nothing worth having comes easy," right? That includes mating opportunities.

Butterflies and porn addiction

Well, now that we talked about how women are presented can negatively affect your perception of them, let's talk about the elephant in the room. One hundred years ago, you would see a 10/10 hot and cute girl maybe only a few times in your entire life. Not having much exposure to it meant that benchmarking most women to that standard would be crazy. To you, the 7/10 that worked as a part time teaching assistant that you ran into once a week after church would have been the prettiest girl you got to see consistently. To you, she was the benchmark. There was no one else to compare to, so she would have been the top beauty in your eyes.

Today? Every 5/10 can look like a 10/10 on the internet. On top of that, every actual 10/10 is taking 1000s of pictures of themselves and posting them for the world to see every single day. Your perception of what is normal is skewed. Add to that the fact that most women in real life will treat you coldly or just ignore you (you are a stranger after all), but the pretty girls online will smile at you and even pretend to be attracted to you. The "hot girl" short term mating strategy kicks in and your brain tells you to spend more time online with "them."

The reality is that this is training you to not like actual women. Scientists found out which colors male butterflies were most attracted to and painted drawings of the "perfect 10/10" female butterflies. The result was that the males only wanted to try, and fail, to mate with the picture rather than even try with the actual real females in their cage. Some even stopped eating all together and died chasing a 2D fake "hot girl." Don't fall for the trap. Keep in the real world with real girls and set expectations more in line with the long-term cute girl. For thousands of years, men would have killed, and did kill, to get a girl as good as her.

There has never been a worse time to go through puberty

You probably noticed, but this sounds like one big trap. After all, the 10/10 hot girls (both real and fake) are not just on adult sites; they are absolutely everywhere. You see them on TV, in every magazine, in every game, on every social media site, and even on advertisements on the bus. "Sex sells," as they say, and it seems like everyone is trying to sell you something. It has always been bad, since every guy knows what will get your attention and has been abusing this knowledge since, at least, the roman empire. However, things seem particularly devious in the modern world. It is more constant, intrusive, and omnipresent. We go to a baseball game and the cheerleaders are hot, fun, lively, and 100% chosen to get your attention and make you want to buy stuff. Maybe a jersey? They do look cute in that jersey. $130? Did the girls make it by hand?

Even when you try to escape it, the temptation follows you. All of the girls around you see this too and notice that all the guys are drawn to it. If they want to be "competitive" many will feel pressured to emulate it, which makes it even harder for you not to notice. Others will do the opposite and try to make themselves as ugly as possible, and will then get mad when men completely ignore them. Or, they will never feel pretty enough, because even when they do imitate it the boys are never quite as interested. Remember the butterflies? There has never been a worse time to go through puberty than right now. You need to keep some perspective at all times and try your best not to get sucked in. Likewise, have some sympathy for the girls around you trying to navigate this as well. Try to find a girl who is trying to avoid the butterfly cycle who can help ground you in the real world. Be that 7/10 for each other.

Once you start, you never stop

I am going to be very honest with you. I will tell you the absolute truth, you will not believe me, and then you will admit I was right years later. Are you ready? You really should wait to have sex. I know your brain is telling you otherwise, trying its very best to get you to reproduce before you die of scarlet fever or get eaten by a saber tooth tiger. I know that your entire motivation to get out of bed in the morning, shower, go to school, and even try to get good grades at all is to increase your chances at, maybe, getting a girl. I completely understand and empathize with you. However, once you start, it does not get easier. For a good chunk of time, it will actually get worse. It will become your entire personality as you convince yourself that this girl will now love you forever and that times will always be this good.

She probably won't and the times certainly will not. You see, once may not be enough to actually procreate, so your brain knows you need to do it at least a few times over a couple of days to maximize effectiveness. To do that, it is going to lie to you about this girl. She is not perfect. She is just perfectly available. Times are not great. It is just a great time that you are having. And now that you have done it once, you will become even more obsessed with it and will start doing things, going to places, and risking it in ways that will make future you very disappointed in your lack of judgment. Again, your brain just thought it was helping. The jerk. How do you avoid this? Actually find the great girl first. Take time to fall in love and actually get to know her, problems and all. And yes, there will be problems. Learn them and build those great times together first before you are having sex. There is no going back once you do. Save future you from having to tell me I was right.

Testosterone dropping as you marry

Now, the fact that your sex drive will only get worse may make you a little worried about the future. If it is this bad now, and will only intensify when I actually start having sex, does that mean I will be a hapless pervert forever? Since the same testosterone that controls sex drive also affects my anger issues and potential baldness, does that mean I will be doomed to be a perpetually pissed-off pervert? Thankfully, no. While bad diet, lack of exercise, and environmental factors can cause you to have low testosterone early, you actually will slowly lower your T by being in a loving relationship.

As part of the cycle of boy - to man - to father, you will actually peak in testosterone in your 20's around the same time you should be getting married and having kids. These life changes will actually cause you to naturally lower your hormonal generation making you less aggressive, less risk taking, and less prone to hump anything you can. This works out for all parties involved, as even with the lower T, you will still be far more physically intimidating than your wife, more likely to take some risks when your family needs it, and more likely to get angry, rather than getting sad, in fight or flight situations.

However, you will also be gentler with your kids, less likely to hurt them or yourself, and be more likely to cooperate with the men around you (to include your sons) than compete with them for female attention. This may go some way in explaining why there are so many 40-year-old perverts who are unmarried or have no kids. They never fully grew up and are now stuck in an earlier life cycle. Likewise, it explains why some guys gave up early and look like unambitious slobs: they lowered T too early from a bad lifestyle rather than naturally.

Date your mom/sister

OK, I know you read the title and started freaking out. Do not worry, it's not what you think. Take a step back. Why do women's advice shows, newspaper columns, and even academics always give the worst advice about dealing with men? Because they are not men and are going purely off of instinct (if you are lucky), or bad past experience that has been twisted into dehumanizing dogma. They are not experts in men. Maybe in some aspects of boys, but not the whole complete picture. Have you made the connection now?

I, nor any of your friends, am not an expert on women. I have a lot of experience with one woman and, even then, I get stuff wrong all the time. You know who knows women a little bit better than all us dudes? Your mom. If you have a sister, her too. You should take advantage of their knowledge and experience while getting some experience of your own. Think of it like training before you go to a warzone, not after. The practice will save a life.

Once you start to become interested in girls, ask your mom or sister out on a "date." Pick a place that you think would make a good date, dress nicely, and let them know about your plan. The whole time, try to treat them nice by being kind and respectful. If you do not have a perfect relationship with them, it will make this an even better test of your ability to be a gentleman even in a bad situation. Also, ask for feedback on everything from location, clothes, conversation topics, etc. Finally, make this a regular thing. At first, both of you will think this is silly and have some growing pains, but that would be true for regular dates. It is better to make some mistakes and learn from them now than on your actual dates, right? Plus, women judge a lot about you based on how you treat the other women in your life, so best to improve these relationships at the same time.

You may think you're untempt-able, but you're not

Every now and then, I will be on a hot streak. I will be 100% in the zone at work focusing on some task and think that I am finally above the temptation of the feminine wiles. Locked in, and incorruptible. I was on such a hot streak in late 2007. I had been put into recommendation for early promotion to Sergeant (E-5) despite not being selected for Special Forces. Heck, maybe because I was not. I came back from selection 20 pounds lighter, but immediately started training again and jumped back into Infantry life full time. I was locked in and, soon to find out, heading to South Korea for my next duty station. I had a buddy talking about how hot the women are there, and I assured him that I was not even thinking about that: I was going there for work first and foremost.

My buddy then insisted on showing me a picture on his phone (we still had flip phones at the time) and assured me it was not pornography. Indeed, it was not, but it might as well have been. It was some random Asian model with long black hair, glasses, and a dragon tattoo up her thigh. I was locked in, alright, but no longer on the mission. In a truly pathetic display of late 19-year-old hormonal angst, I had that girl, and that tattoo, stuck in my mind for the next six months. Now, my wife does have the hair and glasses (occasionally), but no tattoo. It did, however, humble me in the sense that I thought I was above all the testosterone stupidity of my peers, only to then have all that override my brain for so long. I felt pathetic. However, I also felt human. We are all flawed creatures, right? Even Jesus was tempted while fasting in the dessert. If he was tempt-able, why wouldn't we be? Stay humble and ever vigilant.

Maybe, you are the one being seduced

Here is one from your grandpa: be careful of the woman who is trying to seduce you. I never really got the "talk" with my dad, as he had already done it so many times with my brothers that maybe he just forgot. Or, given that I was the chubby theater kid, he rightfully assumed that it was not going to be a pressing issue for me. However, he did give me one piece of advice: think about how you are going to react when you meet a girl who comes onto you. Your pubescent brain has run through the seduction scenario (likely incorrectly) a thousand times by now, but have you ever thought about the reverse? What will you do? I never had this happen. Not even once. I get why he was worried about it, however. He was an athlete on multiple different sports teams all throughout high school. In a small town, I am sure he was many girls' 10/10. Me? Not so much.

That being said, plan your exit strategy for such a scenario. Why would you want to avoid this situation? Well, combine what I said about short term mating strategy and combine it with the ideas of it getting harder to stop thinking about sex once you get it and how you are not untempt-able: give into her seduction and she will become your obsession for half a year. All of her problems will become your problems as you possibly make new ones together. Why is she seducing you? Maybe because you are just so hot. That's what your brain is telling you, in its short-term strategy mode. However, what if she is trying to get out of a bad relationship? What if she is getting over a break up? What if she just gets her kicks from this? That drama will become your drama. Best to avoid it from the very beginning. Have an exit strategy in mind and stay aware of your brain not having your long term best interest in mind.

Buy something you love one size bigger than you need

Finally, some puberty advice that is not uncomfortable tips about being girl crazy. The other big part of male puberty is that you grow so much and so sporadically. You may do all of your growing at 15, or maybe some at 14 and then again at 17. It almost feels random until you get all of it over with and start to come into your own right around 18 or so. However, you have likely gone through a lot of clothes during that time. You get a T-shirt of your favorite video game? You wear it four times and now you have to pass it down to your younger cousins. That $130 baseball jersey you had to have for the big game? You wear it for one season and now need a whole new one. Good luck getting mom to buy you another.

This is something all men go through during these teenage years. Doubly so if your weight fluctuates like mine did. What can you do? Until you stop growing, always buy one size bigger than you need. This allows you time to grow into it and get more utility before you have to go shopping again. I know, some clothes and some styles will not look good on you if they are too baggy, but I promise you that they still look better than one size too small. You feel me? Save yourself some money and your mother some frustration and just pick sizes that you will grow into. This gets complicated with shoes (sizes that are too big may cause ankle rolling or blisters), but maybe half a size here depending on what you will use them for. It's only about five years or so you have to deal with this, so just plan ahead and you will save a lot of time, money, and frustration.

Have at least two sets of nice dress clothes

What about when you finally stop growing for real? Any advice for clothes shopping? I am glad you asked. Whenever you find a perfect shirt, a comfy pair of pants, the best fitting Ts, or the snuggest socks, always buy them in twos. A common habit of many men is to wear our favorite clothes until we die. Or they die. Whichever comes first. I have "lucky shirts" that I wore for over 15 years. They are more faded than fashionable, but I could not care less: I love these comfort fits.

Buying all of your favorite clothes in sets of two helps prevent this, giving more actual life, flexibility, and functionality for clothing that you know you will get a lot of mileage out of. Additionally, you may think that you will just buy a new one later, only to find out that they do not make that item anymore, making you want to hold on even longer to the one that you have long past its shelf life.

Finally, this is useful because it takes a lot of guesswork from your clothing choices. Millionaires have dozens of suits and try to match them for every occasion. Billionaires, by contrast, generally have many copies of the exact same suit (or even just shirt and cargo pants). They know what they like, what is comfortable, and they like not having to think too much about what to wear each day. You are not a billionaire, but you can live that life-style right now. Sort of. Kind of. Just whenever you find a piece of clothing you love, always buy a spare and you will get more out of them in the long run.

You have more in common with a stranger today, than yourself three years ago

Have you ever heard of the Ship of Theseus? It was a Greek philosophy thought experiment. Imagine you have a ship that gets a little damaged and needs to be repaired, so you fix it. New bits of wood, but still the same ship, right? Right. Now, over time, imagine that every single piece slowly gets replaced one by one. At which point does this ship stop being the same one and begins to become a whole new vessel? One more twist: what if every time we repaired the old ship, we took the old broken pieces and then fit them together into a "new" old ship? Which is truly the original? When did the shift happen, if it did at all?

Your answer actually does not matter, because your body actually does this exact same thing about every three years or so (different cells replicate at different speeds, some daily and some by decade). Every single cell in your body slowly decays and is replaced by a new one automatically without you ever noticing. Some take years, others just days, but all are replaced. Are you a "wholly new" person? Maybe on the cellular level, but not on any practical level. Right?

There is one more place where you are very different from the "old" you every three years: you likely have very different experiences, expectations, and views than you did in the past. Think about it this way: how similar was 12-year-old me in 2001 to 15-year-old me in 2004, post 9-11 and the start of the Iraq War? What about 18-year-old me in 2007, a Sergeant and dismount Squad Leader in the army training people for that war in Iraq? They would not have recognized each other. Likewise, who you are at the start of puberty will be unrecognizable to you post all of that experience on both a cellular and mental level. Try to keep all that in mind when people talk about being "true to themselves," or being the "authentic you:" there is no "true you," except the one you create. Do not like the current you? Make a better one over the next three years.

Always be grateful, things could be worse

This will be very hard to do while in the middle of your puberty problems, but always try to be grateful. No matter how bad you think you have it, it could always be worse. In 2024 I ended up reading three very different, but interconnected, books by men whom I found to be very interesting people. Future Vice President JD Vance, Korean American Sociologist Robert Henderson, and renowned Economist Glenn Lowry. While unrelated on the surface (all different jobs, races, and hometowns), what they all had in common were stories about poor kids in bad neighborhoods that eventually escaped them through joining the military, going to university, or both.

What struck me the most was how similar some of their experiences were with mine. Many of the anecdotes about growing up poor resonated with my own experience, down to even memories of trying Dr. Pepper for the first time, wanting to go to fast food but not affording it, or having to get a job very young in order to even afford hobbies. However, there were always two clear differences: none of them had dads in the house, and all of them suffered greatly because of it. Even though on paper we had similar childhoods and even similar paths to success as adults, these two factors meant that my childhood was poor, but happy. Their childhoods were just poor. Even with all the hard work of their moms, it was not enough to avoid the pitfalls of drugs or abuse. No matter how bad you have it, others have survived far worse. Always be thankful for what you have, even as you acknowledge that more could have been useful. Remember: it can always be worse. Be thankful for what you do have, and build a better future.

Give your parents some slack, you are literally not yourself at the moment

It can be hard to give your parents a pass sometimes. Maybe they lose their patience sooner than would be ideal, or are harder on you than they should be. Especially if you have siblings, it will be easy to spot times where they would be given more grace than you were, or are able to get away with what you cannot. Some of this is down to human fallibility. Your parents are flawed fallen humans as well, remember? The other issue is that you might just be a little pain in the butt. Did you ever think of that? But seriously, your shifts during puberty are likely going to make you the worst version of yourself to have ever existed up until that point. Lord willing, the worst version of you to ever exist.

I remember getting mad at my dad once for having taken my older brothers to baseball games, but not me. I could see the posters, T-shirts, and cards that they had showing all of their adventures together at Baltimore Orioles games: reminders that dad loved them more than me. That is, until dad reminded me that he did try to take me to ball games, but I did not like going, thought they were too loud and too hot, and never showed interest in going again. Oops. I was not pleasant to be around during puberty and created the situation where my dad was being "unfair" to me. I was not being myself, so how could I expect everyone else to treat me like myself? Try to give your parents a little slack and treat them with grace yourself. You will only be a hormonal teenager for a few years, and then you can try to both be yourselves again.

J. E. Bassette

This too, will pass

At this point, I have written three fiction books dealing with teenagers as protagonists, with one more in the works. As someone who actively hated that time of my life, I wanted to focus on two themes that I thought were universally true for most teenagers across most cultures: sonder, that is the realization that you are not the main character of the universe, and the idea that young people really seem to think that the present matters more than it does. The past is important because it can help us avoid already proven potholes in the path of life and gives us context for who we are and where we are going. Likewise, the future matters, because you will spend a much larger portion of your life there than anywhere else at this point. The present? Not actually all that long, meaningful, or impactful in the long run. So, why do we care so much?

Yep, you guessed it: survival. Thousands of years ago, recording the past was difficult without literacy, so you have very little of it to go off of. Similarly, the future was very uncertain, with one wrong move now easily costing you your life. Why kind of wrong move? Maybe angering your chief by accidentally hitting on his girl. Or, messing up really bad in front of your hunting pack and now they don't trust you and will leave you behind to starve. Or maybe, you strikeout with one of the only five available mates in your little village and now you are going to die alone. Yikes! But all that pressure was for a "you" that doesn't exist anymore. Your "chief" will forget when you both graduate and move away. You will find a new hunting pack at university or your first job. There are at least a few more than five available women out there. The present will pass. It always does. You are not the main character of the universe, and your problems today are just as temporary as everyone else's. Stop putting too much focus on it, and just work towards the future.

Hey, Sport. It's Me, Your Dad.

Chapter 3: Motivation and Self-Discipline

"There is only one sort of discipline, perfect discipline."

-George S. Patton, US Army General

"The temptation to take the easy road is always there. It is as easy as staying in bed in the morning and sleeping in. But discipline is paramount to ultimate success and victory for any leader and any team."

-Jocko Willink, US Navy SEAL

"But the military taught me that people don't need motivation; they need self-discipline. Motivation is just a feeling. Self-discipline is: 'I'm going to do this regardless of how I feel.'"

-Rob Henderson, American Social Scientist

Learn to do things for yourself

When you were first born, you could do virtually nothing by yourself. Outside of breathing and pooping (and even then, you did both poorly) every single thing you had to do in order to survive was done for you by your mom and dad. And a lot of it was your mom. Hence, babies are able to recognize women's voices even while still in the womb. They can do nothing for themselves and will need protection, nurturing, and care until we are able to grow up. Now, that baby had every reason to need mom's help, but what is your excuse? Why do you need mom to do your laundry, cook your food, clean your room, and even remind you to bathe? When will you grow up?

Women are very in tune to how much work they will need to do as new mothers. Some like to say it was "society" that conditioned this, but one look at other mammals says otherwise: motherhood is a lot of hard work caring for a hapless child who needs all the help in the world. The last thing this new mom would need is an additional, much larger, baby to care for. Namely, you. If you even look like a man-child that will cause her extra work at a time when she actually needs extra help, her desire in mating with you goes down considerably. You are a risk to her and her offspring's safety, so best not to chance it. By the time you are interested in girls, you should no longer rely on one for basic survival. Before you get some lady in the position to become a mother, you should be in a place where you no longer need your own mother. Are you tracking? Do some growing up and learn to do things for yourself to be the kind of guy that girls want and need. You will also learn some self-respect along the way.

Try three times before getting help

Now, you cannot do everything yourself. There will be times when you are faced with a task that you simply cannot complete without some assistance. The difficulty is figuring out which activities are impossible to do on your own and which things just seem like they are too hard because you have never done them before. When you have to do something for the first time and it's hard, when do you know to give up or keep trying?

When I was a kid, I inherited all of my video games as hand me downs from my older cousins. What this meant was that neither my parents nor my older siblings could help me when I was stuck in a game. I had to do everything on my own because there was no one else who could do it. If it was impossible, I still had to try enough times to figure out that it was not possible. Stuck on a puzzle? We had to use the internet at the library, so I could not even look up answers most of the time. I just had to keep trying until it was time to give up.

For my son, I make him try three times before I help. I need him to figure out for himself if it is actually too hard, or if he is just looking for the easy way out of a situation whenever he finds any difficulty at all. A kid that gives up too easily is just as bad as a hapless one. He needs to try and, once we know it is not something he can just overcome by himself with a little more effort, then I will do it for him. Likewise, don't immediately ask your mom for help with something. Try it a few times and see if you just need to give it more time. When you do ask for help, take notes and ask questions so that you can do it for yourself in the future. Be training "future you" to be a better version of yourself every day.

Try to level up a little each day

One thing I really love about games is the sense of progression. It is very easy to feel yourself becoming stronger, smarter, and more capable. In reality, your body works this way, too. Every time you finish your homework, you get a little smarter. Whenever you finish your work out, you get a little stronger. Whenever you eat a good meal and get a good night's rest you get a little healthier. You are actually leveling up your body every single day. So, why does leveling up in a game feel fun and effortless, but "leveling up" in real life feels so much more tedious and annoying?

Part of the problem is time. You are leveling up your body slowly over the course of years, while it happens in minutes in a 40-hour RPG. You can see and feel the results of your effort quickly and immediately, giving you the dopamine rush to keep going and getting stronger. The "grind," as it were. In the same way that the grinder makes the sword tangibly sharper in just a few minutes, you can see your character improving without much effort. In real life, you must work, consistently, for months at a time to see the progress. And even then, it is often done in retrospect as you look at old photos of yourself or read old tests that once gave you trouble.

Finally, it feels different because in a game you are always moving forward. In real life, you can move backwards by being lazy, eating poorly, or partying too much before you even level up. It is possible to go months or years and actually "lose levels," rather than gain them. The secret to getting better is to just make sure you are moving forward, even just a little bit, every single day. Try to level up just a bit and you will eventually see the results. Set goals, ways to measure them, and milestones to check your progress. If you put in the work, you will see the results eventually and get that same dopamine rush of progress.

J. E. Bassette

Set short-term and long-term goals

Let's talk about those goals. Say you want to level up your body and get stronger: how much stronger? How will you know when you have leveled up successfully? The first thing you should do is set goals, a way to tangibly measure success. For instance, how will you measure strength? Maybe you can use pushups. How many can you do now? Let's say five good pushups. How many will you need to do in order to feel "leveled up?" Whatever number you come up with, let's say 50, you then want to pick another number closer to your starting point. Let's say ten. These are now your long and short term goals respectively.

Your long-term goal should be something that is a little out of reach for you at the moment. It should be aspirational enough that you will see it as a major accomplishment, but realistic enough to see through to the end. Likewise, your short-term goal should be something that you can incrementally update multiple times before reaching your long-term goal. In this instance, going from five to ten, then 15, 20, 25, etc. This will help make you feel like you are leveling up more quickly and motivate you to keep going until the end.

This can be done for any task, not just physical strength. For instance, if you wanted to write a book, the long-term goal would be to finish all 200 pages, but you would start with short term goals like five or ten pages at a time. Maybe you want to get an A on your math test? You can start by getting five more points each time you take the practice exams. By setting up these two-tiered goals, you will prevent yourself from the burnout that can happen with only long-term goals, while also making sure you do not settle for less than you are capable of with only little short-term goals. Think of a plan, put it on paper, and post it somewhere you will see every day, like your mirror or the back of your door. Make a plan, execute it, and measure the results and I will promise you that you will "level up."

Success is many small victories

After learning about short-term and long-term goals, you may already be able to piece together that most successful people did not start out successful nor came into successes easily. Likely, they had to overcome years of smaller short-term goals in order to even approach their current level of prominence. Do you even look at a famous athlete and wish you had their level of success? How many total hours of hard work did they need to get there? 10,000? 20,000? Do you wish you had all of that work to do? Well, all of that hard work was how they were even in a position to be successful in the first place. Even if luck played a large role in their achievements, a lucky (but unskilled) person would have fumbled their opportunity. It took both to be a success. When you look at Batman, do you envy his money and strength? It only cost him his parents, decades of training, and virtually every relationship he ever had. You may wish to have their longer-term success, but think about what short-term work got them there in the first place.

When you start trying to define success for yourself, think about all of the work you will do along the way. Do you want to be a doctor? Cool. Start setting up the short-term goals that will get you to the grades you need, then the school you will need, then the study habits that will get you the license you will need, and then the discipline that will give you the success rate you will need, etc. Every success is not the story of one lucky event, but many hundreds of short-term victories. Make sure to take every step along the way. It is not possible to be successful in big things and unsuccessful in smaller things, as it was the slow accumulation of smaller successes that created the big win in the first place.

Coming into money suddenly made me fat

Contrary to what you may fantasize about, people who win the lottery almost never end up happy. Many end up wasting it all (think about the kind of people who often play the lottery and how bad they generally are with money), or they get into gross dragged out legal battles with family that drives them to self-destruct. Plus, over half of it goes to the government in taxes. Yes, it is mostly a scheme for the government to profit off of poor people while cutting taxes to the poor. A back door tax, as it were. If these same people had just taken their lotto ticket money and invested it into anything else, they would likely have been better off.

I had my own real-life version of this. I grew up relatively poor. My folks were good with money, what little we had, so we still got food every day. Some days it was only one or two meals instead of three, but there was never a day with zero food. When I turned 12, I wanted a job at a paper route so that I could finally buy video games. Despite them being my hobby, I only ever got hand me downs from cousins and never played anything new, as mom and dad couldn't afford them. That changed with this job. I had the 12-year-old's equivalent of winning the lottery: 180 bucks a month, every month.

After buying all of the games I wanted, I still had money left over for candy, soda, chips, and everything else we were too poor to afford. Very quickly, I began to put on weight that I would not lose until I joined the army five years later. I had bad habits, so all that money just made me sicker. Work on fixing your character flaws now before you are successful. Otherwise, you will wind up worse than when you started.

Make an "I love me" book

Despite the Army keeping records of virtually everything, it had a very bad habit of losing important paperwork. Records of your metals, awards, and money always seemed to disappear every couple of years with very little effort to try and preserve any of it. After all, it was the soldier's responsibility to keep track of their own stuff. The Army called it an "I love me" book and was a copy of every single important document even issued to you. Smart soldiers had two: one that was the originals and was kept in a fire and flood proof safe. The other was a photo copy of every one of those documents, to include past versions if something was changed or updated. Whenever I had to eventually leave the Army, this book was able to show everything I had ever done for my country, as well as prove everything the country had done to my body. It kept honest men honest.

You should have your own "I love me" book. Even when you are young, you will have very important documents like your social security or citizenship numbers, birth certificate or family records, IDs, diplomas, transcripts, soccer awards, and dozens of other things. You may not realize that these things are important now, but keeping a record of them will likely help save you thousands of hours of work tracking them down in the future. Likewise, it will serve as a reminder of how much you have actually accomplished, both big and small, over the years. That being said, you should actually have four copies: 1. The originals in a fire and flood proof container, 2. A photo copy of everything in a binder or set of binders, 3. A digital copy and scan of everything saved to your computer, and 4. A copy of all those files on an external hard drive. Future you will love it even more than present you does. I promise.

Get a college education, even if you do not go to university

Now making up only 40% of new students, young men are slowly dropping out of higher education as a primary driver of their economic wealth. Is this good or bad? Both, I guess. College is becoming more expensive and less educational year over year. If a product is lower quality at a higher price, the responsible thing is to seek an alternative. The first option is a cheaper school. Going to a good college in a different state or country could cut your bill significantly, give you more real world experience, and become a useful line on your resume. For me, it was also a way to get into a higher ivy league level institution when my home country was less likely to accept applications from people that looked like me or had my work background.

The other option is don't go to school. At least, not a four year one. If the job you want requires a skill or ability, go just for that training. An Associate's degree or trade school may be the only formal training that you are required to attain, so save your money and just do that. Nurse, plumber, cop, and a thousand other jobs are offered for far less time and money investment than a traditional college route. Some high demand jobs actually pay to train you, so always look at the options available for your situation.

Finally, even if you choose no school at all, you can still get all the same information for free. Or, at least for very little. I bought myself a college math book and taught myself algebra for a College Level Examination Program (CLEP) test to save $2500 on the two mandatory math courses. I have a library card, Audible account, and book club that make sure I know all about business, psychology, sociology, theology, and music appreciation all without having to pay a school thousands of dollars for the same information. Only get certified on what you need for your job. For everything else, just educate yourself. Do what makes sense for your short term and long term goals, not just what your friends are doing.

Defining yourself by your job

I always find the question "tell me about yourself" interesting. They normally do not want to know about my love of history, my wife, my son, my tastes in food or literature, etc. This is a question asking about my job. When a girl's friends ask her about her new boyfriend, what is the first thing she tells them? For many young men, your job is your sense of identity, self-worth, and contribution to both your family and society. It makes some sense. After all, your job is tied to money, status, and respect, all of the things women generally like in mates, so it would make sense they kept mating with men who cared about their jobs. Likewise, every one of the world's great religions tell men to take pride in their work and to do it diligently.

However, when I was in the Honor Guard and had to bury dead soldiers, it was rarely men who died in combat. Truthfully, half of the people I put to rest were men who had taken their own life. Not out of PTSD or guilt, but out of a loss of self. You see, it was not 20-somethings I was burying, but 60-somethings. These were men whose entire sense of self was their job. The army was their personality and the service was their life's goal. However, if you are great at your job, exceptional even, doesn't that just mean you can retire early? It is bad to tie your sense of self-worth to an identity that leaves you the better you can do it. Take pride in your work and do it well, but do not make it your entire sense of self. Good jobs last 40 years, but a good family lasts almost twice as long.

Feeling accomplished through your effort

What if you could skip all of the hard work? If your sense of self is not directly tied to your work, can't you just take the easy way out all the time? Wouldn't just inheriting all that stuff you need or living off welfare be just as useful to living the good life? Take a look at your friends who play a sport, have an expensive hobby, or ride a nice bike. I bet you could tell, with only a little bit of effort, which friends had to pay for that equipment themselves and who received it as a gift or just got it for free. Generally, the kids who had to work for it, keep it in better condition. They remember the physical work it took to attain the money to buy it. They fear breaking it, losing it, or having to replace it early because its value is something they can tangibly calculate from their own hard work.

When I was in middle school, I was able to buy my own games and made sure to keep the disks clean, the controllers working, and even dust the console itself. I did not want to have to buy a replacement. In contrast, I was gifted a bass guitar by my parents, one of the most expensive gifts they had ever bought me, and I put in far less effort. Strings were a little dirty. I wiped it down maybe once every few months. I don't even remember when I last made sure to put it in its case after using it. I did not understand its value, as I did not have to produce it myself. Likewise, everything you eat will taste better when you can calculate the work you put into attaining it. Every game will become more precious. Every movie will be more memorable. You will want your car to last forever because you will know the hard work that took to procure every piece of it. Your hard work will make everything feel more like an accomplishment.

You too will die

At least once, you have likely run into the term "Memento Mori." It's Latin roughly meaning "Remember, you too will die." The story goes that when generals would return from successful campaigns, the city of Rome would throw lavish parades in their honor. Going through the streets, people would shower the conquering heroes in praise, flowers, and even gold. It was easy to let it all go to your head. It was not hard for some generals to think that they were the most impressive and important humans alive. After all, they were the heroes in the greatest empire on Earth, right? To combat this, some generals had one of their servants sit next to them during the parade and whisper "Memento Mori" into their ears: "You are not special. You are going to die one day, too."

Whether or not this was real and actually widely practiced or not, the lesson is more relevant today than even ancient Rome. Everyone gets their 15 minutes of fame and finally getting some wind at your sails can make you feel invincible. You may feel like you are ascending into greatness and things are only going to get better for you. Your girlfriend? Ditch her for a hotter one now that you are famous. Car? Upgrade to a Bugatti. House? Time for the mansion, baby! Stay humble. Even if you are on the rise, you do not know when the peak will be. It could be sooner than you think and now you missed a house payment. The car's impounded. You think the girl is staying? Do you really think the first girl is going to take you back? Remember: you too will die. Be humble with your victories and cautious in your successes. It will make you more grateful for them and prevent the backslide when the good times end. Be bold, of course, but if you are cautious and thoughtful in your ambitiousness then you will be humble rather than humbled.

J. E. Bassette

Reject passivity, seek responsibility

For most of human history, the assumption was that men were natural hunters. Whether it was in actual hunting, aggressiveness in the job market, or active and "take-charge" in the dating scene. The conventional wisdom was that young men are naturally forceful and on the move. While that was seen as beneficial in the past, it's now pathologized in the modern world. Hunting? Toxic masculinity that is destroying the planet. Aggressiveness in the job market? Male bravado that is bullying and marginalizing. Active in the dating scene? Sexist and misogynistic. The plan now was to force men to be as passive as possible in every facet of life, but particularly in schools and at the office. Every man was seen as naturally dangerous and bad if not pacified.

However, it worked a little too well. While boys certainly are active, young men seem to take to the passive life a little too easily. No more hunting? I guess video games for me. Cannot be proactive at work? Might as well be jobless, smoking dope at home. Pursuing women is evil? I guess pornography is good enough. We thought that men were naturally active and needed to be taught passivity. We never dreamed that men are naturally passive and were being trained to be active by the men in their lives who wanted competent sons and the women in their lives who wanted proactive providers. You will find many people telling you that passivity is good for you. Schools, politicians, and even role models will tell you that they are trying to make you a better fit for society. The reality is that most of us would be happy to do nothing at all. But not for very long. Only until we die of starvation or get so bored that life is not worth living. You must actively reject passivity and instead seek responsibility, as that will be a path of both growth and adventure. That is the kind of man every society needs.

The price of inaction is always highest

No doubt you have heard of the trolley problem at this point. The famous thought experiment where a train is on track to kill five people, but you have the ability to switch the track and save them, at the cost of one other person. What would you do? It was meant to be a moral dilemma about the nature of action versus inaction. Saving life versus taking life. Passivity versus active reasonability taking. Most laws actually favor doing nothing, so it seemed that this was the position, albeit not officially, of most people and countries. However, when Michael Stevens (you may know him as the YouTuber "Vsauce"), recreated this experiment in real life, he found that a vast majority of people did, in fact, flip the switch. Their rationale? To do nothing felt worse than to do the wrong thing.

I think most of us assume that making no decision is a compromise position. Your mom wants to know which color of sweater you want, but you have no preference, so tell her it does not matter. Either is fine. You are not choosing out of a sense of general neutrality. The reality is that it may not matter to you, right this second, but it is still a decision. It was within your power to make a choice and you chose not to. Maybe it would have been the right choice, or the wrong one. Or, maybe there was no right or wrong choice in this instance. However, you chose to have no choice: you rejected all responsibility for the decision. At the end of the day, no choice is still a choice, and it is often the wrong one. Not because you missed picking the right option, but because no matter how it turns out now, you will have to force yourself to pretend that you never had a choice to begin with. "I could not have saved anyone," you will lie to yourself. In reality, to make a choice and take responsibility for its outcome, good or bad, is the only way to never lie to yourself. Reject that natural passivity and accept radical responsibility even for bad choices. Making no choice, and then lying to yourself later, is the only truly wrong move.

Learning self-discipline

While little boys lean towards activity and young men towards passivity, both are missing out on the one thing that would make them actually great: self-discipline. The little boy will be too active to his detriment, hurting himself, others, and just staying up way too late and now cannot function properly at school. The young man will spend too much time at play, not enough at work, and it will negatively affect his money, stability, and relationships. Both could use the self-discipline to know when to work, when to play, and when to ask others for a little guidance.

So, where does self-discipline even come from? It is not natural; I can tell you that. Despite women preferring well-disciplined mates, it seems they were all men who were born a little listless and gained self-restraint through hard work and experience. I learned it through the army, where a lack of self-discipline was severely punished. Soldiers who cannot control themselves create risks to their squad mates, to the mission, to the civilians around them, and ultimately to themselves. I had these ideas beat into me over months of hard training and forcing myself to do the right thing even when I did not feel like it. Especially when I did not feel like it.

You may not need to join the military to learn these skills, but similar organizations have existed since elder hunters taught self-discipline to new recruits. Today, organized sports like soccer, or martial arts like Taekwondo, or camping and survival groups all teach these life lessons in a way that rewards success and punishes failure. You need both the carrot and the stick if you want the true lesson of self-discipline to stick: it is not just about avoiding the bad, it is also about maximizing the good. Seek out some hobby or activity that will force you to be self-disciplined and your chances for success will increase significantly.

Delayed gratification

A lot of important psychology literature is under scrutiny after the discovery that most of it is un-replicable (testing it again gives different results, meaning its scientific usefulness may be zero). One of the potential casualties of this was the famous "Marshmallow test." Here, children were given a marshmallow and told not to eat it. If they did, they would only get that one treat. However, if they refrained from eating it, they would be rewarded with two marshmallows. The real twist was that the children were being recorded without their knowledge and could even lie about eating it, if they wanted to. The test supposedly showed that children who could be self-disciplined enough to not eat it, and not lie about it, went on to be more successful as students and later were more successful as adults. So, what was wrong with the test? Well, since you are testing their outcomes as adults, it took decades to even test to see if it was correct. Additionally, most kids have low self-discipline, so it was not a great test of their adult performance if some learned this later in life and others never did.

However, let's not throw away the baby with the bath water. Yes, the test may have been flawed, but it did stumble on an important aspect of human nature: those that can refrain from pleasure now, for the promise of even greater rewards in the future, almost universally perform better as both students and adults. Remember all of our talk about sacrificing for the future? Turns out, this helps not only on an individual level, but families who sacrifice for the future, countries that sacrifice for the future, and civilizations that reject momentary pleasure now for better future rewards tend to thrive better. Don't eat the marshmallow. Wait for the second treat after putting in the work to make it yourself. If you can say "no" to pleasure today for a better payout tomorrow, you are already ahead of the hedonistic trap keeping most young men from becoming great men.

Sacrifice your 20s

If sacrificing for the future is so important, do we do it all the time? Is there never a time to enjoy the rewards of your labor? I am going to give you some advice that I never got until it was too late, but I had accidently already followed it: sacrifice your twenties. Ideally, the time to enjoy your rewards would be in your thirties and forties. During those years, you will have great kids to spend time with, you will still be slowly climbing the work ladder (so your income should be steadily growing), and you still have the youth and energy to enjoy life. However, that comes with two caveats: first, you have to already be at some level of success to even do this. Which leads to the second thing: you need to have spent your twenties doing everything you needed to be successful, which means very little time for play.

I joined the army at 17, so I had zero choice but to sacrifice some of my childhood and become a man a little early. In retrospect, I don't regret it. I have met men in their 30's who are still "growing up," while I was a team leader at 18, Bradley Commander at 19, and Sergeant of the Guard at 20. It sucked at times, and was not always fun, but I was sacrificing all of that fun in exchange for money, experience, and the foundations of a great future career. Even with the knee injury and having to leave the army early, I was then able to go to graduate school on the GI Bill scholarship and ended my twenties with a Master's Degree, all of my Ph.D. class work complete, and started a job as a university professor. I had to give up my 20's, but I entered my 30's as a husband, father, and with the most financial stability of any person in my family up until that point. Work hard when you are 20 to have real fun at 30. Do it the other way around, and you will look like a man child.

Hey, Sport. It's Me, Your Dad.

Things could be worse and will be better

It is hard to know where to draw the line when it comes to things like optimism and realism. On the one hand, optimists always seem to outperform their realist counterparts. However, many optimists have crashed and burned when their luck finally ran out. So, how are you supposed to situate yourself for actual success? Being thankful is a good place to start. When you realize, realistically, that you have good things going in your life and that things could be worse, you are more likely to both enjoy the present and have a better assessment about the future. Some people conflate being a realist with pessimism, but taking a completely honest look at your life, as it truly is, requires acknowledging the things that are going well for you.

Optimism is also useful for thinking about how things will be better in the future. Now, there will always be changes and tradeoffs. For instance, your financial situation will likely be better in the future as most people start out near the bottom of the income bracket as teenagers and slowly rise over the next 40 to 50 years before retiring. However, your body and health will likely do the opposite and slowly get worse over time. See? Tradeoffs. Being realistic about how good you have it now (you still have your health, for instance) will help you be grateful and optimistic about the future (I will be financially more stable). Remember to keep some of that optimism for the present (I will see improvements as I continue to work hard), and some of that realism about the future (my knees will get worse, so I need to plan ahead). Both perspectives are needed, but notice there is no place for pessimism. Winners are realistic about their lives, but optimistic about their power to improve it.

I am afraid to try something unfamiliar, but planning helps

With all of the talk in the book about the military, you may have assumed I was really excited about joining. The truth is that it terrified me. Not joining the military specifically, but trying anything new for the first time. I remember getting on the plane to fly to basic training and I had an awful feeling of dread the entire time. I assumed it was pre-training jitters, but the next time I had to go anywhere (this time to Advanced Individual Training), it happened all over again. Almost 20 years on, I still get those same jitters whenever I have to move houses, change jobs, or even go on a long vacation to a new place. Trying something new, without any of my knowledge or experience to draw from, is terrifying to me.

So, what do I do about it? The last time I had to do a major life change like this, buying a new car, I decided to arm myself with as much information as possible. My wife and I looked at all of the options for the price range we had. Together, we made a list of all the features we needed for a long term 12+ year car. We even picked out colors and looked at how well each of them did for things like accidental spills, mud, water spots, and anything else that could go wrong with a car. Then, we looked into how long the whole process of purchasing one would take and what to do with our previous car. By the time we finally pulled the trigger and bought the car, all of the mystery and guess work was taken out. I still had some jitters, but far fewer and much more manageable. Doing some research and planning ahead made everything much more tolerable. With an apartment to buy some time in the next few years, I will be able to test this process out all over again. Planning ahead will help you keep your head.

Decide if you are a work to time
or work to project person

I do not normally like working with other people. Not that I am not a team player, I do love working as a team, just that I do not like sticking to others' schedules. Whether it is in group projects for school or farm work with the in-laws, there seems to be two very different and conflicting personality types. Type one, let's call "work to time" people. Whether it is in time increments ("Let's take a break after one hour") or fitting tasks into time tables ("We don't get off until five, so no need to rush"), time people seem unable to get something done early or even finish before the deadline in order to relax a little. In school work terms, these are the kids who realize that they are on track to finish five days before the deadline, so slow down their work to finish, literally, "on time."

The other type we can call "task people." These folks will work to finish early so that they can either move on to the next mission or just get some extra rest. If it is lunch time, but there is only 20 minutes' worth of work left, the task person would rather eat a little late than to stop, eat, and then have to start back up on that last little bit of work. What a waste of time! As you may be able to tell, I am a task man. I would gladly work over time on Monday if that meant I got to go home early on Friday. I would skip every meal all day long if I could go home two hours early every day. Now, I am not saying that my way is the right way. Some "task people" can push their teammates too far when they just need a little break. Likewise, "time people" seem to be better about pacing themselves and not getting stuck in the "just a little more" loop that can end with burnout. Ultimately, what I am saying is figure out what kind of person you are and make sure you are not setting up your teammates for failure.

Happiness is a motivator, not a goal

The US constitution guarantees the right not to happiness, but to the pursuit of happiness. As a child, my mother explained it to me as "Some people will be unhappy due to their own bad choices. We can guarantee they can try to be happy, but it is up to them as an individual to make it happen." This may be the correct interpretation. Going by what many of the constitution's authors personally believed about providence, this may in fact be what those words mean. However, the older I get, the more I realize that there is a second more profound meaning in this right. Whenever you are happy, how long does it last? A day? A week? A month? When you get a new game, a new console, a new computer, whatever, how long does the feeling of happiness last? I dropped hundreds of dollars on a new PlayStation and I love it. But for how long? When the next one comes out, I am buying it as close to day one as I can. Why? Was the happiness fake?

The happiness was real, but your brain is not designed to feel happy all of the time. Your brain rewards you for doing things it thinks will help your survival, mating opportunities, or status. A new "anything" will be rewarded for one of these reasons. However, your brain also knows that it cannot let you feel happy for too long, or you will not be motivated to keep working hard and improving. You can love your perfectly prepared steak dinner, but that cannot last more than a day or you may not go get more food. Likewise, anything that makes you happy is just temporary motivation to keep improving your situation. Do not despair. Rather, accept happiness for what it is, and keep on the pursuit. If you want a more long term investment in this area, I would focus on "joy." That's the feeling that comes after happiness and stays much much longer.

Invest in habits that help long term

What are the best ways to make sure you can stay on that pursuit of happiness while also increasing your chances at finding actual joy? The first is to get into good habits. The best ones are the everyday tasks that slowly help us over long periods of time. For instance, brushing our teeth. Small habit, but it will not only help with other things like getting a girlfriend or keeping one, it will also save you in the long run from physical pain of teeth falling out, financial pain of fixing all of those problems, and emotional pain that can come from a loss of confidence due to a poor physical appearance. It is a habit, a small one, but the payoff is both short- and long-term self-improvement.

Other great habits? Exercise. Even just a little every single day. It will compound and grow with time, so 15 minutes every day will be worth more than running a marathon in just a year or two. Saving money. Same idea, just a little every day will add up and the habit will allow for more flexibility and peace of mind in the future. Saying "please," and "thank you," to everyone. It helps ease tension and make friends in the short term, but almost always leads to you having a more positive reputation and expanded network in the long run. Any good study habits, like setting aside the same time every day to get work done, will pay dividends. Finally, always being thankful and saying what you are thankful for out loud every single day. There is a reason why most religions require that you pray daily, or even multiple times per day, and say with your own mouth what you are thankful for. The people who do so are genuinely happier than those who do not. It is a habit that will make all of the other ones easier with time.

Always plan actions around your true goal

There will come a time when you have to make a decision about whether to stick to your plan, or change it for the sake of your goal. Let me give you a concrete example: you have been working your butt off to get the money to buy the car you wanted, but this has cost you time that you had originally wanted to spend with your girlfriend. Pause for a second. Why did you want a nice car? If one of the reasons was "in order to get a hot girlfriend," then you are literally sacrificing your goal for the plan. Not a very smart thing to do.

Whenever you start a plan, make sure you are prioritizing the goal over the plan itself. I get it. You put a lot of time and effort into that plan and once it starts to build momentum, it can be hard to stop. However, the goal was always the mission. If you start losing out on the victory because you fell in love with the process, you are heading in the wrong direction.

I think it is easy to see how this relates to the idea of "work being the plan" coupled with "love and family being the goal," but it can pop up elsewhere. If working out is the plan, and your goal is strength and getting healthy, then pushing yourself to stick to your plan past the point that you start injuring yourself is counterproductive. If the plan is going to be to get good grades in order to get into your dream school, then pushing yourself too hard too fast and burning out before the interview is not going to help your chances. When making a plan, make sure it is always in service of the goal.

After winning, we like to start over
(the hedonistic treadmill)

You may have noticed something strange whenever you finish a video game or get to the point of being unstoppable in a sports game to the point that there is no challenge anymore: most of the time, if you want to keep playing the game, you delete your character and start over. This has become so common in games that many developers create extra challenges or missions around New Game+ modes for when fans want to start over again. What gives? I thought the point of the game was to win? Well, once you win, what do you do? What does the dog do when it finally catches the car it was chasing? Your brain does not want you to "win," it wants you to keep getting better. This requires you to keep seeking out new challenges and never stop setting new goals.

This phenomenon is called the Hedonistic Treadmill. Hedonists only seek pleasure and leisure, but even that becomes boring after a while, so new and greater highs (or lows, shall we say) are needed to even feel that pleasure in the first place. You get used to a drug, so you need a harder one. You get used to a girl, so you need another one. You get used to your house so you need a bigger one. While this is to the hedonist's detriment, this process was actually designed to help you in pursuit of positive traits. You will not remain comfortable in your house for long, so you will try to improve it. This drive keeps you moving forward and makes sure you do not slip back into the state of passivity. However, always take a quick pause before you jump back into the grind and be thankful for your successes. Before you hit "New Game+" on a new promotion, new car, new house, or new experience, make sure you appreciate how far you have come already.

Everybody gets only one vice

I have a very unscientific belief that I still hold as a general truism: if you limit yourself to only one vice, you can remain perfectly healthy. I first observed this when I was in the military. Many soldiers smoked, drank, and were glutinous. Soldiers who did all three tended to have some health problems, even though we worked out every single day. Conversely, those that only really had one vice (like they smoked, but never drank alcohol and always ate moderately), tended to operate perfectly fine. I am sure that it is much more complicated than this and that there are more factors at play. However, it was something I witnessed often enough, even in my own life, that I still recommend it to others.

When I first left the army, I was not a drinker, but I did eat far more than I should have. I used to exercise twice a day at the JFK Special Warfare Center, even with my bad knee, so over eating was not an issue. That being said, once I was a civilian and at school, not working out as much, still eating like that, it was a recipe for some health issues. Maybe I could have still made it work with eating just a little less or exercising just a little more. Instead, I added drinking to my lifestyle as a graduate student in Korea. Having these two vices completely pushed me over the edge and I blew up to the largest I have been since losing all of that weight when I went to basic training.

People who obsess over every facet of their health do not seem like happy people. Too much of what is bad for us happens to taste good, be fun, or entertaining. However, they are vices for a reason. Pick your battles. If you are physically active and smart about the other areas of your life, I could see you having one vice and still being fine, health wise. Two or, heaven forbid, three of them? You are going to die early. Again, not very scientific. It's still worth keeping in mind, however.

Boredom compels you to action

Why do humans get bored? It's kind of strange, right? Most animals do not get bored for very long, often finding ways to occupy themselves. Humans, by contrast, not only feel bored very easily, we can feel it even when we know we should not (like at a funeral or in the middle of a lecture). What is going on? The first thing to keep in mind is that boredom is actually a very mild form of disgust. While this emotion is generally used to protect our health from sickness, disease, and death, the boredom version of disgust prevents our minds from wasting resources. Thinking takes calories, so make sure to spend them on something interesting, exciting, or useful!

The ability to feel bored is likely what encourages us to do things like find a mate, build a better car, seek new lands, develop a new skill, or a million other things that helped our ancestors stay alive, thrive, and make more life. It does not feel good to feel bored, but that is what makes it spur you on to go out and do something. It makes you want to take on a new challenge or experiment. This is what helps separate us from animals and allows us to create our civilizations.

You may already see where I am going with this. You are not bored as much nowadays compared to your ancestors. In the past, boredom was a constant and everyday issue. Now? With games, smart phones, streaming services, and even delivery food, we rarely feel bored for more than a few minutes at a time. My advice is to let yourself feel some boredom sometimes. Set aside some time every day to get a little antsy and feel the need to go out and find an adventure. I always do my work quickly and efficiently so that I have the opportunity to feel a little bored at work. This is when I get some of my best writing done. Find a little time for boredom and make sure you are still helping to build that civilization.

Opportunities come at weird times

Less than one month into the COVID-19 pandemic, I was informed that most of my classes that I was teaching for the upcoming semester would be canceled. Since I was being paid by the credit hour, I went from more than enough money for our family to less money than when I was working part time for a language examination company. It was devastating, but I had no time to panic and immediately started looking for another job. I got one at another university, two in fact, but had to make a choice about which school to choose. I did, but only after signing the contract I learned that I would be making far less than they had originally stated. More than the last job post cuts, but just barely. I was in trouble. We burned through our savings as I worked at that job for one year, putting out resumes and interviewing. I even made it to the final three candidates at three different top-ranked universities, only to not get picked for any of them.

That's when I got the offer to be a professor for the government. It was a very rare, and competitive position, that paid more than any of the other jobs I applied for, and it fit better with my major and military experience than the other university jobs. The ironic thing is, I would have never even known that this job offer existed if my first university did not cut my classes. If the second university paid me even a little bit better, I would have likely just put up with it at least until after the pandemic ended. However, opportunity found me at the strangest time in the most unlikely of ways. When you are facing difficulties, see if great opportunities are secretly opening up before you. It is only in retrospect that you can see that a big problem was actually an amazing opportunity. Do not get angry or despair. Instead, stay active and positive as you search for that hidden chance for success. You never know when they will hit.

Do not make your passion your job; people hate their job

All of us at some point have heard some take on the idea that if you "find a job you love and you will never work a day in your life." On paper, that sounds like good advice. People hate their jobs, but have to spend 33%+ of their entire day there. If they only found something they love doing, it would feel good to go to work! In reality, even something you love will become something you hate with enough time, demands, long nights, and deadlines. Notice how game developers only play a handful of new games a year? Notice how movie critics do not like going to the movies for dates? Editors rarely read for fun anymore, and chefs may still eat every day, but how often do they cook for themselves when they do not have to? The fact of the matter is, once something becomes your job you will learn to dislike it, at least sometimes, simply because it is your job. Work is hard, often un-fun, and requires you to be away from the people and places you like. Of course, you hate them, eventually.

So, how do you pick a job? Find something you are good at, even if you do not like it too much. Actual talent and skill is very hard to fake, so if you have an ability or knowledge that people will pay you for, do that. I am a massive introvert who hates talking in front of crowds or meeting new people. Naturally, I became a professor. I was not interested in the work, but I was good at it and people were willing to pay me for it. If you have a passion and it is a skill people will pay for, that sounds wonderful. For most of us, our passion will be turned into a hobby, a side gig, or a retirement job and that is perfectly fine. Do what you are skilled enough to get paid for and use that to fund your passions. You will have to work many days in your life, but they will be days worth living.

J. E. Bassette

But you really need a job

I do not want you to see the advice about hating your job eventually to mean that you should avoid having one. All of us do things we really hate sometimes that end up being really important payoffs down the road. Think about chopping wood for winter: does anyone enjoy that? It sucks, is painful, and you have to do it when the weather is nice and you want to do anything else outside. However, that sacrifice and pain today gets you something very vital in the long run. Think work isn't like that? A lot of young people like Communism because it promises almost no work in the future and everyone can just become an artist. The reality is that 1: most of us will never be good enough to be actual artists, 2: economics does not work this way and always devolves into either totalitarianism or anarchy, and 3: reality shows that having no work ever is not something most men actually want on some fundamental human level.

What happens to people when they actually lose their job? Not only is no one ever happy in this situation, "sad" is the most likely emotion to be experienced. This is doubly so for young men. While being unemployed does correlate with higher depression in women, not having a job literally triples male suicide risk. The only thing that has a higher increase in suicidality in a short-term single event, is the death of a very close loved one (parent, wife, child, etc.). This seems to indicate that a great deal of self-worth, identity, and even dignity comes from work. Even a crap job still gives you something to increase your discipline, gather resources, and have something to complain about with your buddies after a shift. Even a job you hate is better than no job. However, be at a place you hate for too long and you will just hate yourself. Find a place that you like sometimes and challenges you other times. No job will be something that you always love, but as long as it gives you a way to provide for yourself and others, it will help give you some sense of purpose. Get that bag, find another opportunity in a place a little bit better, and keep moving forward.

The bar is so low right now for dateable people, you will stand out by being merely competent

More than half of men on the dating market cannot do five pullups (we had to do a minimum of 11 every time we entered the chow hall at airborne school). Less than a third can do 30 full pushups (the minimum to pass basic training is 42). The average man on the dating scene is slightly overweight, makes slightly less than average, and has less than three years' worth of future plans. Knowing this, it should put you a little at ease when it comes to thinking about your prospects. You have likely heard that 80% of women all compete for the top 20% of guys: "hypergamy." While this is technically true, 80% of women want that top 20%, is it not true that you too are interested in the top 20% of women? Does that mean you would scoff at a kind, funny, caring, and capable 50th percentile girl? Just because you are interested in something, especially at an instinctual knee-jerk level, does not mean that you are stuck there. Look around you: most of those "bottom 80%" of guys are married. Looks like they are doing alright with just a little bit of extra effort.

So, what should you do? Be average or slightly above. Try to run slightly more than average, pullup and pushup slightly more than average, study slightly more than average (about an hour of homework a day), and work slightly more than average and you will blow your competition out of the water. Don't blame women for liking what they like, because in all seriousness, the fact you are alive at all means you literally have the genes to be what women like! Your mom saw your dad and said "Yep. He's hot." Sorry for the mental image, but it's true. You already have the tools for success, just put in the work to be at least competent. There has never been an easier time to stand out as just being "better than average."

Be the best version of you, set intrinsic goals

Is your goal to be the best basketball player of all time? While it may sound nice on paper to set your goals high and aim for the stars, the reality is that poorly thought out and unrealistic goals will guarantee failure due to no fault of your own. Let's take that basketball goal: if Lebron James had the goal of being the best player alive, and was born just 15 years sooner, he would have never achieved that goal. Why? Michel Jordan was, and is, the single Greatest Of All Time. Undisputed. I know I made someone angry there, but it is true. Kobe? Great. But he was not MJ level greatest. These amazing groundbreaking players were able to shine not just because of skill, hard work, and amazing support, but also the luck of being born a generation after the best there ever was. Golf? If Arnold Palmer was born a little later and had to go up against Tiger Woods, he would have a different legacy. If you set a stupidly high goal, and just get bad timing, you doomed yourself to failure for no reason.

What would be a better goal? How about "I want to improve my health, learn good teamwork and self-discipline, and improve my three-point skills by 15%." These are all things that are within your ability to achieve and would result in a better version of you. What more could you ask for? Set a lot of little goals with the ultimate one just being "I want to be a better version of myself." That is something that everyone of us, regardless of skill or timing of your birth, are 100% capable of attaining. You can be the Michael Jordan of yourself: the Greatest version of you Of All Time. While that may not put you on the cover of magazines or in the hall of fame, I guarantee you that it will lead to a proud parent, wife, and kids. Who could ask for a better fan club?

Every action is a wager on the future

Reading through a lot of the biographies of past generals and political leaders, there is an interesting recurring motif that pops up with men as diverse as Napoleon Bonaparte, William Sherman, Glenn Loury, and even George Washington. A lot of young men will go through a bit of a crisis of faith, where religion will no longer hold an important place in their lives, only for them to experience some kind of rekindling of faith in later years. When they were young, inexperienced, and foolhardy, they believed they no longer needed a religion and were better and smarter than all that. After experiencing some difficulties, they would find themselves needing something to believe in. French Mathematician and father of statistical probability, Blasé Pascal, dealt with this very issue. He was devoutly Catholic, rekindling his faith as he began to see math as both the language of the universe and an indication of a creator behind both. Yet, he had many friends who were still in their rebellious phase. They were fine talking and writing about math, but only because they loved gambling and did not wish to think about all of the God stuff.

Pascal proposed a thought experiment about belief in God as a form of betting wager: God is either real, or not. You can believe in him, or not. There are only four possible outcomes to such a game. In it, the bet with the best payout (belief and God is real) also avoids the worst outcome (non-belief, but God is real). Rationally, there is only one choice. A rational gambler would always choose this option. Yet, we do not always make it. When faced with the question of faith, all of us (even the faithless) are deciding with our emotional hearts, not our rational heads. That's fine, since humans are partly emotional creatures. The point was not to say "rational people should just pretend God is real." Rather, it was an illustration that you are already wagering, every single day, with your actions guided by your heart. Either you believe and act like it, or don't and do not. Both are a gamble. Not wagering and avoiding the game is not an option. With that knowledge, live every day knowing you are placing a bet one way or the other, not with your mind, but with your heart and actions.

Under promise, over deliver

I was less than two weeks into being a government official when I realized that my predecessor was a much slower writer and researcher than I was. My team would want a new three-hour class created and say "Do you think you could create this by next month?" I could have done it in a day if I really really really had to, but I knew good research, writing, and practicing it a few times to get timing down would take about one week, so I told them I could get it done in two weeks. This was faster than they expected, but gave me a full week of wiggle room if something went wrong. In the end, I got it done in a week and turned it in to receive many a "wow, that was fast."

From then on, I made it a habit of finding out when they would like it by, figuring out how long it would take me to do it, and giving them a number between the two. If I get it done on time, they are happy. If it takes a little longer than I expected, I still get it done by the promised date. This gets you the reputation of being either dependable or quick: both of which are very positive to have as either a leader or a follower. It is very hard to recover from the reputation of being "late" or under-delivering, so putting yourself in a position to create the opposite impression is a real advantage.

Sometimes they will give you a deadline that you are not sure you can make, but it is important to build in that buffer time just in case something outside of your control goes wrong. Maybe the internet goes out, your computer dies, or you have to wait on someone else to finish their part of the project first. Always have buffer time. If they want it done by Friday, and you know you can barely make it by Friday, tell them Sunday. Get that buffer time. It is best to disappoint them early and then surprise them with an "early" delivery than to promise something and have to disappoint them in the end. Under promise and then over deliver to get the best reputation.

Peter had to kill Maugrim

It is no secret that I love C.S. Lewis. All of his books are Greatest Of All Time tier, but I think his Chronicles of Narnia series may be his most universal. While I think the movie adaptations have been hit or miss, there is one scene that has made the transition from book, to radio drama, to movie screen intact: Peter's fight against Maugrim. For the uninitiated, Peter is the eldest of the family and was set to become high king after defeating the White Witch. He has been dealing with the fact that he was forced to become the "dad" of his family after their actual father went off to fight in the Second World War. He has been struggling with becoming a man and figuring out what that means in a very short period of time with now an entire kingdom resting on his success.

Enter Maugrim, the wolf and the Chief of the White Witch's secret police. He had been hot on the children's trails for some time and finally caught up to them, cornering Peter's sisters Susan and Lucy. As he arrives on the scene, he is not alone and the Lion, Aslan, helps dispatch some of the other wolves. However, when only Maugrim is left, Aslan does not intervene. In fact, he forbids the others from stepping in to help Peter. "It is his fight," he tells them. Whether or not Peter was ready to become a man or not, it did not matter. The situation arose and he would either rise to the challenge or die. He won, of course, and it was the start of his transformation from boy and worried brother, to king and protector. There may be a time when your dad, brother, mentor, or even God himself may make you feel that they are stepping back and letting you handle a challenge on your own. They are (probably) not abandoning you. They are letting you make that move from boy to man. Kill that wolf and take your crown. It was Peter's fight. This is yours.

Assume every problem
is something you can start to fix

In general, there are two ways that a person can view a problem or obstacle: it is either because of themselves (lacking a skill, ability, competency, timing, etc.) or it was the fault of someone/something else (they stopped you, held you back, want you to fail, etc.). We call this "internal locus of control" and "external locus of control" respectively. In absolute reality, most problems likely have some mixture of the two, but it can be difficult for our brains to know all of the details, so it often shortcuts to assuming one or the other is mainly at fault. My personal advice for you to become a capable and productive man is to assume all problems are your fault to some degree and that you, therefore, have the ability to start fixing them. The reason why is, whether it is true or not, people who default to external locus of control are consistently less successful, less happy, and most likely to not fix the problem. Internal locus of control people, in contrast, usually find success in the long run, because they are improving themselves even after something that was never their fault to begin with.

Let me give you an example: I was conducting interviews for an overseas government position and we had narrowed it down to the final three candidates. All three were equally qualified for their own separate reasons. There was no wrong answer when it came to picking a final name, but that ultimately meant that two people would lose out on the position due to no fault of their own. They did everything right, were qualified, and still did not get the job. Now, imagine the two different ways these failed candidates could view this problem. The external locus of control person could get angry at the interview committee, at me personally, at society for only producing one open slot for this position, or any number of things. Regardless, they will not likely seek self-improvement, because it was someone else, not them, who was deficient. The internal locus of control person, in contrast, will immediately start finding ways to add onto their resume, make a more compelling case for themselves, and seek another recruitment opportunity. Only one of them is likely to be successful.

The dream vs career, glint vs purpose

What drives you? As we talked about before, a lot of young men will define themselves by their job. This can be rough then if their job is something like a delivery boy or fast-food worker. Was that your dream? The reality is that I did both of those jobs to get money and experience before joining the army. If my job was my dream, then I may have been disappointed, but I transitioned from thinking about the job to thinking about the "career:" delivery boy and fast-food cook both helped me to become a soldier. They taught me discipline, hard work, being on time, and gave me the money to get by until I was old enough to enlist. In this sense, even lowly jobs were important and something to be proud of. However, does that mean my career should be my dream? Well, six years into that dream and I got hurt and had to change jobs once again.

I learned very quickly that while "career" is a much better dream and sense of self-identity versus "job," both were a little lacking in stability. So, what did I need? More so than a dream, I needed a sense of purpose. I need to feel like I had a mission to accomplish and my sense of self which came from being useful to others. From delivery boy, to burger cook, to soldier, to sergeant, to husband and father, the one thing that connected all of them together was a sense of purpose and the feeling of success that came from helping others. Many of us can get this purpose from our jobs, but others will get it from family, friends, or helping their community. I do not mean "community" in the abstract identity politics version of the word; I mean the actual people around you in your daily life. Helping them thrive and be successful will make you feel like your life has purpose and will give you a self-identity you can actually be proud of. Neighbors, co-workers, church members, and local coffee shops are all people you can invest in and create that community.

Chapter 4: Leadership and Being a Productive Follower

"Everyone who's ever taken a shower has an idea. It's the person who gets out of the shower, dries off and does something about it who makes a difference."

-Noland Bushnell, Founder of Atari / Chuck E. Cheese

"The supreme quality for leadership is unquestionably integrity. Without it, no real success is possible, no matter whether it is on a section gang, a football field, in an army, or in an office."

-Dwight D. Eisenhower, General/US President

"I'm no leader; I'm a little humble follower."

-Mahammad Ali, American Boxer

Get a part time job as soon as you are able

There is a lot about the world that you never learn until you have a job. Simple things like the value of money, why over taxation is a problem, how to relate to and work with coworkers, and the dynamics between a boss and employees. Not every job is equally good, and low skill part time labor (which will be you as a teen) is infamous for its relative difficulty and lack of fulfillment. But that's OK in the long run. This work is not to be the start of your career, rather it is to get you real world experience, a baseline to compare future money and employment opportunities, and get some financial freedom to learn how to use and save money.

I had a colleague at graduate school who had not worked a single day in her life. She went from high school, to university, to graduate school with the only break being to take a holiday on her parents' money. When discussing tuition scholarships, she commented that I, as a "white male" should be excluded from scholarships because I was "rich and privileged." After explaining to her I was not rich and my scholarship came from my seven years in the army, she then claimed that being in the military only made me "more privileged" and that I deserved my scholarship even less. This was a woman who had no idea what the real world was. She had no clue what any normal person thought, believed, or experienced. She was the most sheltered a rich European professional student could be.

The only protection against being an ignorant punk is to educate yourself. Live and get both experience and perspective. The fact that you can do that and get paid for it should sweeten the pot even more. Leave high school with more practical experience than your peers and you will not only have more money in your pocket (your money, and not your dad's), but you will be able to understand the world in a way that professional responsibility dodgers never could.

A man focused only on himself has a small world

There is a bit of warning I must give you about striving to be the best version of yourself: if you are the center of your own world, then you live in a very tiny galaxy. "No man is an island," but many people feel content looking out only for themselves, or only caring about others in the abstract ("the poor," "the marginalized," "minorities," etc.) rather than actual real-life people that they would have to put ahead of their own needs. This can create a very small world for you to inhabit and cause you to miss out on potential relationships, experiences, and opportunities to gain a real sense of purpose. That is not to say never focus on yourself or always put others needs above your own, but you should be being that most of the time.

Think of it this way: what is a sure-fire way to determine a cult versus an actual religion? There is some joke about religions just being successful cults or old cults, but that is missing the forest for the outlier trees. The big difference is that a religion (be it Hinduism, Christianity, Buddhism, or even Daoism) often asks you to sacrifice your own wants and needs in service of someone and something greater than yourself. A cult will promise you everything you want, in exchange for sacrificing things to a person, someone as equally flawed and broken as the rest of us. A religion asks for money in order to do things that glorify their God. A cult asks for money to glorify their human leader(s). Again, big world versus small world mentality. Politics is starting to sound a lot like cults, right? Indeed. Don't be a small world person. Open yourself up to being a big universe guy, even if that is just to your family and friends.

Hey, Sport. It's Me, Your Dad.

Every leader is an example of what to be or not to be

I had some truly amazing Noncommissioned Officers when I was in the army. Some of these men literally kept me alive and were stellar mentor figures during my time in uniform. Others, however, were complete garbage. I remember one Staff Sergeant at Ft. Benning who never knew the answers to any question I had about basic Infantry things. No matter the question, he always just looked blankly, said "I don't know," and then berated me for asking "dumb questions." I quickly figured out that, despite being in the Army for only half a year, I had already been taught by good leaders and educated myself beyond what this guy knew. Rather than be embarrassed by his lack of general knowledge, he just berated those asking the questions.

I had other leaders who were at least much smarter, but were selfish, prideful, discriminatory, or just plain lazy. They would screw up basic things, make us stay late at work for their mistakes, or just waste our time because they personally had nothing better to do at home so were in no rush to leave the office. It frustrated me that they got to be paid so much more than I did to be so much worse at their jobs. It did not seem fair. It wasn't, but life has never ever been fair and never will be. It's run by people and people are flawed, after all.

So, what should you do? First off, be thankful for all of the good leaders you get. Learn as much as you can from them and use their examples to shape the kind of leader you want to become. Second, be thankful despite your bad leaders. Learn as much as you can from their bad actions to understand what to avoid when shaping the kind of leader you want to become. Every single supervisor you meet will inform you of either who you want to be, or who you want to avoid becoming. Learn from both examples.

Do it right the first time

Eventually, you will be faced with a task you absolutely do not want to do, but know must be done. For example, let's say the lock on the bathroom door is busted, so you must buy a new one. It's a bother, but you finally find the motivation to get it done, so you drive down to Home Depot, buy the doorknob, and drive back home. You then put off actually fixing it until you have guests coming over and now must do it as fast as possible. You got the wrong one and it now locks on the outside. Crap. You go back to the store and buy the right one. You put it tougher in a slapdash fashion that is loose, and does not lock well. Or locks too well when you do not want it to and it locks you out of your own bathroom. You finally break down and look up a tutorial video on YouTube about how to fix it. Time, money, and effort were all wasted for no good reason.

Instead, imagine you could go back in time to when you first realized that the lock was broken. Now, think about if you took that task seriously and looked up the video first thing. Maybe you could fix it without needing a new lock. Maybe you would see the reminder to get a lock facing the fight way. Maybe you would hear tips about avoiding loose locks or over-sensitive ones that lock you out of the bathroom. Regardless, taking a little bit of time to plan ahead and do it right the first time would have saved you a lot of time, money, and heartache in the long run. Every mission is worth doing right, and every mission is worth doing right the first time. Take the time to save "future you" a lot of time.

Leave the world better than you found it

I remember hearing as a child that you can "tell the measure of a man by how many people come to their funeral." It made some kind of logic on paper: people often take good folks for granted until they are gone and would like to pay their respects in the end. However, my dad pointed out two flaws in this logic: firstly, dictators have quite a few people show up to their funeral, as do celebrities, or deaths of people politically useful to some cause. Secondly, most great people are humble and do good in private, so do not have the opportunity for anyone to even know their greatness. So, how can we know the measure of a man? By whether or not he left the world around him a better place than he found it.

The world will never be saved. Wars will never be completely ended. Justice will never be perfectly served. However, if you came into a world that had a rodent problem, and you left after making your neighbor's farm rat free, then your life was a net positive. Maybe for just that one person, but likely more. With less pests, your neighbor was able to bake more bread, saving many from hunger, while also making him enough extra money to put his daughter through veterinary school, etc. In a "It's a wonderful life," style fashion, we often impact others in ways that we could not even imagine. It is often only in retrospect that we realize how much good we actually did. Some of us. Many folks, especially those with big funerals, often leave this world worse off than when they found it. The celebrity who abused kids, the activist that led to more crime affecting their city, the politician who caused more people to go hungry with bad policy. As long as you leave this world a better place than you found it, I would say you were a pretty good guy.

Don't define yourself by just your job

I wonder if the FIRE movement will still be popular whenever you are reading this. It was an acronym for "Financial Independence, Retire Early." The idea was that people, often in the tech world, would bust their butts and sacrifice their teens and twenties to have one perfect idea, technology, or company and sell it off to retire by the age of 30. It once was called "speed running life," or "min-maxing capitalism," but the takeaway for me, personally, was that the better at your job you are, the quicker your job will leave you. If you "win capitalism," then you will have your career for less than 20% of your life. How foolish it is, then, that many men view their jobs as their entire identity or sense of self-worth.

I already mentioned my time in the Honor Guard burying good men who lost their sense of identity when they retired and just gave up on life. I will not belabor it here, but I will mention the retired soldiers I met who did make that transition successfully. Like the FIRE people who actually did it and not just immediately wasted all of their money or started up a new company two years later, many of the thriving veterans all had families to care for and communities to serve. Most had "husband," "father," "grandfather," "pee-wee baseball coach," "volunteer nurse," or a plethora of other hats to complement their previous identity of "soldier." Whenever you retire, if you even retire at all (Dr. Thomas Sowell is still writing books at 95), just make sure that who you are as a person is not one identity, but many. All of the aspects of yourself that have contributed to the better world that you will one day leave behind.

Spread positive rumors

When I went from a combat forces job in the army (100% male at the time) to education (my field was almost 78% women at the time), most of the differences were things I kind of already expected. Joshing and teasing was no longer encouraged, talking about sex was far less frequent, and the game of "screw, marry, kill" was seldomly played. However, there was one thing I was completely unprepared for. It was common to take little 10-minute coffee breaks in the afternoon with a colleague or two. I had originally thought these were a time to touch base on an ongoing project, ask about each other's kids, or just to say nice things about the other person's hair. Instead, a very common use of this time was gossip. In retrospect, I realize that the fact they were sharing this with me was a kind of symbol of affection, as women tend to gossip with people they see as allies. But I never liked to talk about people I did not know, especially behind their back.

I eventually found a solution: whenever someone not in our current group was brought up for the first time in a conversation, I would immediately pay them some kind of compliment. "Oh! Speaking of Yujin…" "Ah, Yujin is great. Did you see how well they ran the joint program with the Egyptian team?" This worked to quickly dissuade negative gossip, because now the conversation had shifted to their positive points immediately. Second, my colleagues quickly caught on that I would always do this, and would not bring up anyone's name that they did not want to hear a compliment about. Finally, I started to gain the reputation of a guy who always says nice things behind people's backs. It actually encouraged people to spread nice gossip about me. For a majority of men in female spaces, this is a great reputation. Be the kind of guy everyone says nice things about, by being the guy with nice things to say about everyone else.

Men's spaces and learning to hunt

There are some things I miss about being in a mostly male space. I think it was to my benefit that I did things in the order that I did, because a younger me really needed some male guidance. And, an older me brought up in a mostly female world moving to a male one would have likely ended with someone calling me a mean name. Many times. The idea of having a place where men go out together to work and young men get both mentors and practical experiences is not just in hunter gatherer cultures. This has been the norm in most of human history with family business, apprenticeships, and military conscription all being used at various times throughout history and in every culture. This is not even exclusive to humans, as many ape species have males working in bands, elephants have adolescents working with senior males, and even wolves will have fathers taking their sons out on hunts to train and toughen them up.

Sadly, a lot of this has been taken away from you for various reasons. Schools are primarily women run now, so most of your day is spent far away from positive male influences. Most male spaces have been banned, like the boy scouts or even intramural sports, as a way to be seen as inclusive. The boys who wish to be in girls' spaces are, rightfully, seen with fear or derision. Girls who wish to be in boys' spaces, however, are celebrated. It's not super fair to you guys, as we benefited from our male spaces only to then deny you yours. You may have to make your own spaces, through pick up soccer games, gaming night, book clubs, or what have you. Make sure they are a good crowd, but find a male crowd that has at least a few guys a little bit older who are trustworthy and have your mentorship and best interests in heart. One day, be that guy for some other young men.

Hey, Sport. It's Me, Your Dad.

Try to look your best, first impressions matter

Why do you need to look nice for a job interview? For church? For school photos? For a date? How you look on a special occasion is generally the best you are ever going to look. Take a glance at someone's wedding photo. Do they look better now, or then? 99% of the time, that was them looking their very best. Likewise, if you go into an interview with messy hair, a T-shirt, and flip-flops, they will assume that this is the best you could possibly look and will be unimpressed.

I worked for a language examination company for about 15 months while finishing my Ph.D. courses and getting my job as a visiting professor. While I interviewed in a suit and tie, the dress code was a little more casual. They wanted someone who looked very "American," so my work outfits were clean blue jeans and polo shirts. I looked "OK," but I would not mistake me for a graduate level educator. When I finally got that professor job, I interviewed in my suit, but went to work looking like "An American." I got called into the dean's office and was told that one of the other professors lodged a complaint about my appearance. "It looked like a student was leading the class," they said.

Rightly or wrongly, people will judge you based on how you are dressed. Low minded people may judge you based on what brands you wear, but normal regular everyday people really only care about you looking like you are put together: clean, neat, thoughtful, and competent. A little bit of effort will make a much better first impression whether that is on a date, at the interview, or in the classroom. Try to look your best, as people will assume, regardless of how you look, that this is your best.

Separating your heroes from their villainous side

I had a paper route as a kid and sometimes delivered on foot, while other mornings (especially in the winter) I would have my brother or father drive me. There were not a lot of choices on the radio at the time, so we kind of just listened to whatever was playing. One of my favorites was Ravi Zacharias' program "Let my people think." It would cover a theological idea, concept, or principle in nice short segments that felt like the early precursor to Tik Tok or YouTube shorts. I loved these so much that I not only read most of his books, I even donated to the man's charity for almost a decade. Following his death in 2020, it was revealed that he was a serial sexual harasser. In much the same way I felt after discovering the fact that Martin Luther King Jr. was a serial adulterer, I was heartbroken. I trusted these men, and looked up to them for spiritual guidance.

In much the same way that their good works (and they did a lot of them) did not justify their sins, their shortcomings as people do not erase all of the thoughtful material they did produce. In fact, since humans being sinful, evil, fallen creatures is an idea central to their theology, their shortcomings actually confirm their hypothesis. What I had to do about it, was try and separate what they were experts in (Christian apologetics) from what they were obviously not (experts on sexual fortitude). No one's heroes stand up to scrutiny. Every person is ultimately flawed and their sins will work to undermine their message. Part of being a smart follower is knowing that your leader will ultimately disappoint you at some time in some way. Try to hold on to the good and the truth they were able to produce, while also acknowledging their fallibility. Because every hero is a human, at the end of the day, every one of them has a villain inside somewhere. Separating the good from the bad is part of your role as a responsible, truth seeking follower.

Choose your experts wisely

One of the harder lessons I had to learn when becoming an adult was that many people in charge are not very bright. As a child, you see most adults as knowledgeable and competent at their positions, because they are... compared to you. I would hope that a police officer, even the worst one, knows more about the law than a five-year-old. However, as you start to become more experienced yourself, especially in one or two areas that you are really passionate about, you will start to meet adults with the title expert, but without any of the knowledge, talent, or expertise you would expect from someone in their shoes. I met officers who couldn't read a map properly. I worked for government officials whose understanding of American culture came exclusively from TV shows and newspaper articles. I even talked with "experts" in war, whose only qualification was that the university needed to name someone an expert and they volunteered because "I've always thought war was kind of bad."

The fact is, given how difficult it is to be good at even one thing, most experts are out of their depth when forced to do anything else. However, because they have the right title, background, or education, we just assume that they know what they are talking about. I was not alone in thinking Dr. Neil Degrasse Tyton sounded like an expert when talking about space, which was his field. Yet, he sounded just as sure of himself when declaring that women are not biologically real and just the result of the societal invention of makeup and dresses. Neil was not an expert on women, I assure you. Ultimately, even professional athletes are going to be great at some things, and awful at others. I would trust Charles Barkley to hit a three-pointer. I would never trust his take on military operations in the Balkans. Linguist Dr. John McWhorter is peerless in his understanding of the English language. All of his talks on Christian apologetics sound like they come from a 12-year-old. Try to understand where an expert's expertise ends and only fully trust them up until that point. That way, they can never disappoint you. And once you are great at something, do not make their mistake and assume you are great at everything.

Your leaders will eventually fail you

It was not an easy job to be a Templar Knight following the crusades. Starting out as a religious order of monks turned warriors, these volunteers had no private property outside of equipment, could not marry, and had to live in one of the most dangerous parts of the world. It was their job to protect pilgrims in the holy land and defend it from some of the most impressive, and brutal armies in history like the Saladin's Arabs, the Turks, and even the Mongols. What did they receive for all of this sacrifice? French King Philip IV became desperate for money after a failed currency reform and thought snatching land and gold from the Jews there would be enough. It was not. He then set his sights on the Templars and all of the things that were donated to them across Europe and the Middle East for their years of sacrifice. To do this, he accused them of heresy, sodomy, and being devil worshipers. When they defended themselves, he burned them alive. Even the Pope and other kings of Europe went along out of convenience rather than justice. The Templars deserved better.

Even in a great company, a wonderful country, or a fulfilling community, you will eventually have leaders who fail you. Power often attracts the worst of us, so it is inevitable that some bad actors will find themselves in a position to punish you for doing a good job. It is unjust, but that is part of life as a human with flawed manmade institutions. The foundational principle of all great religions is the idea that we are broken and fallen creatures. The things we build will contain the imperfections that make up our personhood. When you are on the receiving end of these injustices, remember to keep your faith. We still remember the Templars and those that died with heads held high. Even if this world remains cruel, do your best to be a man of integrity that others will want to follow. And, when you get into a position of authority, try your best to be a righteous and just leader for the sake of those below you. Be a Richard the Lion Heart, rather than a King Philip IV. We still make paintings of the former. The latter died of a stroke before he could even fix his country's financial problems. Most Templars even outlived him. A small justice in that.

People exaggerate for fear or power

In 1968, the book "the Population Bomb" was released and convinced the world that all human life was about to end due to having a population over one billion. It surmised that all food would run out, all fuel would be depleted, and all life would end unless we decreased the number of humans to under one billion. As you may have guessed from the fact that we hit over 8 billion and human life is actually living better with less starvation now than in the 1960's, it was complete horse poop. However, the person who wrote the book and the crazy environment cultists that believed him were not mocked nor punished; they were promoted. A lot of the end of the world doomsday headlines and warnings about the climate and the environment are literally the disciples of this once discarded neo-religion. Rather than say they were wrong, they just change the mechanism (from population to fossil fuels) and the timeline (all dead by 2000, to death by 2015, to apocalypse by 2030.) When they are wrong again, they will just change both and keep going.

Why do something like this? For many of the followers, they think they are actually doing good and are too overwhelmed by their sense of righteousness to realize they are being used: "Red shirts" in someone else's crappy revolution. It can happen to all of us (just look at crazy sports fans or regular folks during an election). For the people at top, it is because it gives them more power, authority, respect, and money to lie than to be honest. Humans are damaging the environment, but the ways to fix it are boring and involve very little money or power transfer to activists and politicians. Better to just exaggerate about the scope and timeline to make people scared and give me stuff, right? It is human nature to respond to incentives, and if lying and exaggerating gets you more of what you want, then someone is going to try it eventually. Try not to get suckered into it. A good rule of thumb is that if it is a new buzzword, it is likely crap. From global warming, to climate change, to climate crisis: the new buzzwords are all about new hype and new money, not any new science.

Beware of Bubbles

During the COVID-19 era, I fell into a trap a lot of the "laptop class" of people did. I had a job that could be done mostly by remote, as I was a professor who already liked making lecture videos of my classes. I could grade papers, do tests, give feedback and everything for my work from the comfort of my home on my personal computer. Even my son, only being in kindergarten at the time, was able to do his work at his own pace with his mom and our great high speed internet. Weeks into the first semester like this, a group of students sued the university I was working at along with dozens of others. They argued that they were missing out on a good education and needed the in person instruction to maximize their learning. Even my wife's cousin, in her final year of high school, ultimately had to drop out and get her GED as the online classes were causing her to fall behind. I never thought about how hard this change was for them, because it was not hard for me or my immediate family and friends. I was trapped in a bubble.

This trap can be easy to fall into if you live in a very rich or very poor area, as both groups are unlikely to interact with each other in a personal way. If you work exclusively with white collar or only blue collar people, you will start to misunderstand the other group. If you only consume one type of book, one genre of movie, or a single style of game, you will be unable to empathize with fans from another group. This will ultimately make you a less thoughtful person, as you will view all of your actions, beliefs, and values based on only the limited information you have available. I have heard colleagues refer to Americans from any state other than New York or California as "not worth talking to." I have heard some say that anyone who does not get into college does not deserve a job. One man stated that soldiers were the "least moral people on earth: worse than serial killers," and that was why he "never associated" with them. This man was an exchange student to Korea, where all men serve in the military. This man's bubble kept him dumb, un-empathetic, and missing out on possible friends. Stay out of bubbles.

Humans require narratives

How can so many young people be caught up in these neo-religions so easily? From climate cults, socialism worshipers, and vegan animal obsessives, it seems that the less religious we become as a society the more zealots we create. It's because people are hardwired for grand narratives. We love stories, which no other living creature on the planet does. It is something that makes us human and binds us together. Some stories are true, while others only serve as a way to bring us together into communities, cities, countries, and people groups. For instance, George Washington really was a great general and leader who turned down a (very brief) opportunity at being an "American King," preferring to make a country without monarchies. It is not true that he cut down his father's cherry tree and told him the truth because he refused to lie. After all, this is the guy who snuck behind enemy lines on Christmas Eve to kill them all in their sleep. He was not above a little deception.

When America was young, it needed its own narrative: who were the people who made our country and what does that tell you about us as a group of humans? You can see the narrative shift, as now Washington is portrayed as a slave owner (true) and a racist (not true). He actually was very non-racist by the standards of men at his time and even secretly released many of his slaves early with money for farms of their own in free states. However, the people who want the narrative of "America is evil" must lie in the way that "America is always honest" people did. The narrative matters more than truth. Ultimately, the truth should always matter the most, but understand why people lie to themselves: they are trying to keep their narrative alive. Make sure your own narrative is as close to the truth as possible and do not put stock into people who value their narratives over the truth.

Realism versus idealism

If truth is so important, does that mean realism is better than idealism? Most of the time, yes. However, that does not mean realism will always be correct and idealism wrong. For instance, it is realistic to say that women would not like to date you if you have no job. This is objectively a good piece of advice to give to any man who is interested in getting a date post high school. However, is it objectively true? If you are a realist and have no job, so decide to not look for a date, is that not just a self-fulfilling prophecy? Are all jobless men without girlfriends? Obviously not. Sticking too rigidly to your realism, to the point you are self-sabotaging opportunities, is not actually the pursuit of truth, but of likely possibilities; two very different things.

That being said, the worship of idealism and optimism, without regard to the real world, is even more damaging. Most of the truly vile things done to fellow humans in this world were done by idealists. If someone believes that they are changing human nature for the better, they can justify some horrifically damning remedies. From eugenics, to genocide, to communism, to fascism, to even recent ideas like euthanasia, net zero, gender-transition, open boarders, and others have started from people who believed they were making a better world. They had big ideas and stuck to them even as the pain, death, destruction, and erosion of trust made the lives around them worse, not better. Realism is closer to truth more often than idealism, but neither is the truth. It is best to be a realist who is smart enough to get out of the way of their own success, then to be an idealist who only occasionally lets the real world stop them from hurting others.

Men want to feel power and respect

While I cannot predict if this will still be the case in the future, as of writing this book, there seems to be a very big push for everyone to be in therapy. It is seen not only as "normal" to need psychiatric help, some even seem to take a level of pride or self-identity in how much they need it, how many medications they take, or which mental conditions they have collected like Pokémon cards. As someone who went to therapy during my time in the army, I can tell you that some people needed it, others did not, and anyone who tells you everyone needs it is getting the wrong kind of head treatment.

The real downside of this therapy culture is that almost all of the ideas, treatments, and medication is based around the hard work of female doctors for female patients. For real. Go into a psychiatrist's office today as a young man and talk about your issues with school, work, or relationships and what will they tell you? 90% of the time they will tell you that you are good enough, you shouldn't push yourself so hard, and that you need to learn to love yourself. All great advice to young women, but completely worthless to young men.

Most young men want to feel respected and powerful rather than loved or efficient. Not to say you do not need those things, you do, but if you feel hopeless because you cannot find a job, would you prefer to be told that "you are good enough as you are," or be told where you can find a job, work hard, and then be told "Wow! You are really doing great!" Being told we are "enough," when we know deep down that we are not doing enough just yet, feels like a lie rather than comfort. Try to find friends and mentors who are willing to tell you how to gain that self-respect and sense of personal power that you need to feel like you have accomplished "enough" to be loved. That is the best way to gain and feel actual respect.

J. E. Bassette

Like crabs in a bucket, loser friends hold you back

I never had a pet crab, but I have had two turtles for a couple of years. Despite their reputation as being slow, these suckers loved escaping their little water buckets. They would slowly climb up and even on top of each other until one escaped. We eventually got a terrarium designed to prevent this, but the lesson was learned: even slow and clumsy creatures can achieve quite a bit with enough time and hard work, or a little help from friends. Crabs, in contrast, rarely escape buckets. As long as you have more than one in there, his buddies will always make sure he never gets out. It's quite fascinating, but as soon as one climbs up high enough to escape, another crab will grab his leg and yank him back down. Likely, he was just trying to climb up using his buddy, but the end result is that none of them are getting out.

Bad friends or garbage leaders can be like that sometimes. I have seen colleagues put themselves on the right track and get a promotion or go back to school, only for their friends to tell them that they are "working too hard for the man," are "wasting their time," or are a "sellout." I had one soldier who did not like to go home on leave because his mostly black friends would say that his hair and clothes looked "too white," and that he should quit the army and hang out with them again. This was despite our, very black, Sergeant Major having the same clothes and haircut and was the coolest guy I personally knew. I saw one soldier get the opportunity to go to Ranger School as a Private First Class, only to have his own Sergeant talk him out of it because "If I couldn't make it, you definitely won't." I secretly got our very cool Sergeant Major to approve the training slot without either of them knowing. Some people fail and want others to fail with them to not feel alone. Do not let those crabs pull you back down.

Imposter syndrome as a leader

There are two times in my life when I felt completely over my own skis: when I became a Bradley track commander and when I became a professor. The two have something in common. In both cases I was a student one day, and then expected to be a master the next day. I started out as a Bradley driver when I first enlisted, but rather than become a Bradley gunner next, which is generally how you progress, I was made a dismount team lead and then squad leader. I basically changed roles within the unit, but I did really well there, even becoming an instructor for dismount drills and tasks for some of the other NCOs. However, out of the blue I was told I was the next track commander, as we had lost an E-6 to Drill Sergeant School. Suddenly, I was now in charge of a vehicle that I only knew how to drive, but not even shoot. Professor was equally jarring, as I had finished my final comprehensive exam for my Ph.D. course less than three months prior, but was now "Professor?"

In both cases, what got me through it was making sure I was "good enough" by studying as much as I could. I would read everything I could get my hands on, ask my colleagues questions, and ensure that I either knew every answer or knew where to look up every answer. Eventually, the feeling of "imposter syndrome" started to disappear as I began to run into colleagues who started to know less than I did. Once I had raised myself to above average, I no longer felt that I was a "fake" or a "fraud" simply for moving up a level in responsibility. When you get a leadership position and feel like a fake, educate yourself to the point that no one could mistake you for anything other than the real deal. If you never feel like this? You may be one of the actual frauds and should double check your knowledge. Stay humble, king.

All young men end up in the army or gangs

Let's combine some of the different topics into one overarching idea: if men naturally seek groups of men to learn and compete with, wish for power and respect, and are inclined to father/son or apprentice/master relationships, then most young men naturally want to be in a baseball league, or something. Indeed, whenever there is a new sport, technology, hobby, or industry, there will soon be groups of guys hanging out together talking about it or working on it. Happened with horses, cars, boats, books, video games, etc. Why this is so important to you is that some of these groups are great and can give you a real sense of purpose while providing strength, guidance, and opportunities for your future. Think, the army, soccer club, or bible study group. However, others will take from you just as much as they give and put you in a worse place. Think gangs or cults.

For my positive example, the army was a "gang" that gave me a steady paycheck, the chance to go to college, a healthier body, and a cool uniform. While I never fell into the bad kind of gang as a teenager, many of my colleagues in the military did. They had a place to feel powerful and gain respect, but also hurt themselves, their loved ones, and their community. Those gangs took even more than they gave. The army took a lot from me too, in terms of my time, effort, and my bad knee. However, when I look back at what I got in exchange, especially in the area of self-respect and financial freedom that brought pride to my family, I consider it an overall win. It is perfectly natural for you to want to find a place to fit in and a "gang" to join. Just make sure it is one that will make a better version of you, and not a worse one.

Men need a mission, a dragon to slay

The visual of the young knight taking up his sword, training hard, and slaying the dragon may feel very specifically European, with some critics even citing the story archetype as a symbol of "white" culture. Would it surprise you to hear that, actually, young men in every culture like this "hero's journey" story? It's true. Turns out, this innate drive to rise up to a challenge and win the girl is something that can be seen in virtually all other males. Even if they do not have the story or cultural narrative to underpin it, the cycle of "boy works hard to become man in order to find victory and love" is a fairly universal male experience. The women who push back on it do so from a lack of empathy and a little genuine fear. They may feel that men looking for dragons to slay, and finding none, are likely to use their violence elsewhere. Likewise, if women are to be saved from the dragon, where is their agency in this? Both miss the point: the fight nor the dragon have to be actual fights or dragons. Additionally, something worth fighting for is rarely an actual object nor is it ever viewed as one.

The dragon can be any challenge, from finding a good career, making it into a good school, to even just fixing up the local community center. Any problem that needs someone to take up the responsibility and work hard to accomplish it would suffice. Similarly, most of the things men want to protect and save are rarely "things," but rather ideas: country, family, peace, hope, love, security, etc. Some women hear that they may be seen as a prize and think they are being compared to an object, not realizing that liberty, justice, and glory are also "prizes" men are willing to fight for. I do not think anyone would honestly compare those to mere "objects" in good faith. Find a dragon to slay, a princess to save, and do not let anyone tell you not to.

Never use people as a means to an end

Immanuel Kant, the German philosopher, could be seen as the "Confucius" of his time. Both men were living in eras where wars were pretty common and had tasked themselves with finding a way to create a mechanism for perpetual peace. Since at least two new wars have been started since you began reading this book, it is pretty safe to say that they were unsuccessful. However, both hit upon an important issue that often goes unaddressed by the more idealistic of foreign policy makers: states are made up of the people within them, so how can we expect peace between countries if there is no peace between citizens in that nation? For Confucius, the answer was to create a perfect hierarchy where everyone knew their place within it, and everyone could be both juniors to some and seniors to others. How well this system works will depend on who you ask (Confucian counties do seem to have better rule of law than others, but also fought a whole lot of wars), but Kant's idea is a little more interesting.

Immanuel Kant believed that everyone should view all of our interactions with others through the lens of "Am I using this person as a means to an end?" He believed that if the answer was "yes," then we should view our actions as amoral and selfish. For instance, if I were to buy my wife flowers that would be good, right? Well, if I did it just because I wanted sex or to avoid her nagging me for something else, Kant would argue it would be amoral. Stop to think if you are interacting with someone for their benefit, other's advantage, or just out of a sake of fondness or respect for the person. Kant believed if everyone at least tried to do that, we would still get our "ends" taken care of by others who were looking out for us the way we looked out for them. A bit too idealistic, but why not try? Stop and think if your actions are because of love, respect, and kindness, or if you are just using them as means to your own end.

Beware of fad diets, money making scams, or trendy policies

Humans love "new things" more than "old things." There is even a psychological phenomenon around it called "Recency bias." It makes sense that things we are already familiar with are probably safe, so easier to ignore, while new things could be dangerous so should command more of our attention. The problem with this mental shortcut is that it makes us assume that just because something is new, and therefore interesting, it must be better or truer. Case in point: fad diets. This has been a problem facing humans since the invention of food, with "snake oil" even becoming the catch-all terms for this kind of trickery. Some come from a scamming place, others from a sincere but misguided place. In all cases, a fad diet promises you weight loss, or muscle growth, or a cancer free body, or all the above if you just eat the handful of things that they tell you to. They may look to work in the beginning, but they never stick. Because they were new, our brains told us they must be important.

This also happens in the job market or politics. Some new money-making opportunity pops up on the internet or some trendy new policy idea will start to get pushed by newspapers. Whether it is drop shipping or drug legalization, they all eventually implode in on themselves. They make people feel special or smart for doing or liking something before everyone else, because our brains are stuck thinking that new always equals better. In the end, the scams lead to losing money and the bad policy ideas lead to losing money or lives. While new technology, science, or techniques do come along and are a version of new equaling better, it is always best to be wary of a new idea that is promising to change the game forever: it fails more often than it succeeds.

Don't become a red shirt
in someone else's crappy revolution

Authoritarians, by their nature, do not like to get their hands dirty. From monarchs, to terror leaders, communists, or fascists, the people at the top always want others to do all of the hard stuff for them. Osama Bin Laden, the mastermind behind the 9/11 terror attacks, was a spoiled rich kid who went to university where he learned a modified communist theory that justified wanting to kill all Americans and Jews. How many did he manage to kill himself? How many suicide vests did he wear or planes did he fly? The same amount as Hitler, Stalin, and every other two-bit tyrant. Their job was to radicalize others into being their red guards or brown shirts in order to kill, die, and destroy the world around them. Maximum kill counts with minimal effort. If you are being told to fight by those who cannot or will not themselves, they may not have your best interest in mind. You already have non-combatants to prioritize who love you, your family, so no sense taking on someone else's crappy revolution.

When teachers, politicians, or charismatic leaders talk about the need for violent resistance, yet offer none themselves, this is a sign that they are just recruiting disposable red shirts to die on their behalf. When finding a cause to follow, find a leader who is there not because they want to be, but because they were the best man for the job. Find someone whose words and deeds always match. Maybe even become that person for others. Remember: Leaders lead from the front. They lead by example. They put their men and their needs above their own. None of these qualities can be found in the tyrant. Whether at your school, in your daily life, or online, avoid the revolutionary recruiters who have guns for you, but white gloves for themselves. Remember, the fate of every petty tyrant is guaranteed eventually: the same six-foot holes reserved for all of their disposable followers.

The Parable of the two sons in the vineyard, words vs deeds

In the 21st chapter of the book of Matthew, Jesus gives the parable of two sons who were asked to work in their father's vineyard. Their dad asks them to help with the work, but the first son says "No," because he does not feel like it. The second son says "Yes," and promises to go. The first son changes his mind and ends up going out to get the work done. Likewise, the second son changes his mind and ends up doing nothing. Who is the better son? The one who says the right thing or the one who does the right thing? Obviously, the one who actually helped his dad is the better kid. So, why do we seem to favor people who say good things instead of those who do good things?

Look at politicians. In no other profession can there be such a massive mismatch between words and deeds and you can still keep your job. Imagine if a plumber, a doctor, or an office worker said they will do something, but never ever get it done. Who would still keep their job afterwards? It seems that some professions and some people are given a pass on the disconnect between what they say and what they do. Many activists who were given praise, money, position, and power turn out to be criminals, sex pets, and thieves. Yet, we still name charities, buildings, or holidays in their honor. It does not seem fair, and isn't, but do not see this as an excuse to be a "Second son" kind of guy. Be a man whose actions always speak louder than your words. When they can match, so be it. When they cannot, your actions will always matter more to me and the people who actually love and respect you. This is doubly so for a leader who is only worth their salt if their actual actions accomplish missions. No motivating speech alone can get any actual work done.

Fix problems first, find who to blame later

It is very easy to find someone else to blame for a problem. While this is true for things that are not your fault, some of us are especially good at finding someone else to blame for things that are actually our faults. Shifting blame likely was a very useful social skill thousands of years ago in order to prevent being kicked out of villages and being banished: a death sentence for most. However, this knee jerk reaction is not very helpful during a crisis and can only prevent any actual problem solving. It does not matter whose fault it was during the "reaction" phase of the issue. Your job should be to fix it right away, as best you can, and then deal with blame later.

I was the Sergeant of the Guard during a military exercise once that included guarding the bunker where all of the major flag officers (Generals) were working for the two weeks of training. To make matters even more stressful, the high-profile nature of this annual event meant that protesters always knew when and where to show up and create bad PR for us. To help combat this, we would put up blue tarps on the chain-link fences, making it harder for them to tie on signs for their protest photo ops. I was told what to do and where to find the tarps in a supply shed and... nothing. Someone skewed up and did not put them back in the right place. It was not my fault, but who was I going to complain to? I was the Sergeant of the Guard. I was, literally, the person in charge of this situation for the next 24 hours. We quickly found an old lady's house nearby who had blue tarps in her yard, and offered to rent them for the next two weeks. I paid for it out of my own pocket. But you know what? Not one general even knew there was ever an issue. We fixed the problem first and dealt with blame later.

Greek gods vs Judeo Christian God

Have you ever played the computer game "Sid Meier's Civilization?" It is a fun game series where you start with a country during the stone age and slowly build them up into the modern era. Good times. What I always found interesting was the order in which technology is discovered, with some prerequisites making sense (discover gun power before making cannons, for instance), but one I always took umbrage with was religious practice. In order to discover monotheism (one God), you had to first discover polytheism (many gods). For the Abrahamic religions, they obviously believe that monotheism was first and that these two practices came up side by side post the fall of man. But in the general narrative of anthropologists, it was easier to think that everyone had many gods and over time some groups just narrowed it down to one God. Accuracy of this aside, there is one major way in which monotheism is an important evolution over polytheism: the nature of deities.

There is no better way to explain this than to look at the only remaining great religion which is still polytheistic: Hinduism. In past many-gods religions, deities were basically just powerful humans. In the Greek and Roman tradition, gods were sexual deviants, murderously jealous, petty, vain, lustful, gluttonous, and had every basic human fallibility imaginable. On the one hand, it made them relatable. On the other, why worship someone who is just as broken and flawed as you are? Hinduism solved this by shaving off a lot of the rough edges of their gods, them now representing cosmic ideas rather than just super powered humans. A goddess of justice is much more worthy of our attention if she is the actual embodiment of justice, rather than a powerful woman who just sometimes cares about it. What the monotheistic religions all share is that God is not a flawed human. He is someone, and something, greater than any person is capable of. More loving, true, just, and merciful than anyone of us could ever be. He is someone aspirational, and this is the kind of thing that sticks in the hearts and minds of humans in the long run.

J. E. Bassette

Old Testament God versus New Testament God

A common observation is that God in the Old Testament (Yahweh, Elohim, Jehovah, etc.) is a much angrier sounding deity than God the father in the New Testament. One seems very strict, demanding, and even self-described as "jealous," while the latter sounds more like a loving or concerned parent. While some armchair theologians would argue that this means they are different gods or that the nature of God changes, I think a much better way to think about it is as a reflection of time. As I discussed before, gods of many ancient religions were just powerful humans in terms of their desires, personalities, and flaws. Abrahamic God, in contrast, is best understood as a parent. God has the love and kindness of a mother, but also her vengeful protective streak. God has love for an orderly life and the discipline of a father, but also his temper. The twist is that we humans can use these traits unjustly where God cannot. We can love someone to the point of enabling their self-destruction. We can get angry and lash out. We can be disciplined to the point of totalitarianism. We can be kind to the point of allowing evil to continue rather than stopping it. God is not us, but more powerful; God is us perfected. An impossible goal to inspire awe and worship.

Then what changed in the New Testament? Nothing. The Old Testament covers three thousand years of history, and whenever the Israelites screwed something up and made God mad, it was a common catalyst for writers to start their records. The New Testament covers less than 100 years, with only one major Israelite screw up and the rest being a relatively peaceful time for his chosen people. In both cases, we can see the parental instincts of man (but perfected), play out with God not being angry or vengeful for no reason. We see examples of his love and orderliness, but never to the point of enabling harm. We even see forgiveness and willingness to sacrifice that all parents must have, but done in a way that no human could possibly match. A good leader could never match the Old or New Testament God, but it is an example worth aspiring to. You were never meant to reach that goal, only aim for it.

Hey, Sport. It's Me, Your Dad.

People have trouble following their own advice

If you know me in real life, then you know that I have sometimes failed to uphold some of the items in this book. For the lessons I learned the hard way, this is understandable. But for the ones that I screwed up after already knowing what I should do? What excuse do I have? Some of it is just human fallibility. Think of all the advice I will give you in the next couple of chapters about women: I have not been the best when it comes to women. Not a womanizer nor abuser by any stretch of the imagination, but still not always sticking to plans I knew would work. Sometimes it was a failure to override the instinctual and flawed part of my brain with the logical and more Christ centered one. Regardless of the reason why, you will see that many folks who have good advice can still struggle with following it to a T.

You can see this a lot with addicts. Whether it is gambling, smoking, or even shopping, these people know they have a problem and can tell you why living like them is bad, but still do it anyway. This can come from years of building bad habits that make doing the right thing a daily struggle rather than a one-time choice. This can also stem from their lack of motivation to change. Remember that people respond to incentives, and most of us are motivated by mating opportunities and family ties. If you do not have either, or have tricked yourself into thinking you don't, then it can be hard to take your own advice and do the right thing. As a leader, try to be mindful of how it would look if you could not keep to your own word. As a follower, try to see why they would fail at their own advice and try to learn from their negative experience. Following good advice is great, but you can also learn from the people who fail to follow that same guidance.

Chapter 5: Sex and Romance

"The romantic love we feel toward the opposite sex is probably one extra help from God to bring you together, but that's it. All the rest of it, the true love, is the test."

-Joan Chen, Chinese Actress

"If in order to obtain sex, men must marry a woman, or become pillars of the community, or lie, or amass riches, or be romantic or funny, then they will do precisely that. If men need to simply be in the right place at the right time at 3am in a nightclub, then they will meet these standards appropriately."

-Chris Williamson, British Podcaster

"She's beautiful, and therefore to be wooed; She is woman, and therefore to be won."

-William Shakespeare, British Playwright

Humans as plants and spreading seeds

It is no coincidence that humans started using flower and plant metaphors to talk about reproduction. For one, plants growing, spreading, and re-growing is a birth, life, death, and rebirth cycle that we all get to see played out every single year. Historically, humans have had to be very familiar with plant reproduction because we did not eat otherwise. It made it very easy to explain to our children, "You know seeds, right? We plant them in the ground and more plants grow. Well, boys make the seeds and girls are the ground. Kind of." Of course, it is not a perfect metaphor, what with the role that parents play being even more important than, say, the farmer in this analogy. It's not like the seed producing plant has much to do after insemination, but a majority of good dads have quite a bit to do after that point. Doubly so for the ground versus moms.

That being said, it is useful to get the very basic gist of sex. Why do we have it? It helps keep our species going, just like wind blowing seeds onto the ground every fall. Why is it so much more… involved than with plants? Because mom and dad need to bond together because our kids take longer than just one spring and summer to ripen. Metaphorically, of course. Why do plants do it automatically without even thinking about it, and humans have to spend so much of their waking hours thinking about it? Because, for humans, not all seeds are created equal and not all ground is of the same quality. By having a more complicated and involved system, we often produce much better offspring than ourselves. For plants, we have to get involved and force breed them to improve them. For humans? Us just competing with each other has done all that hard work for us. By definition, our actions around coupling and mating means our children have the potential to be better than us. Sex is just like plants. Kind of. Sort of. But a little messier. And that messiness can lead to a lot of pain and heartbreak, or a strongly bonded team.

The drive to reproduce before death

You will spend a lot of your mental power thinking about sex: who to do it with, how to do it, why it is not easier, etc. The moment puberty hits, it becomes a very important part of your personality, with your grooming habits, fashion choices, hobbies, haircut, and even the way that you speak changing to maximize (you hope) your mating opportunities. They will, hopefully, all be failures. You are too young to be having sex and thinking about continuing the species. If so, why does it strike so early if no one is actually ready for it?

Part of this is due to how hard our ancestors had it. Over 1/3 of all humans that ever lived died before five years old. Half were dead by fifteen. When you read about the average life expediency in the middle ages being 35, it was not that most people died then. Rather, you either lived to 80 or died at two. This created the "average" life of around 40. This was the reality for many humans regardless of where they lived. Compared to these conditions, we live like kings now. But that does mean your brain was designed to help keep humans alive a 1000 years ago, not today: so, start procreating by 15, because it may be the only chance you get before you die.

Obviously, that is not the case anymore, but your brain does not know that. The people who had children young were the most likely to actually have children before they died, so they were our ancestors and passed down their genes to us. That includes the strong desire to procreate when far too young for it. Really think about it. You, with your mixed grades at school, video game addiction, and complete obsession with side boob: would you make a good dad right now? Just be patient. You will be a great guy one day, so do not let your brain get you into trouble now. Become great dad material first before putting yourself in the position to be a dad. Earn that position.

Historically, most men were reproductive failures

Speaking of "averages" that are mathematically correct, but a little deceptive out of context: the average man never had any children. Obviously, this is nonsense to some degree, but where does this statistic come from? Well, thanks to modern technology, we can look into our DNA to see variants in our male and female ancestors. What we have found is that we have a little over double the number of mothers in our collective genes versus fathers. There were several points in our history where war, conquest, and violence led to a surplus of women after many young men were killed off. After a war, women were taken and men were executed. Add in the fact that women and children require fewer calories to survive, and even things like famine led to these sex imbalances. Also, some cultures allowed for bigamy (most in the distant past), so it was common for successful men to have many wives and unsuccessful men to have their balls cut off. Seriously. That's what eunuchs are.

We, thankfully, do not live in that world any more. Most young men will not die young in a Viking raid and will have the ability to eventually become husbands and fathers themselves. However, again, your brain is designed for a much more brutally competitive world. You are likely a descendent of one of those raiders, conquers, or bigamists. This is going to make you very competitive with other young men; even the ones you really like and call friends. If you find yourself showing off in front of a girl, sabotaging a friend's shot at a date, or getting very jealous when some guy you do not know gets more female attention than you, our past and fallen nature are the reasons why. Try to both understand your feelings and why they are not necessarily useful in the 21st century. Hopefully, your brain eventually gets the message.

The one man/one woman compromise

While bigamy and wife stealing may have been our past, it is obviously not our present. With some exceptions aside, like some sects of Mormons or half the Middle East, there seems to have been some consensus created around the idea of "one man for one woman" in the modern dating market. Part of this was the spread of Christianity which was the first of the Abrahamic Religions to preach monogamy. Its successful spreading to most of the globe did have an impact in this area. However, there were similar shifts happening throughout most of the world. China, for instance, did have a harem system where Emperors and members of his court were allowed to have many concubines. However, this was a privilege of the very upper class, with most men expected to have only one wife. Confucianism even taught the practicality and utility of only having one wife as a way to reduce conflict with other men (fighting over women) and within the household (wives fighting against each other).

It is also worth mentioning that the push towards monogamy also included women themselves. Having to share a husband brought many potential issues (the youngest wife would likely have more power in the family because she was prettier, but the older wives had children that needed protecting) and children in polygamous relationships were far more likely to suffer abuse or even death than in two parent households. Regardless of the exact reasons why, the one man/one woman compromise has been very important to reduce conflict between men, between men and women, between women and women, and reducing risks to children. But you will still see men ruin their lives and break their families apart trying to have more than one woman. Understand where this instinct comes from, but never let it ruin your life or your family. It is never worth it.

Your sexuality should never be your personality

There is a very seriously negative trend that started in the 1960's and has only accelerated in the English speaking world: the idea that your sexuality is your central identity. For most of my childhood, I never knew anything about the sex lives of the adults in my life. At best, I could guess based on if they had kids. I sometimes would hear a joke about it if they had a lot of kids, like my mom and dad. However, that was the end of it. I definitely could not guess kinks or anything else. Fast forward to the present, and I see people bake their sexuality into the clothing they wear, bumper stickers on cars, forced government holidays, written in people's bios, and even the first words out of their mouth during a self-introduction. Not only is it obnoxious, it is very performative. It feels fake and forced in a way that actual personality is not. No one who is punctual, kind, introverted, extroverted, loyal, clever, or a million other things would choose clothing or flags to represent this. They just are those things.

For a lot of these people, their sexuality is their religion. Again, it even has its own holidays, symbols, mantras, prophets, and heretics. Considering how diverse and interesting a person's actual personality is, how sad is it to just be boiled down to "guy who has sex while dressed as an animal" and then making that your only personality trait? No one, outside of their fellow cult members, will ever bother to get to know that actual person, because they made that kind of thing their core identity. They are more than that. Or, should be. In much the same way, do not make girls, and the fact you like them, your only identity. Frat boys are obnoxious too, in their own way. Sex is something that motivates you, and brings you together with your wife to create your family. It is a part of you, but should never be all of you.

Women's priorities are different; they must be pickier

I am sure you have heard of, or maybe even experienced, the dreaded "friend zone." This is the phenomenon where the man is romantically attracted to a woman, but she cannot see him in that way. He may be nice enough to hang around with, but not enough to actually date. This could hurt your feelings and make you feel like you were betrayed. But why is there such a disconnect? You could see you two as a great couple, so why can't she?

Remember that men view most women as beautiful and, since that is the highest valued trait for initial attraction, you could feel like you would make a good couple with 80% of women your age. You kind of have low standards, naturally. She is alive in the first place, so her dad found her mom attractive. Women in general are pretty for that very reason. But what do women find initially attractive about men? You may think looks, height, jawline, skin, or a dozen other things, but you only think that because that is what you care about when first meeting a girl.

In reality, she has a lot more to risk with coupling than you do in terms of time, resources, and physical danger should your mating be successful. Women carry more risk in reproduction, so have an obligation to be pickier with mates. Try not to take it personally. It may actually be a case of "it's not you, it's me," as her brain is telling her to look for a guy that compliments skills she is lacking, rather than be with a guy she is more similar with, like you. There are "friend zone escapee" success stories, lots of them, but I would not put all my hope in that and respect the fact that your capability will not always match hers. She has the right to be picky, given her risk. Respect her choice and find a girl that is compatible with you from her own desires. She is out there; you just have to keep looking.

Women look for potential in their mates

So, if not looks, what do women look for in mates? Looks can be helpful in terms of things like being healthy, so taking care of your body is a good start. Women look for potential that they can invest in and develop over time. That is why they always fall for "I can fix him," bad boys in the fiction they love. Think about it: a bad boy tends to be physically strong (good protector), a little troubled (is willing to push back in a bad situation), risky (will fight that tiger and save the kids), and often commands the respect of other outlaw types (access to support and resources). The only problem is that he is an ass, so just needs a pretty girl to warm his cold heart and make him all better, right? Not usually, but there is a reason why such novels are seen as the "porn brain" butterflies for girls.

In reality, what she needs to see is that you have healthy genes that will make strong babies (whether she wants to have them or not, her brain is still looking out for them), an ability or skill that will make you useful to the community to earn money and resources (athletic, artistic, musically inclined, etc.), and can help elevate her status. Note, only half of these things are about who you are. The other half is about what you could theoretically do if given the time, resources, and motivation. Women like potential and someone who looks like they can achieve it. Try to show girls that you have something that you are good at or passionate about. This can be anything from writing, to martial arts, to even the drums, or calculus. While some of these skills may seem more "cool" or "sexy" in your mind, only young girls think like that. Most women just want to know that they are investing in someone who can be special at something if given the chance. Find that thing you can be good at, and show it in a way that shares your true potential.

Do women actually like bad boys?

Google has kept search data on users based on demographics like ages, sex, and location since their website first existed. While privacy laws are more restrictive now than in the past, they have given talks and seminars on some of their more interesting findings over the years. Of particular note was that men were much more likely to have searches that involve visually explicit content (no surprise), but that women were more likely to seek out written explicit material. This material also seemed to follow a very specific theme: pirates, vampires, werewolves, bandits, and other violent characters who are seduced and charmed by the female romantic protagonist. Literally, she "fixed" the bad boy.

It should, hopefully, be obvious that it is not the "doing bad" that makes bad boys attractive. Rather, it is the dual signals of power and the will to use it. By "power" I mean either enough authority to get away with bad things, or enough resourcefulness to not fear the effects of their rule breaking. And by the "will to use it," I do mean that ability to rule break. Women want to feel safe, so they are not usually attracted to lawless men. However, depending on what kind of life they have lived, the idea of someone willing to break some of the rules, and get away with it (for her in particular), could be a very attractive proposition. Imagine if she had an abusive father, heartless step mom, or overbearing teachers that created cruel and arbitrary rules. A bad boy could look like a kind of savior there. And her ability to "warm his heart" and change him? Proof of her loveliness and his admiration for her.

This is a fantasy, of course, and rarely works out that way. It is best to not try and save the "I need to fix him" type of girls. Also, don't try to fake being the bad boy and do not find your self-propelling mission and identity thorough just being defiant of others' rules. Be your own man and a good girl who admires that is sure to follow.

Do not let her fall in love with a fake "you"

There is a lot of pressure on both men and women to act differently on a date than we would in real everyday life. Kind of like how we are on our best behavior at a job interview or at church, we are presenting a more refined version of ourselves. I think that is pretty normal and probably for the best. However, do be thinking about the long term implications if this "best version of you" has nothing in common with actual you. If you lie about your job, hobbies, interests, family, or values just to impress a girl, that can only end in heartache. Even if she falls for it, and you, there will always be the nagging feeling that you are both a fraud who will be found out, and that the real you is not worth loving. After all, fake you got the girl, so real you must be a loser, right?

Both pick up artists and "cuttlefish" men deal with this reality every day. For the pick-up artist, he thinks that any lie (about himself or her) is justified if he gets the girl. In the long run, he will always feel like a failure because girls only fell for the character he was playing and not him as a real man. No amount of sex, especially from strangers, will make up for the idea that no woman loves the real you. Likewise, cuttlefish men are the guys who pretend to be the least masculine guy possible thinking that it will make women lower their guard around them. An actual cuttlefish will be as small and feminine as possible, so that rival males do not fear them or pay attention to them, while the bastard secretly mates with females. The human cuttlefish pretends to love everything she loves, believes all of her beliefs, and hates everyone she hates. He might get "lucky," but she does not love the real him. And the real him definitely does not love himself. Be on your best behavior on a date, but show her the best version of the real you. Never let her fall in love with a fake you, for both of your sakes.

Think about if you could be with this girl every day for the rest of your life

This may seem like putting the cart before the horse, but it is important to ask yourself this very early on when romantically pursuing a woman. Could you really be with this woman forever? Your short-term mating strategy brain will always tell you "yes," but it would also say this about a cartoon character. Be completely honest with yourself. If you had to wake up next to this woman every single day, trust her with all of your money, rely on her to pick you up from the airport, be patient with her mood swings, laugh at all her bad puns, not take it personally when she did not laugh at your bad puns, and love her when she gets old and gray? It may sound like I am taking it a little too seriously. After all, you just met her. How could you possibly know all of this? The point is to try and ask those questions, and actively seek the answers.

The fact of the matter is that your brain will do its very best to make you think any girl you fall for is the right one for you. It has to. Remember, it is convinced that you could die in a bear fight or duel with an invading samurai any day now, so you must fall in love and reproduce as soon as possible. Our species depends on it! Thanks for the vote of confidence, brain, but very few of us will die at 15 anymore. Even if this were going to happen, would it be fair for you to make that baby, die in a wrestling match with a tiger, and then leave mom and the infant all alone? Maybe you did not have a choice 2000 years ago, but you have one now. Be honest with yourself. Do not fall in love and think that the present will last forever, because it won't. Is this girl the woman you can live with until the day you die? Remembering that the day will be closer to 80 and not 15. Be honest with yourself, because both of you deserve that.

Women need someone they can talk too

Women and men use gossip very differently. While you may think that you do not gossip as a guy, you are just doing it in a male fashion. Yes, you may not be talking about Suzy's new secret boyfriend, but you are talking someone's ear off about why the Roman Empire fell, why you still call Istanbul "Constantinople," which WW2 Tank is the best, and which Japanese Samurai Clan had the coolest battle flags. Men like to show off knowledge, the more obscure the better, to people we just met. With your best friend, you fight about which variant of the AK47 has the coolest buttstock, but you don't try to impress them. With strangers, you feel the need to ramble random trivia. Why? Because men feel the need to show that they are useful when we meet someone new. We have to convince them that we are the kind of guy they should trust on the mammoth hunt or to marry their daughter.

Women do the opposite. To strangers, they reveal as little as possible. Surface level things only, and never show off or brag. Bringing too much attention to yourself to someone you do not know yet is inviting scorn, envy, or skepticism. No, women only gossip with people they trust well enough not to look sideways at them for "showing off" their hidden knowledge. This disconnect with how the sexes communicate has led to the insane ideas of "Man-splaining" for confused women ("why is he sharing so much? He must think I'm dumb."), and the impression that women talk too much for men ("Why is she still trying to share with me? I already trust her, so she must just like blabbing."). As a good date, try to not over explain when first meeting a girl, and as a great tenth date, be ready to be a sounding board for all for the hidden knowledge she wants to share. Just pretend she's talking about troop strengths of 18th century European Navies. You'll do fine.

On a date, do not try to brag

This is directly related, but try your best to not be a braggart too early in the relationship. Your brain is telling you to prove your usefulness to the stranger, and it emphasizes the need for it to be extra cool because the new potential friend is a pretty girl. This leads to a lot of oversharing of accomplishments, hobbies, interests, and dreams. All of these things are important, and many girls will be interested and even impressed by a lot of it, but not on a first date. Her brain is telling her not to show off, be modest and cautious, and to only selectively reveal truths about herself. When you come on so strong, she may misread it as you trying to look down on her, you lying to impress her, or you not having a filter at all. A failure to cross sex mind read.

So, what should you share? Start with factual bullet points and slowly go deeper if she asks more. Where are you going to school? Tell her the name, what year, and maybe one additional detail, like if you enjoy it or not, or how pretty the library is. That's it. Two, maybe three sentences at most, and then pass the question back to her. By being modest, factual, and open, you will seem much more genuine and in line with her expectations from sharing personal information so early into the relationship. Also, you get the added bonus of opening up more on future dates with actual interesting information about your skills and usefulness which will get you a "What? I didn't know you could play piano? That's so neat!" sometime down the line. Makes you seem more mysterious, layered, and capable in all the right ways. Pro tip: keep track of what you have shared and how much, but also remember what she chooses to share. That way, you know when she has moved from cautious to comfortable with giving you her "secret knowledge."

On a date, use stories to show interests

Humans love story tellers. Across every culture, religion, and country we can see that people who are good at sharing engaging narratives are favored in our societies and communities. This is a trait that women find attractive too, and it can be an effective way of sharing your interests and hobbies in a way that sounds more natural and less boastful or forced. Let's say your hobby is reading books. To start listing novels that you have completed this year can just sound like you are bragging or trying to impress her rather than sharing something personal about yourself. Instead, if you shared a short story about a time in your life that a great book impacted you and used that to share your interest it would be more engaging. Don't lie and make up a story. Just be honest, while still keeping in mind that you want her to empathize with "past you" and how much that book meant to you as a window into "present you."

I was on a very rare date once when I was in the army. I had not had a date in almost two years and was only doing this as a wingman for a buddy. I talked about army stuff and video games, because those were the only things I had going on in my life at the time. The poor girl was bored to tears. In contrast, when I was on a date with the woman I eventually married, I used a story about helping one of my soldiers to segue into talking about my work in a way that sounded much more interesting to her and cause her to ask follow up questions and show her genuine interest. Video games, I saved until a future date. No sense scaring her off too early. Moral of the story, have a story when talking about things you love and you will come off more charismatic and interesting to your date. Everyone loves a great story teller.

On a date, talk about family you admire

Similarly, it is easy to sound a little dry or route to list off your family members. Mom, dad, brothers, sisters, etc. Without any context, she has nothing to grab onto with this information and often not even faces to go along with the names she has just heard for the first time. Would you care? A much better way to talk about family is through a quick story that shows off a quality you admire about that person. It's one thing to say that you have a brother who is a firefighter. Rather, if you shared a story that shows off your brother's strength, bravery, or willingness to help others and use that to segue into his work as a fireman, it would be much more engaging and say something about you as a person if those are the qualities you admire.

It is also important to include women in your life that you admire and why. This is very important to your date for two reasons: first, you can often tell a lot about the quality of a man by how he treats the women in his family. If he hates his own mother and sister, how is he likely to treat a complete stranger? Showing that you have a good relationship with at least one close female family member will show you are very capable at treating at least one woman very well. The second thing this shows is what kind of qualities you admire in women. This is going to be an early indicator of whether or not you and your date are a good match long term. If you admire your sister for her kindness, faith, and great work as a mother, and your date questions why those are the qualities you picked, you know that your date is not interested in being kind, faithful, nor a mother. Use this as an opportunity to share a bit about your values while also getting feedback about hers.

On a date, talk about your dreams and plans

Remember that girls love potential in mates? How can you show potential without bragging about your skills, abilities, or accomplishments? Talking about the future often allows people to gauge, at least, theoretical potential. Many young men are so concerned with the present because their brains are working under the assumption that there may be no future and you could die any day from a wildebeest stampede. Don't think about the future! Only think about procreating as quickly as possible before you die! Of course, women's brains do not work like this, so she is unlikely to sympathize with you when you say that you have not thought too much about the future yet. She has no choice but to think long term if she wants to survive. She expects you to have thought about it at least a little.

Think about what your skills, passions, and interests are. What would you like to do with each of these? Is there a career you have in mind that covers at least one of them? Anything you are working on as a hobby that you hope can help you in the future? This can be an opportunity to share more about the things you like and care about in a way that shows off your future potential. It also looks mature to have thought about at least some short-term goals and how you wish to achieve them. This is especially important to young women who may have their own plans and short-term goals and will find comfort and compatibility if yours complement hers. I would try to think about the near term (one to three years) and the medium term (three to five years) when coming up with a good answer. Bonus points if you can point to hobbies, work, or studying you have been doing that are related to accomplishing some of these goals.

Find a girl that cares about others more than herself

I fell in love with my wife long before we were married, of course, but I do have a story from about two years into our nuptials where I felt the most in love with her. It started at a coffee shop chain that we frequent together. I got the large triple shot iced Americano, as I always do, but half way into my drink I discovered it had a little extra bonus in the cup. Nothing gross, but there was a metal handle, likely from one of the tools in the coffee shop, that broke off and fell into my cup. At first I did not want to say anything, I was unharmed and it did not affect the taste any, but I knew that the 17-year-old working behind that counter was likely looking for it.

My wife saw the dilemma playing out on my face and asked what was wrong. I told her, not wanting to lie to my wife, but was afraid she might cause a scene. She took it from me and loudly said that we had to go back there right away. I sat in the car the whole ride over, worried that she was going to yell at this kid, demanding to see a manager, expecting a free drink, or something. As we made our way into the shop my wife checked to see if there was anyone else in the store before asking him if he was alright and to make sure that the broken tool was not the result of some accident. She then gave him the broken piece, explained where we found it, and double checked to make sure he would not get into any trouble. The entire time, my wife was worried about the kid too.

Some people were never the 17-year-old in this situation, making some dumb mistake and getting chewed out for it, but my wife and I were. We knew what that was like and wanted to make sure he would be alright. I realized that, more so than anything else, my wife not being "fake compassionate," but actually caring about other people in a non-virtue signaling way was a very attractive quality. It made me realize that she would be a great mom and I was lucky to have her. Find a girl that cares about others. Not in a self-righteous social justice way, but in a real basic human way. She's a keeper.

Different girls like different muscles

There was a popular set of pictures going around the internet of two guys at the gym with a big debate about who looked to be in better shape. While there were lots of opinions, one extremely clear conclusion was happening in real time: men had the general consensus on which of the two they thought was stronger and why, while the women disagreed not just with the males' assessment, but even amongst each other as to the reasons why. For the men, they thought the man who was taller, had larger biceps, triceps, and pecks was the guy in better shape. These were all muscles that men themselves work on, "glam" muscles we might call them, because we think they make us look good. They do, kind of, but what they actually signal to other men is that they could beat us in a fight. That's it. That is why men think they make us look good or look healthy, because they are how men gauge the lethality of potential rivals.

What about women? It was more complicated. The thing that connected all the women's choices were indicators of "hand grip strength," but what these indicators were exactly differed slightly from woman to woman. For some, it was forearm size. Others, it was shoulder muscles. Others, it was hand thickness. Still others found six packs or even neck muscles as more attractive. This discrepancy may explain why the guys that women find to have the most attractive bodies rarely include body builders, as the muscle groups being focused on do not always overlap with a woman's preference. And where do women get these preferences? Often from their fathers or other prominent male figures. One study found that whatever prominent muscular features a girl's father had, that tended to be what they found as healthy and attractive. What this means to you personally is to not get hung up on having one particular body type, because as long as you are healthy, you are likely some lady's type. Focus on your strength and the rest will follow.

J. E. Bassette

Why men like T&A: A biological perspective

A long-term study of men in over 90 different countries found two very interesting observations about preferences for female body shapes. I say "interesting," but the average 14-year-old boy could have told you just as easily. Men liked women with a "coke bottle" shape of hips and breasts larger than their waist. In all 90 counties, when asked to draw their ideal body shape, every one when added together came out to around 1 to 1.6 waist to hip ratio. It makes sense: women who have larger hips literally were more likely to survive childbirth, and larger breasts and buttocks indicated a high chance of surviving in calorie scarce situations, which was something that many humans found themselves in every winter. A thinner waist also made sense, as it implied a non-pregnant woman, so someone who was not already taken and could lead to conflict with another guy if you pursued her. Additionally, excess belly fat could indicate health problems that would become worse with pregnancy. Everything you like about a woman's body is because they are the things that will keep her and your offspring safe and alive.

Now, it was their second finding that was more interesting. Remember how each country averaged out to 1 to 1.6 hip/waist ratio? It did, but you may have figured out that this ratio is possible in different configurations. A small waist and thin round hips would do it. But so too could large hips with a medium waist. Do you see now why your ideal girl may be different from your friend's? All these different configurations of breast, waist, hips, and buttocks across all people groups are capable of creating this 1 to 1.6 ratio. For some ethnicities, thin waste is easier, but for others it would be large hips. This diversity in configurations means that not only were our ancestors good at picking out body types that would survive childbirth, but that even physical beauty comes in unique shapes. What you like, be it an "A," "T," "H," or whatever, this is probably a reflection of this cultural uniqueness within the human experience. Don't leer at these poor girls, but also know that what you find attractive is both biological and logical.

Girls are not naturally gold diggers, they are nesters

Think about how much the role of children and childbirth plays into understanding male attraction to the female body. Virtually everything you like is something geared towards the safety, care, and survival of children. Now, I want you to imagine taking children out of the equation completely. What was once reasonable and perfectly understandable ("I like breasts because a woman with them is more likely to survive childbirth and then keep that child alive") becomes something that feels a little more base or gross: "I like breasts just because they are hot." One feels practical and sensible; the other feels objectifying. Many modern women have taken children out of their assessment of male preferences and decided, in a shocking lack of empathy, that all men are just gross.

Now, before you judge them too harshly, remember that you may be just as guilty. Think about "gold diggers:" the women who are interested in your money and are very keen to only date up the economic ladder. She likes a guy with a fat wallet, fast car, and freakishly big house. What a base and gross woman, right? Now add children to the equation. She wants a fat wallet because she wants to make sure your kids get fed every day. She wants a fast car because symbols of socio-economic status means that your children are more likely to find mates themselves in the future. She wants a freakishly big house because she wants to make sure all of your children stay safe and warm at night. Taking children out of the equation makes both men and women look a little base and gross. Keep this in mind when you are judging the preferences and desires of the opposite sex and try to be as empathetic to them as you would like them to be to you.

Your type may not always be your type

No battle plan survives the acid test of war. Meaning, you may have a great idea about how you would do something, but until you actually do it, you are working off of a lack of knowledge. This is very true when it comes to having a "type." Whatever kind of girl you are interested in, some of it will be natural and instinctual (men have been finding women pretty for a very long time, after all), but a lot of it will be thanks to your environment. Movies, popular culture, a crush at school, even your mom will all be things your brain sees and will begin to latch onto specific things that you find attractive in women and will begin to build your "type."

I had a type growing up. Living in Japan and having a lot of female friends at the time, I had an image of femininity that I think many boys in my shoes had. Being in the late Showa era as well, the petite, slender, bright eyed, smiley girl was something you saw everywhere. In the movies I watched, friends I played with, and idols I listened to, this kind of girl solidified in my mind as the kind of girl I was going to marry. I, in fact, did not do that. My wife is short, but not petite. She is very large chested, and would not pass the "slender" description due to her curves. She is a little more "tough eyed," than bright eyed. She smiles, but is just as likely to scowl, cry, joke, and talk smack. She was nothing like my type. She was better. A real "top-heavy tomboy." I never knew I liked that until I met her.

What happened? Life happened. It turns out that, regardless of the type I had in my imagination, as soon as I met a girl who was pretty, smart, kind, and helpful, I fell in love. My lack of experience created my type, so an increase in experience changing my heart does make some logical sense. I am not telling you not to have a type. Only that your type may be built on assumptions that may prove to be untrue in the acid test of real dating experiences. Do not miss out on the "best girl" just because she does not meet all of the items on your "checklist." Keep a slightly open mind. Or, heart, rather.

Why women like flowers

Flowers seem like a kind of cliché gift, but something similar is found in most cultures. Men giving little gifts to women to show their interest and affection is so common, even penguins do it. But why did so many human cultures settle on flowers? The first is that flowers are pretty. Associating her with beautiful things ("I saw something lovely and immediately thought of you") is never a bad parallel to make. It is also why women tend to be more price conscious, as association with something that is expensive (or "worth a lot") makes her feel precious, valued, and rare. When coffee and chocolate were more expensive, those also became common choices. Same when books were pricey, or even fruits like bananas and pineapples. Anything uncommon and showed beauty, worth, or uniqueness gave the impression that you associated her with those things.

The second reason is that they are, practically, worthless. This seems like the opposite of the point I just made, but it is not. A gold ring is worth a lot of money, but what is its actual utility? What is its worth outside of a status symbol? Virtually nothing. A man who can spend money on pretty, but dying, plants that will be thrown away in a week is a man who has extra money at his disposal. He is well off enough to be able to waste money. Why does she like the more expensive steak place, when the BBQ spot next door tastes way better? It was never about the food; it was about what the restaurant represented: "I have more money than is needed just for survival. I can keep our offspring safe and well fed." The next time you buy a gift, think about what association you are creating with it, and what the ultimate message is that you are communicating. Not every girl is going to want or need the gold ring and steak dinner. But she likely does want to feel worthy of one.

Men won't trust an easy girl

There is a sad irony built into the short-term and long-term mating strategy psychology of humans. Once young women notice that leaning into "hot" rather than "cute" gets them more attention, some will prioritize this as a way to meet men. Oh, they will. Many men will show interest in her, but very few will stick around. Why is that? Our brain tells us to try and take advantage of a short-term mating opportunity during the short window it is available, so you will be interested in her. However, as soon as you have her, your more logical side will kick in and say "If she was this easy to get, then surely she will be that easy to lose." You will not fully trust her, thinking that she will seek other short-term mating opportunities in the future, so you should not get attached to her. Little did she know what made her so instantly attractive to guys would be the same thing that drove them away. Ironic.

There is a biological imperative to this. While women risk far more than men in terms of physical resources when having a baby, men risk a lot of material resources. You will have to feed, care for, and protect this kid for around 20 years. Doing this to some stranger's kid could be a waste of resources if they are scarce. It would only make sense to invest in a child you are 100% sure is your own. This concept is called "mate guarding" and is so common in mammals that female chimps and lions, if pregnant with some other male's baby, will give birth in secret as to avoid the new jealous male from eating the baby. Gross, cruel stuff. Thankfully, human males are not so cruel, but it is still important to us mentally to be sure that our children are ours. This is why guys who voluntarily adopt and care for others' children are seen as good men, as they are working against this very ingrained impulse. If you get a girl easily, it is harder to trust that the baby is yours. Truly unfair to the child, but as we saw from the example of chimps, lions, and even dolphins, nature is never kind to children. Be better than your own nature, but it is best to avoid easy girls all together. For both of your sakes.

Women won't respect an easy guy

Do not think this absolves you of "easy" behavior, young man. If young women use sexual availability to get young men's attention, only for it to backfire long term, what is the male equivalent? What is an "easy" man? A simp. Coming from the shortening of the term "Simpleton," a low IQ individual, simp culture has always existed in some form, but exploded in visibility during the E-girl internet age. A man who is quick to part with his money with the hope of getting a girl's attention will work, at first. You shower a girl with tangible signs of material wealth and access to resources, and she will be more likely to be interested in you in the same way she may get your attention with a revealing dress. However, both scenarios will end up the same way in the long run. In the same way that you will not be able to trust her to be faithful, she will never be able to respect you as an actual provider. After all, money is easy come, easy go. How can she be sure it will last? Does she know anything else about you besides your money? What is there to respect?

Now, do not get it confused. Some things that are called "simping," are absolutely not. Being nice to a girl? Not simping. Buying her dinner on a date? Not simping. Flowers as a gift? Not simping. Good rule of thumb, anything a guy would have done for a girl in a 1950s Disney movie is probably not simping. Girls want to know that you are kind, are able to be a provider, and are thinking about them in a romantic way. However, do not focus on the money and do not be quick to part with it for just anything. There is a give and take in any early relationship. Giving her access to all of your resources is what husbands do for wives, not what dates do for near-strangers. She will have access to your store of goods eventually if she sticks around and is faithful. Likewise, you will have access to all those matting opportunities as a husband if you stick around that long. Build that trust and respect first, before giving anything away.

J. E. Bassette

Sex as a motivator for self-improvement

There are two semi-popular anthropological theories that propose that all of human civilization was made for two possible reasons: access to alcohol and matting opportunities. There is a clear dividing factor between agricultural people who settled and created farms that turned into cities, and those that stayed nomadic and even became raiders. In most of these cases, it involved the cultivation of alcohol, and the opportunity for young men to find women in a less dangerous profession than big game hunter or marauder. It may sound a little un-romantic, or ignoble to have such motivations, but think about how useful it has been to human progress.

You likely did not care about your hygiene until the thought of repelling women became important to you. Same with being mature, taking responsibility, getting a job, wearing deodorant, caring about your local community, etc. Women and the pursuit of mating opportunities likely drove you, even if subconsciously, to be a better version of yourself. It drove me to lose weight and likely prolonged my life for 20+ more years. It helped me get out of my comfort zone and join the army. It motivated me to get stronger and be more physically capable. It convinced me to travel to another country, learn its language and culture, and to get a job working as a professor. The pursuit of matting opportunities eventually put me on a path to a great woman and creating a great family.

The flip side, of course, is that the ease at which some find mattering opportunities, short-term strategy types, means they are not motivated to accomplish much. Pornography and general titillation in the media and advertisements also means many young men are not motivated to be better versions of themselves. Do not let that happen to you. As ignoble as it sounds on paper, wanting women, and not having them readily available to you, is what will motivate you to create a better civilization around yourself. Sex is a powerful motivator. Make sure it is compelling you to be a better you, not a baser you.

The political divide between the sexes

One thing I have been very happy to avoid, because I got married when I did, was the sharp political divide between men and women in democratic countries the last generation. Now, men and women have always had different priorities and interests when it comes to political matters. For instance, women were more sensitive to issues of physical security, health, and children while men were more attuned to issues of taxation, labor, and national defense. Makes sense, as these were things each sex was more likely going to run into on a daily basis. However, something began to change over the last twenty years, greatly accelerating since 2015: men and women started to care about "everything" and often came to opposite conclusions.

There are some reasons for this, but a major one was the pathologizing of men and male interests in the political sphere. Anything that men liked (to include even just being attracted to women) was immediately decried as "Toxic," "Regressive," or "Harmful." Little girls started to fear men who were just normal little boys interested in boy things, and this drove both parties to move away from each other. Boys stopped caring what their teacher said, because she came off as a misandrist shrew. Girls began to think that everything wrong in the world could be attributed to men, so they did not need them. Politicians on both sides of the aisle took notice and began to use the split to their advantage.

The truth is that anyone who tells you that men do not need women, or that women do not need men are cheats, grifters, and liars. For the entirety that humanity has existed, absolutely every single thing we have created, accomplished, and preserved is solely due to men and women working together. There is literally only one religion in the world where the relationship between men and women is not sacred and central to your life: politics. Do not let bad policy, lazy scientists, and bitter old people keep you two apart.

Date within your values, but try outside your culture

It is important to date a girl that cares about the things you care about. I do not mean in terms of hobbies or interests, but rather in the realm of values. Do you love kids? Marrying a girl who hates them is not going to end happily for either of you. Do you think killing all cows in order to appease the sun god and slow climate change is kind of dumb? Then do not date a girl who tells you that burgers are a form of toxic masculinity. This is mostly for big things, but there could be some deal breakers for you that you need to figure out early into a relationship. For my wife and I, family was very important. I ended up, at different times, housing my younger brothers and my sister. Her sister and our nephew have been living with us for a decade. If either of us did not share this particular value, it never would have worked between us.

That being said, do not confuse "values" and "cultures." While it is true that many values derive from culture, they are not mutually exclusive. For instance, my wife and I having this deep interest in helping out immediate family is something we share despite being from different cultures. Indeed, the subtle cultural differences in how American Christians through Protestantism and Korean Christians through Confucianism think of this family issue has led to both of us understanding our own personal values more deeply. By experiencing different cultures, I could see how things like geography, history, and religion shape the values of a place and put my own values in order. There are plenty of Americans who do not hold my values. There were plenty of Koreans who did not hold my wife's values. Didn't it make sense for us to date each other? Always date within your values, but do not be afraid to date outside of your culture.

Women are the default; men are the exception(s)

There is no female Mozart or Shakespeare. There are great female musicians, millions of them, and Jane Austin is peerless, but none are as freakishly outstanding as the outlier men in our society. Indeed, it is important to remember that, yes there is no female General Patton or Albert Einstein, but virtually all men also fail to reach those heights. Outlier men seem to dominate all areas of commerce, science, military, and economic pursuits. While some see this as proof of a conspiracy to keep all women down, there is another much more statistically sound explanation: there is also no female Jeffery Dommer or Adolf Hitler. Looking at self-made entrepreneurs, it is overwhelmingly male. But so, too, are prison inmates. Men dominate every single sport, but also every single mental disorder except bi-polarism. If you made a chart of personalities, income, disposition, prison sentences, or anything else you wanted to measure, you will find that the normal distribution of women is more clustered at the center than men. Both the very top and the very bottom of any rank will be dominated by males. What is going on?

This phenomenon is called the "male variability hypothesis," and posits that while what is desirable in a mate for men stays fairly consistent (the 1 to 1.6 waist to hip ratio, kind, pretty, etc.), what women look for in a mate may vary based on current circumstances. Do women want a smart mate? Naturally, but what if you are in the middle of an ongoing conflict? Maybe a less intelligent, but strong, husband would be better. Naturally, a kind husband is ideal, but if you need protection from a violent family member, maybe a husband with a more confrontational disposition could be useful. What men like stays the same, but what women want may have changed or fluctuated even during their own lifetime, creating a very diverse gene pool for their sons. Keep this in mind if you have something about yourself you do not like: some woman at some point in your history found that trait very useful to her own survival or that of her children.

J. E. Bassette

Keep honest men honest

Mike Pence is the former Vice President of the United States from 2016 to 2020. What he may be best known for during his time in office was his refusal to meet one-on-one alone with women. His argument was that, as a married man (but also just as a man in general) it would be best to never put yourself or any woman in a position where something untoward could ever happen. While his political opponents tried to frame him as "sexist," the reality is that he was smart. The US Army had been able to greatly reduce the number of sexual assault cases by following, what my Sergeant Major liked to call, a "keep honest men honest" strategy. No woman would be assigned to an all-male unit by herself. Instead, they would always be assigned in pairs. No female drivers or assistants to superior officers without another woman working in the same office. No one-on-one counseling between male and female soldiers. No putting women on a barracks floor without at least one other woman as her battle buddy. Etc., etc., etc.

While there was some pushback, mostly from women with absolutely no military experience who were willing to put other women in possible danger just to make a political point, most soldiers saw it as good life advice. You want to make sure to minimize the possibility of putting either yourself or her in a position where anything untoward could happen. This is very true if you are already in a relationship and find yourself socially out with another woman. Do not put her in a position where gossip could start, and do not give yourself the opportunity to even have temptation be a possibility. Keep yourself honest and it will make keeping others honest just that much easier.

If you wouldn't live with her forever, no sex

I have another army story for you, but to be honest it could have come from any NCO. A lot of junior soldiers, away from home for the first time, with steady income for the first time, and having sex for the first time, meant that a lot of them ended up marrying strippers and prostitutes. It would happen like clockwork: a group of enlisted men are about to go off post for the weekend, I give them a safety briefing not to have sex with a sex worker or they will fall in love with them, they would tell me I am crazy, and then I have to sign the paperwork for their marriage four months later. The divorce papers, about four months after that. And then I have to remind them that they have to pay her alimony. I hope that weekend was worth it. Remember when I talked about how once you start having sex your brain will convince you that you are in love, whether you are or are not, in order to maximize the chances for conception? Well, imagine that happening with a woman who you certainly have no future with.

These soldiers are young, most of them teenagers, with very little real-life experience. I want to say that I cannot blame them, but the reality is that their mom likely already warned them not to sleep around. It is a recipe to end up with someone you do not actually like being around very much. You thought you liked them, in the beginning, because your brain was trying to make sure you procreated before you died. Well, mission accomplished, but now it is with a woman who will just take your money and start it all over with another guy. Again, her brain is telling her that maximizing alimony payments from various dumb young soldiers will increase her survivability. Well, mission accomplished, I guess. Just do not have sex with any woman you would not want to spend the rest of your life with. Because even if you divorce her, those checks every month you will write her name on are going to keep her in your life forever.

Don't live with her until you marry her

Now, you might think of yourself as somewhat clever: you think you found a loophole, right? Just move in together and not get married. Boom! No alimony payments! Putting aside the concept of a "common law marriage (where you become legally married after living together long enough in some states/countries)," this is likely to cause someone heartache. Most couples that cohabitate end up not getting married, so even choosing this option is giving a vote of "no confidence" in the relationship. Knowing this, I hope that you are the kind of man who can be honest with a girl and not string her along in a fake doomed relationship just because it gives you access to her body. I hope that you are a better man than that. Equally important, if any children end up in the equation, cohabitating parents that are unmarried have significantly more disciplinary and development issues with their children then those that are married. Putting your child at a disadvantage just because you wanted to avoid commitment is not only selfish, it sends a very poor message to your kids.

In 2013 I had a decision to make. I was in the middle of my second year of graduate school and living in a very tiny one-person apartment. It was enough for me, but my then girlfriend was living with her sister who had just become engaged. The sisters had always lived together, making their more comfortably sized house more cost effective. But with sister one and two now moving out, my girlfriend could end up alone and paying for that big place by herself. Living together made sense, financially and practically. However, I remembered a cousin who moved in with his girlfriend, against his family's advice, and she turned him into a vegan loser for half a decade. I knew the right thing to do. We would not have enough time or money for a wedding until 2014, but in May 2013, one month before her sister's wedding, my wife and I got married. Making that commitment, and doing the right thing even though it was not easy, started our life together on the right foot.

Women care a lot
about what their friends and family think

Speaking of her sisters, I made a good choice in befriending them before my wife and I got engaged. It was already nerve-racking dating into a family as a foreigner, with no full-time job (at graduate school at the time), and about two socio-economic levels lower than her family. However, before I ever met her folks, her older sister and younger brother already knew me. I even spent a summer together getting to know them. This created what sociologists call "social capital:" it was resources I was earning and could spend socially to help my position. In this case, my standing within her family. While this is helpful to men, it is vital for women. Historically, social capital was far more important than material capital for surviving as a woman. Having grain could keep your family fed, but having access to people who had lots of grain was even more useful for your family.

This is why when most guys ask about your girlfriend, they just want to know how hot she is. That is the only thing guys care about in terms of social approval. Women, on the other hand, need their friends and family to like their boyfriend. They need them to vet their decision and praise them for a good choice or warn them away from a bad choice. This is why getting them to know you and like you is so important to long term stability. It is also why abusive men always isolate their girls from these people, because he does not want to lose all the influence over her to friends and family.

It does not even need to be relatives. I remember getting into a little argument with my wife over something. I do not even remember what the fight was about. However, I had to give a lecture that day and my wife and son tagged along. She was shocked to see over 200 people waiting for my class and then staying afterwards to shake my hand and ask questions. Seeing all of these people praise and validate her choice in a mate made her feel happy. We stopped fighting and had a great conversation on the drive home. Women really need people to like you just as much, or more, than she does.

Chapter 6: Relationships and Being a Better Boyfriend/Husband

"Love is patient, love is kind. It does not envy, it does not boast, it is not proud. It does not dishonor others, it is not self-seeking, it is not easily angered, it keeps no record of wrongs."

-1 Corinthians 13:4-5

"My most brilliant achievement was my ability to persuade my wife to marry me."

-Winston Churchill, British Prime Minster

"A great lover is not one who romances a different woman every night; a great lover is one who romances the same woman for a lifetime."

-Chinese Proverb

Men make more money after marriage

There is a persistent misconception that getting married and having kids would lead to having less money. While it is true that married women, especially mothers, do end up earning less than their unmarried counterparts, the amount extra earned by married men actually replaces that. Two 30-year-old men with the same education level and background, but one is married with children and the other is single, may differ by almost 50% higher annual income or even more depending on the sector. Total life earnings, the married one will more than double, sometimes even triple, the single guy. Why is that? Women tend to make less money after marriage and children simply because they tend to work less hours and, therefore, make less in average income. It makes sense, as many would prioritize extra time with children over additional working hours. In contrast, the man will not only take on extra overtime after having children (on average working 12 hours more per week than married women with children), he will also be more likely to pursue promotions, take on riskier positions for higher pay, and even change careers to something more lucrative.

Do note that this is not me telling you that you should do these things, only that you most likely will want to do them yourself. As a single guy with disposable income, there is not much driving you to work harder once all the video games, pizza, and beer are paid for. Once you get comfortable, what will push you to move past that zone and intentionally make your work life harder just for more money? Women (access to mating opportunities), self-worth (that comes from providing for your family), and a feeling of accomplishment (that you are setting a good example of hard work and diligence for your kids). Do not be afraid of getting married thinking that this will drain your bank account. In reality, you will likely find the motivation to fill it right back up, with interest.

No, half of marriages do not end in divorce

A statistic that I heard a lot growing up was that half of all marriages end up in divorce. Sometimes that was a way to comfort someone whose relationship ended prematurely, while others used it as an excuse to never get married. It always felt off to me, though, as with all the increase in divorced couples and families on TV and in movies, they always made up way less than half of my friends. The numbers always seemed a little sketchy.

Indeed, the number was never 50%. While numbers fluctuate every year, the highest they ever got in the western world (which has significantly higher divorce rate than other places) was closer to 45%. Close to half, but never actually half even at its worst. Most years were likely to be closer to around 38%. What was going on? You have to keep in mind that changes in divorce law and dismantling perception of it was always framed as a feminist issue in these countries. This was due to most divorces being initiated by women (around 70%), so it was seen as "pro-women" to try and make it seem more normal and common than it really was. Also, these numbers included people divorced multiple times, so they wished to make themselves feel more normal by pretending it was "half of everyone" and not "a minority of relationships, and those that do get divorced are likely to do it multiple times which skews the numbers."

The reality is, not only do far less than half of marriages end in divorce, but that number has been slowly dropping every year since it peaked in the 1990's. Do not let these dishonest actors psyche you out of a great relationship because of their bad experience. Find a great girl you can trust and build something together that will last. Even if you come from a family of divorce, you are the perfect place to start again with something stronger and better. Do not let anyone take that from you: especially not yourself.

Make sure her family loves you

I already mentioned that having the approval of her family and friends is very important to your relationship. The social capital generated through these connections will make not only your relationship smoother, but the stability of your family more secure. I have personal experience with this. While I was married in 2013, we could not afford to have the wedding ceremony until early 2014 after I got my Master's degree. It was a stressful time, as money was a little tight even with all of the generous help of our families. We decided to have two small weddings, one in the US and one in Korea, so that friends and family could all come. My wife and I had felt the pressure building, but did not want to talk about it. Eventually, after getting lost driving back to our hotel late at night trying to find cup ramen for her family to eat, I exploded. Not at her, at myself and the situation. However, she still felt like me yelling "around her" seemed like yelling "at her" and she refused to go to our room, instead going to her parents' to vent. Likewise, I felt like I was not in the wrong, and neither was she, so fighting was stupid. I bought a bottle of cinnamon twists flavored vodka and decided to vent with my family.

Something magical happened that night: her family took my side and my family took her side. While both of us expected to vent to our "team" and just get affirmations, they had a different plan in mind. Her family reminded her of how much I had sacrificed to make our relationship work. My family reminded me that I was not the only one stressed and that my wife likely wanted to yell at the situation too, but was being courteous and holding it in until after the problem was solved. Having both of our families in each other's corners that night meant that we did end up staying in our room together. Imagine if her family hated me? Or, mine hated her? Would we still be together? Make sure her family likes you. It's good to have them get your back in a fight.

Infant mortality and the blessing of the modern age

In Korea, most babies have nicknames while in utero. These tend to be cute things, like our son "Dreamy." Even after a proper name is picked, this nickname tends to stick around even into early childhood, but is especially used up until the baby's "100 day" birthday. Why? Historically speaking, most babies did not make it to 100 days. To help spare the mother the heartache, it was best to not give the child a proper name, and get too attached, before you knew they would survive. This was not exclusive to Korea. This was the norm for most humans throughout history. Why do you think cats and dogs have litters of eight or so kittens and puppies at a time? Because most won't make it, and the species had to work hard to continue. But continue, they did.

There are some young people today that say they do not want kids, don't like kids, or think they are somehow being altruistic by not "bringing kids into a world like this." The fact of the matter is, virtually every woman born throughout our thousands of years of civilization would have killed to be able to have a child and just know that it would have a 99% chance of making it. The peace of mind that would have brought. The lack of fear and dread that you couldn't even pick a name too early and risk loving the thing, as they likely would be taken from you too soon.

Be thankful that you live in these times, and do not take them for granted. Both my wife and her mother have heart conditions that complicated their pregnancies. Thankfully, we took precautions and neither them nor the babies were in danger. However, it is only because of modern medicine and the grace of God that this was the case. If we lived 200 years ago, there would be a very real chance both of them could have passed away. Because of how rare the hardships of the past spring up in our modern lives, we take our good luck and fortune for granted. Be thankful and make safe beautiful babies for a safe beautiful future.

No woman wants a baby for a husband

Now, while some women debate the merits and timing of having a baby, there is complete consensus on where they never want to have a baby: as a husband. There is a stereotype in Korea of the son who never has to grow up until going off to the army. As a baby, he is strapped to his mother's back while she tends the rice paddies. As a child, he clings to her skirt and never leaves her side. As a student, she serves his every meal, and every whim, as he sits at his study desk. From cooking to laundry, to paperwork, to phone calls, and even school interviews, the poor boy never has to do anything for himself until finally leaving mom. Now, this is not always the case, with it more likely for only children rather than just for all boys, but there is a nugget of truth here. Because it has happened just often enough to be a stereotype, it has grown into a concern for women.

Imagine, you are a young woman looking for a potential husband, father, and provider, only to discover that he is a man-child who expects you to become his substitute mom. Not only is the "mommy" role not very sexy (at least I hope not), but it makes her think that a relationship with you could be a liability. If you have children together, she does not get a partner who is going to help support them and keep them safe, but rather just a doubling of mom responsibilities. See why this could worry her?

To avoid this, learn to take care of yourself a little. Help your mom cook, clean, do the laundry, and whenever you have to do something new or difficult (like start a part time job, make an uncomfortable phone call, or fill out paperwork), try it yourself and ask for help only with what you cannot figure out. Teaching yourself some self-reliance will go a long way in convincing a young woman that you are interested in finding a wife and not just a new mommy.

Real men keep their promises

Women lie a lot. I do not mean this as a dig at them, or to say men do not lie (they do it all the time), but think about just how often women feel the need to be dishonest in their daily lives. They lie about their friend's outfit, a new haircut, about how much time it took them to get ready, about not feeling hungry when you order fries, whether or not she feels like going out tonight, etc. Remember that women naturally deal with more neuroticism and negative feelings than you do: especially fear. While some of this stems from just being physically smaller, so they lie to avoid angering someone who could beat them up, you may have noticed that this is not the most common lying situation. Not by a long shot. Women fear being ostracized. As scared as they might be of someone bigger than them, they are much much much more afraid of having no friends and no allies to help them out of a bad situation. That is why most of their lying is to keep friends happy and to avoid others judging them. She wants the fries, but is afraid that you will think she is fat. You will not, but her brain tells her to worry and that lying will protect her. Poor thing.

What does that have to do with men and keeping promises? Think about it from her position: "Here is a guy who does not have my size disadvantage and will not have to lie to his friends to keep them on his side. He has no reason to lie, so I need him to be honest with me." Now, that does not mean she does not want you to lie about liking her haircut or new shoes (she still wants those lies), but it means that she will not sympathize with you if you lie in order to break a promise or responsibility that you had between each other. The others? She has to fear them backstabbing her one day (even if they never will). But you? You were supposed to be the only one who never would. The one person that if she asked you a favor, and you said yes, and would fulfill it 100% of the time. Being a promise keeper is about being her rock in a world of waves. Do not break that trust. It's really hard to ever get back.

Men need to be dependable

Now, being a promise keeper is a two-way street: Not only does she need you to be her rock, but you as a man want her to need you as her rock. Let me explain: you know the feeling of being in an online match, and one of your buddies goes "Oh, let him have that weapon. He's always a great shot with it." Or, your soccer team captain says "Make sure to pass it to this guy at mid-field. He's the fastest guy on the team." Or even when a friend asks you for help before the midterms because "I know you are the best in our group at history and I need your help." This feels awesome. The dopamine producers in your brain reward you when people recognize you for a skill, ability, talent, or utility. It makes sense, as 3000 years ago, you would want to take someone on the hunt with you that had at least one thing that made him reliable and dependable. "Let's take him with us on the mammoth hunt: he's the best long-distance runner we got."

In World War 2 during the long years of bombing campaigns in London by the Germans, many young men were injured and ended up in hospitals. After such relentless destruction over such a long time, many suffered not only physical scars, but mental ones as well. They had become nearly comatose and unresponsive, as if stuck in a daze and not wishing to come out of it. That is, until a bomb hit nearby and people cried for help. Many of these men got up from their beds and rushed into danger to save their friends, neighbors, and complete strangers because it was something they could do to feel useful. To feel powerful. To feel capable. To feel dependable. For thousands of years, women selected mates that were dependable and wanted to feel dependable. This is our legacy as men and a deal where both sides get what they want. Real teamwork. That does mean being someone who keeps his promises and rejects passivity, as that is what will make you dependable.

Get a girl that compliments your weakness

Part of being a good team and being capable of good teamwork, is that you should find someone who complements your weaknesses. Many couples seem to make two equally bad choices: you either date someone exactly like you, or someone very different from you for "balance." For the former group, this means doubling down on whatever you are bad at. Are you bad with money? Well, that's now twice as much debt. Bad at planning ahead? Well, now you stumble into every problem unprepared. Love dogs too much? Now your house is a literal kennel. See what I mean? Now, someone who is the opposite of you may sound like a smarter choice then, as you can avoid the double weaknesses. But now you will always be fighting over where to eat, what to do on vacation, how to discipline the kids, etc.

Like with a lot of things in life, you want to be somewhere in the middle. Honestly assess your three or four biggest weaknesses: the things that you simply cannot do well or are byproducts of other positive qualities (For instance, your great, spontaneous, fun-loving personality is the reason why you are bad at planning ahead for the future). Then, figure out your strengths and what you bring to the table in a relationship. What are you offering that can help cover for her weaknesses? Then find a girl who compliments your skill set. I am a feverous planner who cannot drive very well due to joining the army so young. I married a very skilled driver who cannot even plan a weekend picnic. Together, we make a great team.

Compromise goes both ways

This may seem obvious, but compromise can only happen when both of you do it. There is a reason we call a one side compromiser "hen pecked," or a "doormat." Subconsciously, we humans all know that men and women are supposed to be working together and that our differences often make for better decision making. For instance, if you got your way every time, how often would the house go uncleaned, money would be wasted on entertainment, or important weekend work put off due to a sports game? Likewise, if she got her way every time, the kids would be little slaves in the homework mines and every meal would be whole wheat and broccoli. Compromise, a little of you and a little of her, often makes for the smoothest of well-functioning households.

Now, does that mean every issue is always met half way on everything? Heavens no. There likely will be some things that will be 60/40 decisions, or even 95/05. For instance, if the choice is on buying new school pants for the kids, who has the most knowledge and experience on that topic? Is it really 50/50? I doubt that. The goal is to always be open to compromise, and to have the total average be half her and half you, but with the wisdom that most issues will lean towards the more experienced party. Case in point: when we bought the new car my only input was that I wanted a hybrid (as the price difference was very low and virtually zero after tax rebate), an SUV with at least a little more room than the current one as the family was growing, and that was it. She was the "car guy" of the family, so she got to pick out the model, year, color, options, everything else. Conversely, when deciding how to talk to the boys about puberty, well, I got to decide 99% of that. Know your strengths and weaknesses and compromise the rest.

J. E. Bassette

Women need to worry more than men

I have mentioned before that women suffer more from neuroticism, but men suffer more from risk taking behavior. While I have already alluded to the reason before, I think it is time to address the fact that this is by design. Women have negative thoughts, especially worry, significantly more often than men. So much so, that the term for greatly believing a fear that is not actually real or greatly exaggerated, hysteria, was believed to be caused by having a uterus (coming from the Greek word for "womb"). It's actually caused by estrogen and is in the brain, and such unwarranted worry is not exclusive to women, but the association stuck for a reason. Women do, in fact, worry more than men and this includes worrying about things that are not real or actual problems (just look at politics).

Don't think men are off the hook, though, as our risk-taking behavior derived from our testosterone fueled brains may make us attempt daring feats of skill and bravery, but it also makes us stupidly blind to actual and real dangers (just look at how many young men there are in an emergency room at any given time). Women fear more than they should, men fear less than they should. The reality is likely in the middle. But why are we like this at all?

Think back to 4000 years ago: you hear a sound in the middle of the night that may be a tiger, or may just be the wind. The reality is that it could be either, or a thousand other options between them of various danger levels. What is the most efficient course of action that will maximize the safety of your children? Well, one assumes it is always a tiger, and gets the kids out of there, and the other assumes it is just the wind and checks it out. If it turns out to be nothing, the man laughs and calls his wife hysterical. When it turns out to be a tiger? Well, thank God she got the kids out of there. To believe all neurotic thoughts are equally true is as dangerous as thinking none of them are. A good team works together, with him protecting her from jumping at shadows and her protecting him from foolishly getting himself, and the kids, killed.

Men need loyal women

Being faithful in a relationship is very important to both men and women. No matter what some TV show or garbage newspaper article may try to convince you, jealousy over cheating is not some invention of Christian puritans or just western culture. This is universally found across the globe. It hurts to be cheated on, so don't do it to someone else. That being said, there is one reason why disloyalty, despite being awful for both parties, hurts a little more for men. In the case of a disloyal spouse, most women have backup kin networks that can help with immediate emotional, financial, and logistical needs. It is heartbreaking, but help is available. For men? Right now, if my wife cheated on me and took my kid, who would I call? Even my strongest support network outside of them is literally her own sister and son. Who is there to help me? She is literally my best friend and confidant. Who else is there?

I think this is one of the issues keeping men from committing to women. There is the more base self-serving reason (being committed to her means no more mating opportunities with other women), but another great fear is faithfulness. I think the widespread examples of cheating in TV shows, social media drama, and dumb think pieces by unfaithful women have tricked young men into thinking that they are only one bad fight away from her leaving for another guy, taking the money and the kids, and not even giving him the dog. The fact that a majority of laws in every democratic country favors the mother in this situation (even if she is the cheater), and you have a recipe for guys not wanting to say "yes," to marriage. I get it. I really do. But part of being an adult is doing your homework, making a plan, being as thoughtful as possible, and then taking a little leap of faith. Without that final step, you may never get hurt, but you will also never find someone who would be worth that risk in the first place. With all this talk of "cheating," make sure you do not cheat yourself out of a great relationship.

Why women like you giving them your coat

When we talked about gifts last time, namely flowers, the two important takeaways from it were that women like displays of excess wealth/resources and to show that you associate them with things that are beautiful or worthwhile. There is a third category of gift that you will encounter much more often: the loving gesture. Imagine you are out on a date and while you brought your coat because you are not a nincompoop, your date did not. Now, it is not that she did not know that it would be cold later or does not understand how weather works. She did not bring her coat because she wanted her outfit to look perfect. She was willing to take a risk of her personal comfort to show you how pretty she is. A little short sighted? Yes. However, here is your opportunity to reciprocate the acknowledgement: she sacrificed for you, so are you willing to sacrifice for her? Give her your coat.

Remember that young women are looking for signs that you will not only be a good date, but a good future husband, father, and provider. Women test these in various, and sometimes even subconscious, ways. She will see how you react to bad news like an accidentally broken cup or computer monitor. Maybe she will ask you a seemingly stupid question about loving her if she was a worm. Perhaps she starts a fight with a stranger to make sure you would come to her aid (maybe view this one as a red flag). Regardless of the test, she is doing this for her own safety and peace of mind. You are supposed to be her rock, remember? The coat scenario, or walking on the side of the sidewalk closest to the road to prevent a puddle from splashing her, or carrying her up the stairs when her heels blister all have the same subtle goal: is this guy willing to make small sacrifices for me? Remember, she already feels like she can make little sacrifices for you (like those high heels that gave her those blisters). Show her that you both care about her sacrifices and that you can be depended on to make sacrifices of your own.

Men's vs women's work

I think even the mention of a concept like "men's work" or "women's work" will likely get you sideways stares from many people. It is important to keep in mind that voluntary selective breeding, as our species is for the most part, would lead to certain traits and dispositions to be more common than others. As just a random example: a woman who is able to cook (not even well, just at all) and takes a keen interest in making sure family members are fed, is more likely to successfully find a mate, produce offspring, and keep them alive. Same for men who prioritizes using their height, muscle, and throwing advantage to kill something to eat. Does that mean every mother had to be a cook or every father a hunter? No, but just from the process of elimination, many would be. I say this as a guy who likes cooking, has a very hard time killing animals, and is married to a woman much more athletic than I am (although I am much much much taller and muscular, thank you very much). Exceptions will always exist to some degree on a spectrum, but that in no way negates the average or the most likely.

I think some of this umbrage about men's versus women's work is the past sexist belief that men's work was more important, and the current sexist belief that men's work is more important. Let me elaborate: in the past, men would hold themselves as the more important of the pair by showing how they did all of the hard hunting work and women just did the easy gathering jobs. Once women's suffrage came around, some started to pretend that women had always done the men's work (like hunting) and should be recognized as the better sex (or that sex itself does not even exist at all). Both lost sight of something important that even modern hunter/gatherers intimately know: both hunting and gathering are important. Just hunting is not enough food to survive and just gathering will not get enough resources like leather and cured meat to survive the winter/dry season. I think, regardless of who does which in your personal circumstances, it is important to acknowledge that men's work and women's work are both vital. We have always been a team.

A great woman is like a horse
helping you pull your cart

Now, if you did a double take at the title of this section, please let me enlighten you. How much weight can a horse pull? If they are healthy, a carted horse can pull about 6,000 pounds (or about 2722 kilos). That's quite a bit, and could even be higher if they build up their strength and core muscles. What if we add a second horse to the same cart? How much could they pull? Logically, you would add them together for about 12,000, right? Actually, the number is closer to 18,000, or three times their individual load. What is going on here? When working together with another horse, things that could cause them to stumble, slow down, hit a snag, or tire out are all reduced as their teammate shoulders that load. Intuitively, you may have already seen this in action. Think about carrying something not only heavy, but awkward, like a couch. Doing it by yourself is not only hard, but very slow and tires you out easily. In contrast, even having just one buddy makes the whole process easier, faster, and much more manageable.

There will be days when you think that you may not need a girl ever. You got your video games, anime girls, and enough pizza and ramen to hold you over the winter. You can do this all on your own. The reality is, no matter how good you got it, a great girl will help you do three times better. Even the rewards and legacy that come with family and kids aside, just the process of being a better you becomes that much easier when you have help pulling that cart. I cannot count the number of times I had to deal with a problem at work, with my health, or in general and just having my wife there to help me through made a difficult task feel like a breeze. You are capable of a lot if you work hard. No doubt about it. However, you are capable of so much more together than apart.

How women fight vs men

At all times, as a man, you are aware of how much bigger or smaller someone is than yourself. If you are having a conversation and another person appears out of nowhere, your brain immediately tells you if you could try and take them in a fight. Now, your brain is often wrong and males' tendency for risk taking means you overestimate yourself quite often, but it does a good job of at least noticing the outliers very quickly: the very small guy you would easily push around, and the very big guy that you should deescalate with at every opportunity. As a man, your physical size and ability to solve many problems with your body is not just something that you learn from the other men around you, it is something deeply ingrained and selected for by women for thousands of years.

Women, by contrast, are keenly aware that they are almost never the biggest person in the room. Even our nine-year-old son already has a bigger shoe size than my wife. In much the same way men are always vigilant about what threats they can and cannot take out with their fists, women already assume they cannot win by force and must use their heads. A guy has beef with another guy, he beats him up, if he can. A woman has a problem with another woman, and she will pretend to be nice to her, find out her weaknesses and biggest secrets, and use those to spread rumors and turn the rest of the group against her. Men see a problem and want to punch it, but women will try to remove it from the environment completely.

What this means for relationships is that women fight dirty. Your wife will bring up problems from 10 years ago, or try to make you hate the next-door neighbor by telling you that they hate fried chicken, or something ridiculous. In her mind, she has to eliminate a threat and if she is feeling threatened by you, it may cause her to hit below the metaphorical belt. Try to understand why she does this, but also set some ground rules together. After all, you agree never to hit her, right? She can compromise her biggest weapons in order to fight fair.

Men and women need each other

I think, of all the great things given to us by the modern age, there is one very pervasive falsehood that is destroying countless lives every year. Historically, men and women needed each other on a very basic survival level. Remember men's work and women's work? Just one was not enough to make it through the winter. And even if you did, how long of a life would you want to live without the other? Coupling was a matter of survival, but it also gave each other meaning, purpose, and drive to get more out of life. However, this tying of coupling to just material survival in our minds ("you have to find a man or you will starve!") created the false sense that if those material needs were met elsewhere, then coupling would become unnecessary.

Enter the welfare state. No longer will you need a husband, as the government will be one for you. Security? Food? Shelter? Care? Why, we can give you all of it! Oh, you still want a husband for social status and a feeling of pride? Why not just get that job and social position yourself! Be the man you wish you had! Obviously, this messaging appealed to women more than men. It is kind of cruel for men to just "be the women we wish we had." *Shutters* However, even for the woman in this equation, it was a deal that only got them half of what they wanted.

My wife's cousin bought into the messaging quite a bit. Even stopping dating men all together thinking that there was nothing that she wanted or needed a guy for. Men's work? No such thing. She was going to do it all herself. The anxiety attacks had always been there, but greatly increased as she entered her thirties, still single and determined to not need a man. I offered to carry her bag, only for her to shoot back that "Women can carry bags just fine." This was the same night I had to walk her home because her panic attacks made the trip impossible. I feel so sorry that she was lied to about not needing a man, because her lack of father and husband in her life has left a visible mark on her. Sport, you need a girl and a girl needs you. Do not believe anyone who tells you differently.

If possible, be near her family

Growing up in a military family, it was very common to have to move every two years or so. You saw extended family about once a year, or less, but this set up seemed very normal to us at the time. Even after I got out of the service, the idea that I may have to travel far from home for work, and my wife would accompany me far from her family, seemed like a pretty normal situation to have. It was only after I read about nomadic tribes that I realized how unusual this set up is, historically speaking. Most people in a village or tribe configuration would have lived near their family. It makes perfect sense when you think about it, but I just never did. While the women would normally move into the man's house and be closer to his family, her folks were rarely far away. It was nomads who first had to decide how to handle this situation, as it was important to keep bringing in outsiders through marriages to prevent inbreeding.

However, this situation is not ideal for women. Think about how big of a role her mother, sisters, and friends play in the life of the average woman (doubly so during childbirth). Women were not designed to be so far away from their kin networks, and female psychology showed this. Turns out, these women who married into nomadic tribes tended to be more obsessed with finding and maintaining allies, became far more skeptical of new arrivals, and even resorted to killing rival women or children in the cases of polygamous families. Without her support network to keep her grounded, it all came down to the husband to be her mother, sister, and best friend all rolled up into one. Not an easy task. A lot of women are strong and have made due in the past. However, if at all possible, try to live near her family.

Menstrual cycles and women's emotions

I probably do not have to explain what a woman's period is, but know that the sheading of the uterine lining once per month is not a fun experience. It has an important biological function, and not just the one you were taught in school. Introversion and extroversion are two ends of a continuous spectrum of personality dispositions, both referring to how social and outgoing someone is, as well as how mentally draining or recharging these social activities are. Wherever you fit on this spectrum, know that there is no right or wrong personality in this case. The fact that the spectrum is pretty varied, with even the most strict categorization of introvert and extrovert having around a 45/55% split, it is likely that all types are useful at some point or another. However, what if I told you that you are not strictly one type and actually kind of move around the spectrum slightly due to things like health, mood, temperament, and even the weather? It's true! It is even more true for women.

Before the whole uterine lining situation, there is a period of time when a woman is ovulating. The PG version is that this is the period of time when it is possible to conceive a baby. Now, if you were designing a human brain, and you know that this is the only window to procreate, what would you do? Maybe make her a little more social and extroverted during that time? What about right after, when she will either be pregnant or about to experience abdominal pain and discomfort? Maybe have her be a little more withdrawn and introverted? I hope now the mood swings you experience from her make more sense and you can see her situation with a little bit of empathy. She is hormonal for the same reason you get hormonal sometimes. Your brain thinks it is helping. Just try to help her out when you can and be understanding the rest of the time.

Tell her that you love her everyday

Due mostly to my personality, but also to the fact that I was an early promotion to Sergeant and Staff Sergeant, I often hung out with older soldiers. The median age of my friends was easily 15 years my senior. Because of this, it was little wonder why I quickly befriended a much older NCO when I was at Basic Noncommissioned Officers Course. He was old enough that he had children that were enlisting in the Army. He was a decent guy and did not drink much at a time where I did not drink at all, so we would hang out when others went to the bar. I remember him getting a phone call from his wife one time and after a bit of back and forth between the two, he finally said, "OK. Bye," and hung up the call. I was shocked. "Why didn't you tell her that you love her before you hung up the phone?" In my world, husbands always said "I love you" before they hung up. Always. "She was nagging me. I didn't feel like I loved her, so why would I say it?" His answer made some sense to me, but it still felt wrong. I told him to try and say that he loves her anyway. I mean, he once joined the Army in his 30's to make a better life for her, right? That sounds like love.

For the rest of BNOC, he said that he loved her at least once a day. And you know what? He started to feel it more. I do not know if this had any material effect on their relationship. However, I do keep this in mind every morning before I leave for work. I think about it when I call my wife over lunch. I also keep it in mind whenever I come home late at night. Even on days that I do not feel it, I know that I love her because my actions tell me that I do. Why not say it out loud then? Every day, tell the people that you love how much you love them. It costs you nothing but time, and could be the best thing that they hear all day.

Why women cheat versus men

Cheating is bad. I should not have to tell you this. The most common cause of spousal murder, higher than the next three reasons combined, is unfaithfulness. We are hardwired to hate it. For women, it means either losing a provider (which puts you and the kids in jeopardy), or having to split resources with another woman and her family (again, putting you and yours in a bad spot). For men, it means the possibility of using time, money, and resources on a kid that is not yours. While there is honor in being a dad to a kid that needs one, even one that is not yours biologically, there is still a great biological imperative to avoiding that situation. Not even to mention the psychological, emotional, and spiritual toll such a situation takes on each other and especially the children. Cheating is bad. Tracking?

However, men and women often cheat for different reasons. In a survey of couples who experienced infidelity, it was found that men were most worried that their wives had had sex with another man, while women were worried that their husbands were in love with another woman. I think these different concerns show an important distinction in priorities. For men cheating is mostly physical. The same brain that told them to mate as soon as possible before they get killed in a Mongolian raid is the same brain that rationalizes "Oh, you are not dead yet, and there is a pretty girl, so you better do it again just to be safe." While you could imagine the utility of that mentality for a small village beset by marauders 3000 years ago, today it makes you seem like a real jerk. Your brain thinks it is helping, but it is not. Women, in contrast, often cheat for emotional reasons, possibly thinking that their husbands are not invested in the relationship, so are a flight risk. Complicating this is the issue of the aforementioned situation of women being far from their families. If she has no mother, sister, and friend to rely on, she may be putting all of her emotional needs on just you, not getting those needs met (you are only one person after all), and seek it elsewhere. Both cases are not healthy and only hurt all parties involved. Try to head off both possible problems before they arise.

Women need self-less men

We talked before about how expendable men are in terms of how our species organizes itself. If one of you has to die in a war, eating poisoned mushrooms, getting a disease, or just dying off from a heart attack, it would make sense for it to be you and not her as to keep the babies alive. I know such a position as a young man can feel unfair sometimes, but women really need a guy who would be willing to hold off the invaders while she and the children escaped. Even if she has convinced herself this is not true, women's mating choices say otherwise. In every study on what can cause a woman to lose attraction to a man, the one universal item across every culture, age group, religion, and demographic was when a man did not try to help or defend her in a dangerous situation. She needs to know you have her back, and by extension, your family's back.

I once was in a discussion with a young woman who was convinced that a man was not needed in this equation. Surely a government or her friends could provide that safety and willingness to sacrifice? I disagreed. No government has loved any of its people to that degree. No friend has loved another friend quite to that degree. I have had army buddies I would 100% die for, but even then, none that I would die for to quite the same degree. When a man loves a woman, there is a primal spiritual sense of duty that is kind of hard to explain. It is hardwired and was bred into us over generations of survivors. When Hector of Troy left his wife and son to fight to his almost certain doom, he did so hopeful for a peaceful future for his family. His son would likely have the same thought one day towards his own wife and child. Fair? Of course, it is not fair, but it is why any of us are here at all. She needs you to be self-less, because she too will sacrifice for your children and needs to know you will have their backs all the way to the end.

Liars and lazy men are dangerous to women

For as much as women lie to themselves and their friends in order to maintain good relationships, you would think that they would be OK with men being a little dishonest. However, nothing will make a relationship fall apart quicker than a dishonest husband. Well, maybe a lazy husband. Believe it or not, these two things may be more connected than you think. Remember that the biological reason for women to feel negative emotions more often than men is the self-preservation of offspring. Even their "little white lies" about their friends' dress size or hairstyle choices are in service of keeping a social network around her to maximize safety. You should be a key pillar in that safety net, but with a much more hands on position. You see, her friends must like her in order to help her and your children, but you must be willing to even put yourself in danger for them. Maybe even die if it comes to that.

Because of this very serious role you play in her mental image of physical safety, the last thing that she needs is any sign that you may be unreliable. Imagine if you had a security guard that had a habit of lying to you. Would you feel safe with him watching your place at night? If he was a bit lazy and just did not come into work some days, or kept putting off security sweeps because he "didn't feel like it," would you keep him around? Your position as the guard dog of the home means that any indication that you are not up to the task is a reason for her to be afraid for her own safety. It seems like a small thing, but lying to her (especially about money, other women, or physical dangers) sends up mental red flags that are hard to tamp down. Same for not taking initiative and being lazy. Both tell her that you cannot be trusted with the role of guardian of the household. Take your responsibility seriously.

You need kids, but you'll love wife more

Becoming a parent is one of the coolest things in the world. It is hard work, and very tiring at times, but it literally rewires your brain to become a better version of yourself. All of puberty, all the weirdness, awkwardness, and development was leading you to the moment you get to become "dad." It's the best. Looking back at everything I like about myself (going back to school, getting back in shape, becoming a professor, learning to cook more, writing fiction again, etc.) was mostly due to his arrival and my need to take being a parent seriously. For women, the physical change of pregnancy is mostly biological, with the baby's DNA literally making its way into her body and the two helping each other change, grow, and adapt. For fathers, the change is very real, but it is physiological and slower, so it does not feel as immediate. Mom becomes mom literally though the baby. You become dad mentally through interacting with them, thinking about them, preparing for them, planning for them, etc. Both powerful, but fundamentally different experiences.

Why this is important is that your wife will almost certainly love them more than you. How could she not? They literally shared a body and still share DNA. Crazy stuff. You, in contrast, will still likely love your wife more than your kids. I mean, they are awesome, do not get me wrong, but assuming that your wife is still your main confidant, lover, team mate, and drinking buddy (now that the baby is born), it makes sense that you would still feel a greater attachment to her. Please try not to feel jealous or angry of her love of the kids or your wife wanting to prioritize them over you. It makes sense for their survival that mothers would prioritize the kids over the "expendable tiger fighter" of the group. She still loves you, but has to make sure that these kids, your offspring, make it. Most didn't in the past. Just try to empathize with her position.

You will need to schedule sex/romance after you have kids

It sounds very unromantic, but if you do not put down a time and place on your calendar to be romantic, it is just not going to happen. There is an old joke that women marry their husbands hoping they will change and men marry their wives hoping that they will never change. Guess who is most likely to get their way? I think it is in the realm of romance that this is most true. As you both get busy and tired, there is a compromise that gets made in your head: the small defenseless infant, who will literally die if we do not help him, should get some level of priority over having sex. Good call. Very mature of you. However, the second half of that compromise never seems to materialize. You both agree to default to the kids' needs, but never seem to swing back around to each other. This is doubly true if you are living "Asian style" with your kids literally sleeping in the same bed as you. Even the moments of spontaneous opportunism are very unlikely to happen in such a scenario.

Despite having these limitations, my parents managed to have seven kids. What gives? Well, I was deep into my 20's before I figured it out, but my parents had just scheduled it. Every Sunday after church, all of the kids were allowed their weekly soda (we could only afford it once every week back then) and got to pick out a movie to watch as mom and dad took a nap. Or, so we were led to believe. We were bamboozled. Oh, well. Good on them for making a plan and sticking to it for all of those years.

Learn from that experience. It is important to keep romance alive in your marriage, as she will want to feel pretty after the pregnancy and you will want to show her that she is pretty, so do it. Literally. However, both of you will just continue to make excuses unless you pick a time, place, and plan it all out together. It sounds unromantic, but is there anything in the world more romantic than "I have been thinking about you all week?"

Love your wife, as Christ loved the church

I remember getting into a mild argument with a girl when I was in high school. Like many young women, she felt that religions, Christianity in particular, put too much emphasis on the need for women to obey their husbands. Now, putting aside the role of subordination women play in, say, Viking Pagan cultures as war booty, there seemed to be a disconnect between perceived levels of responsibility for husbands and wives. In their minds, men got to be in charge and women had to be servants. A quick glance at how human couples actually operate would show this to be a little simplistic, but even biblically you had a lot of women who were strong and made a difference in their families and communities while still not trying to belittle their husbands. Think about Ruth, Easter, and even Mary herself! Godly women were hardly doormats.

But there is something to their observation that men do seem to get to play the "leading role" in many cultures, to include antiquity. Some of this is due to just how history was written (most records were about kings, wars, and trade: all dangerous and male dominated endeavors), rather than directly trying to ignore the vital role women must play in all societies. Likewise, there is the phenomenon of women tending to couple with men more powerful, dominating, and take charge than themselves, so by their own mating choices they will be naturally "overshadowed." Even Taylor Swift only wants to date movie stars and professional athletes (congrats on the engagement).

Finally, there is the issue of what responsibility men have to their wives. If the biblical command is for women to submit to their husbands, what is the man's role? To die for his wife. To "Love her as Christ Loved the Church," to be precise. In the same way that "submit to your husband," sounds impossible or unfair, "Love them as much as Jesus," seems like a very steep standard. That's by design. We both have impossibly hard goals to aim for and the act of trying will make you a better person today than you were yesterday.

Chapter 7: Being a New Father

"Being a father has been, without a doubt, my greatest source of achievement, pride and inspiration. Fatherhood has taught me about unconditional love, reinforced the importance of giving back, and taught me how to be a better person."

-Navven Jain, Indian Entrepreneur / Businessman

"It is the primary duty of parents to make their children socially desirable. That will provide the child with opportunity, self-regard, and security. It's more important, even, than fostering individual identity."

-Jordan B. Peterson, Canadian Psychologist

"God chooses ordinary men for fatherhood to accomplish his extraordinary plan."

-G.K. Chesterton, British Author / Apologist

Have a kid (slightly) before you are ready

Do not be having children out of wedlock. Do not do that to yourself and those poor kids who deserve loving and married parents. However, once you tie the knot, there is a subsection of humans who are completely convinced that you have to be 100% ready before you start having children. While it is admirable to want to make sure you are physically, mentally, and financially prepared, the truth is that you will never hit that 100% ready mark. There will always be something more you could learn, a little bit more money you could make, or a few more life milestones to achieve before you conceive. You will forever find excuses and put it off until both of you are at an age where real health concerns arise for the baby, mommy, or both. It is not fair to them to put things off so long.

Historically, almost everyone had a kid before they were "ready for it," and were still able to make everything turn out OK. As long as you have the basics covered, you should be doing better than any of them. So, what are the basics? Married. Non-negotiable. Even cohabitating parents are three times more likely to split versus married ones. That kid deserves a two parent household, you understand? Second, at least one of you with a full time job. If she is working while you are finishing school, or both of you are double part timing it as you transition careers, or whatever, that's fine, but there needs to be a steady income. How much is needed is so case by case specific I will just say "Enough that all rent and utilities are paid, three meals are covered, emergency money set aside, plus 15%." I have seen plenty of young couples start there and end up perfectly fine, as long as you are willing to make the right sacrifices. Finally, she has a support network in place to help with the baby. This can be her family, your family, friends, coworkers, whomever. But there needs to be more than just you to help out when things get a little tough. While I have seen just mom and dad alone being each other's support network, remember that for most of human history everyone was dirt poor, but they had family to help with the baby. That network is worth more than money.

You won't feel like a dad on day one

My older brothers often talked about how much their worlds changed when their first daughters were born and that they loved them even more than their own wives. This was my expectation on May 12th, 2016, just days after my third year wedding anniversary. At a small maternity hospital located above a Korean spicy rice cake shop (yes, really) I saw my son for the first time. I expected my whole world view to shift and that I would become like a completely different, and better, human being. But I didn't. I thought he was super cute, but I did not feel too dissimilar from who I was 15 minutes earlier. It would be a few more hours before I would be able to hold him, so hoped that it would click then. It didn't. I thought he was even cuter close up, he had my chin and nose after all, but I still felt like a husband more than a dad. Was I just a bad dad?

No, I was just mis-calibrated. Being a dad is a process, not a singular event. My journey was not only just starting, I had a lot of growing up as a dad to do, but I had already learned and changed a lot even before this due to having great dads in my life. From my father, to my brothers, and many of the better noncommissioned officers from my time in the military. Even before I met my wife, the men in my life were already preparing me for my future role as a father. For your wife, her brain has literally been changing the past nine months to prepare her for this job. Secretly, your life has been doing the same for years. You won't feel like a dad on day one, most likely, but you will eventually and not even remember a time before you did. It is a truly life changing experience, but it takes time and will not be an overnight metamorphosis.

Everyone has an opinion,
and they all have their reasons

You will get a lot of unsolicited advice as a young parent. Your folks will likely tell you things that you never even asked about, but every single person you meet will suddenly become an expert on burping, when to start using a bottle, where they should sleep, when to let them cry, and a million other things. This entire chapter is going to come across like that, and I completely know how it feels to suddenly have the judging eyes of a billion former parents telling you how to do your job. But, like with most things, it comes from a good place.

Having a lot of wars, and a much higher mortality rate with childbirth in the past, meant that not having your parents as direct examples for raising kids was a, sadly, common occurrence. If we were to survive as a species, strangers would also need to take sudden interest in the parenting habits of everyone around them. This was likely to help keep them safe in the long run, because you could then help their kids in the event of something happening to them.

Likewise, humans like to stick with what we know works and justify past choices. This means, whatever they did as a new parent (if their kid lived) is cemented in their mind as the "right choice" and any deviation is a potential risk. Once you realize their strongly held opinions about C-sections, cloth vs disposable diapers, and when to potty train are not actually about you, but are about themselves, you can see the good they are trying to do. It may come across as judgmental or busybody work, but in the end it is just one reproductive success trying to share with a new reproductive success. The circle of life, baby. Take the good and leave the bad, but always appreciate the place where that advice is coming from.

J. E. Bassette

Make a bug-out bag

About two months before the baby is due to arrive, you should prepare everything you need to take to the hospital with you. We call this a "bug-out bag," from the practice of military units having all of their essentials in one place, so that if they had to make an emergency evacuation ("bug out"), they could just sling it across their shoulder and leave. Speed, literally, saves lives in both of these scenarios. You should have two, one main one with everything you need, plus some extras, and an "essentials only" bag that is already stored in the car. This second bag is in the case of a middle of the night water break, or if you are on a trip away from your home when you get the message that the baby is on their way.

Essentials likely include all paperwork for the hospital already filled out, a few changes of cloths for both of you, extra underwear and socks in case those at the hospital are uncomfortable for her, birth plan, lip balm, lotion, a pillow that she already likes and has broken in, phone charger, eye mask, and ear plugs to help her sleep. How many or how much of these things will vary based on your stay, but have at least two days' worth in the car bug out bag, and three more days' worth in the regular bag.

Speaking of which, what should be the extras in the regular bag? Entertainment for both of you is useful. A few books, extra phone chargers, a tablet with movies and shows she likes pre-loaded, etc. Food is also useful, so bring snacks that she likes and are comforting to her, while being something that would be OK to eat after surgery. Finally, something personal that reminds her of home, be it a bear, shirt, blanket, or some tchotchke that makes her feel at ease. Your priorities are to maximize comfort in the same way the hospital is maximizing safety. While her input should be used when packing them, these bags are your responsibility. She will already have enough on her plate as is.

Have the emergency plan memorized

Your wife is doing millions of things to prepare for the new baby: physically, mentally, emotionally, financially, etc., etc., etc. Ideally, you too are doing these things as well, and most of them together. But much in the same way that only she can do the physical portion of this process, only you can do the execution of your emergency plan. You two should make the entire step by step process together, from the route you will take to the hospital (with back up), birthing plan with doctor's contact information (with back up), bugout bag location and check (with back up), contingency plan if the baby arrives far from the planned hospital (with back up), and so forth. However, despite doing all of this together, it will be up to you to effectively execute this plan. Your wife is a very capable lady, but she is kind of busy at the moment. She is trusting you to know the plan forwards and backwards, have the route practiced, and be able to account for all the possible contingencies.

I say all this, sadly, from experience. I was not the "bag man" for our big day. Granted, I was in Seoul at work and my mother-in-law had everything covered. However, when I got the text message telling me that they were en route to the hospital, and another one just a few hours later that was a picture of my newborn son, I realized in that moment that we would have been screwed without my wife's mother. She not only came in clutch for our main plan, but was able to perfectly execute the complete back up plan version of it. She was a real hero that day and I am eternally grateful for her. However, I do feel like I learned the limitations of my planning just a little too late that day. Learn from my experience. Be the bag man she needs that day, and have a backup plan even for the bag man.

J. E. Bassette

Decide what you will do about work during labor

As a continuation of that day of my son's birth story, you noticed that I was at work when he arrived. I was working at a language examination company at the time and only had office hours from 10am to 4pm. When I got the initial message from my mother-in-law about my wife's water breaking, we decided I should finish up my classes and then come down. The logic was that I only had three hours of work left and both of her sisters have deliveries that lasted up to 12 hours, so I could teach, grab a bus, and make it to the hospital at around the halfway mark. Well, he was born only two hours later. My wife is a champ. Our plan, and the backup plan, kind of ran into a brick wall, but everything worked out in the end. Would I do anything differently now? Likely. There was no plan in place for a substitute teacher, a remote lecture, or anything else in case the baby was arriving sooner than expected. I also had not worked out if leaving early would count as a sick day, part of paternity leave, or be docked from my pay. These are all things that should have been long worked out before game day.

When you are around month seven or so (babies can come early, so make a backup plan for that too) sit down with your boss and have these conversations. What if the baby comes at 6am? What about 2pm? What about if the hospital trip is at 7pm after work, so you think you do not have to call off the next day, but the labor ends up taking 16 hours? Have all of these possibilities laid out and come with your thoughts for possible solutions. Bosses do not like problems, but are much more accepting of them if they come alongside some potential solutions. Not every boss will be perfectly accommodating, but most will be and your chances for their kind cooperation will greatly increase if you come to them early enough to make these contingency plans.

223

Decide when it is best to use your paternity leave

This is an issue that will affect people very differently depending on their job, country, position in the company, etc. For most of us, you should have some form of paternity leave, but the decision on how to use it, and when, is important. In my case, I was given three days paid leave and used it all on my wife's first three days in the hospital after our son was born. It seemed logical at the time and, with only a few days available, there was not much flexibility at our disposal. However, I found that I was far less useful at the hospital than I expected. Day one I could be a big help with providing comfort, getting her things she needed, and... not much else. The nurses did all of the hard work, the baby was sequestered away for 18 hours a day, and the wife needed rest more than anything else. On the second and third day, I only really worked as an errand boy and conversation partner when my wife was awake.

So, what would I have done differently? I think being there day one is an absolute must, even if most of the work is being done by someone else. She needs you, emotionally if nothing else, and you would really regret not being there to see the baby. However, for the rest of the hospital stay, you may be less needed then when she has to leave it a few days later. In contrast with day two and three at the hospital, the days she first came back home had a lot more that needed to be done for both mom and the baby. With no nurses to do the heavy lifting, simple things like cooking, cleaning, helping her to and fro, etc., were all ways I could have been a real hero when she needed one. In our case, mother-in-law came in clutch again and did most of this for the first three weeks. If you can arrange this, or maybe a sister or two, this is not a bad plan. Just don't make them do everything. Talk with your wife and figure out when you will be most needed and plan most of your leave time around then.

Maximize your empathy capabilities for 48 hours

The ability to procreate is nothing short of magic. It's crazy how much women are capable of doing and keeping our species going. On top of being a miracle, however, it is best to also think of it as being akin to surgery. If you had a friend going into the hospital for a heart transplant, how much empathy would you be willing to give them? Now, imagine surgery when your body is, literally, the most hormonal it has even been. This is not a pretty set up. She needs you to put up with whatever madness may be going on in her head, because however much you have been her rock in the past, you need to also be her empath now.

Try to put yourself in her position and then add a dash of hormones. Do you think the doctor will care if your wife's legs are unshaven? Do you think he does not know that women have hair on their legs sometimes? It does not matter. Your wife cares. She is already not feeling her best, is a nervous wreck, and is afraid of making a bad impression at a time where there cannot be good impressions. Help her out. Hair, makeup, comfy underwear; none of it will actually matter, but if it does to her at that moment, then it is your duty to help give her those little comforts.

My dad famously got really hungry during the birth of my older brother: the longest labor of all the children by a wide margin. In his hunger-based delirium, dad decided to let my mother know that he was hungry. Big mistake. Empath, remember? His duty was to maximize empathy with her for 48 hours. By not thinking about her and what was going on in her head at the moment led to a very angry outburst and a cautionary story that I get to pass down to you. For two full days starting from when that water breaks, you are her rock, empath, and whatever else she needs you to be. Pack sandwiches for later.

Be her black-market dealer while in recovery

After arriving at the hospital and getting to see my son for the first time, I very quickly realized that I had little to do. Between the nurses, her mother, and both of her sisters rotating in and out of the hospital, all of the hard stuff was already covered. However, there was one thing I could do that her sisters would not: Break the rules. Nutrition is very important during recovery for not only mom's general health, but also for milk production for the baby. Mom needed vitamins, minerals, and lots of fruits, veggies, and protein. Excellent. The nurses were on it. However, spice was not on that list. Because the food has to be palatable for any mother who just gave birth, safe and bland was the order of the day. In a country like Korea, it took real talent to make their food bland. However, there was a perk of being at a rural maternity hospital in Korea: we shared a building with a Deokbokki (Spicy rice cake) shop. I knew what to do.

Now, you should never give her something that would put her or the baby at any risk. Always, smartly, get this information out of a nurse without giving away your intentions. Think of it like a spy mission. Guys love spy missions. Once you know that the thing she wants is in the clear, you need to be the secret black market dealer for the new mother. Her comfort is a priority in this situation and you are uniquely qualified to provide a certain brand of comfort. This may also include sneaking in things for her to do during recovery to help relax. Just keep her neighbors in mind when you do, and maybe share the love when possible.

You can have one cigar

I am not a smoker. Outside of the health risks, there are cheaper vices that do not make running harder or make your clothes and car smell like ash. That being said, I have smoked two cigars in my life: one on my wedding day with my groom's men and one with my brothers-in-law when my son was born. Lord willing, I will get a few more in some time in the future. It has nothing to do with the actual experiences of smoking at all. Rather, it is about reminding myself that dads have existed since the beginning. We have always been here, doing our dad duties, and moving on from boy to man, and bringing more into the world to start all over again. Creating ritual and reverence around the usual is not a bad thing. Think about the first drink on your birthday, the "bug juice" punch at the end of basic training, the blood wings at airborne school, and a thousand other things that are not special or unique to your experience, but rather link you to a long line of other men like you.

It does not have to be literal cigars, it can be anything you wish to mark the festivities with, but you need to do something special to mark your passage into the ordinary. You are joining a long fraternity that dates back to Adam himself. Every man, woman, and child alive today had a dad. It is the most ordinary thing in the world. But it is through participating in the ordinary that you can join something extraordinary and, literally, life affirming. There will be plenty of times in life where you will mark special achievements, milestones, and events that are solely your own. However, it is through these shared milestones that you will be connected to all of the great fathers of history and to your own children in turn. Celebrate this passage into the club of extraordinarily ordinary dads.

Use your time in the hospital to plan your next moves

While I spent most of the first day in the hospital talking with family, seeing the baby, and getting a chance to catch up with the wife when she was not resting, it was on the second day that my laptop came in handy. My wife and I had talked a lot leading up to the birth about my need to change careers. I really liked working for the language examination company, as just 30 hours a week while getting a comfortable entry salary was a dream job straight out of college. But that was the problem. If I was single, this would have been perfectly comfortable. As a married man? Still not too bad, but the lack of ability to "rank up" or get higher responsibilities or pay made it only OK. Now as a new father? I needed to find something that gave us room to grow. While she got the rest that she needed a few feet away from me, I found and filled out job applications for more than a dozen different positions. They were in various fields, but they all had one thing in common: I would have slightly less starting pay, but with a much higher long-term income ceiling.

Ideally, you have had the talk about short- and long-term plans long before you are literally in the hospital, but the idea is that you should use this time to be serious about making those needed changes. Actually, put everything down on a piece of paper, with a few caveats and back up plans, and then actually put out those resumes and applications. Just this action alone will make a lot of these plans begin to seem more real and doable, while also showing your wife that you are very serious about your new lives as parents. The timing worked out for us that our son was born in May and summer was the big recruitment time for most of the fields I applied for, but any time can be good for future planning. Make that next important step together with your gaze firmly aimed towards the future.

Do not buy baby clothes

I often joke that I was very lucky to have a son as my first born, as the abundance of cute girls' clothing would have likely made me go bankrupt. Kids clothes are adorable, and in anticipation of having my own little kid to dress soon, I bought maybe a dozen onesies ranging from joke ones about having the best dad, a few video game ones, and some that I just thought would look cute on a newborn. However, out of all the clothes I specifically bought brand new for my son, he wore exactly none of them. You see, friends and family like to buy you gifts to celebrate your big day with you. What is a good gift to get a newborn baby who has nothing, not even clothes on his back? Lots of clothes for said back, of course! It also did not help that our son was boy number four for his generation, so a lot of baby hand-me-downs were readily available. It just made more sense to wear out the hand-me-downs first, try on the gift ones for at least one photo to show the folks who bought them for us, and then he was already too big to fit into any of the clothes I bought him. Those just turned into gifts for the next newborn.

What should you buy instead? I would recommend getting one sentimental gift for your child (I got a teddy bear that records a message of me saying "I love you," which he broke his first month back), and then spend the rest on your wife. See what she still needs after all of the gifts and baby showers and get her something that will make her life easier. I bought her air conditioning after refusing to install one for three years. Maximize her comfort and, in turn, your friends and family will maximize your child's. You will have plenty of opportunities to buy them cute clothes later.

Learn at least five of her favorite dishes

How much cooking will you need to do when you first come back from the hospital? It's hard to say, as women recover at different speeds, you may or may not have a mother or sister to help you, and maybe your wife will want to prioritize other things over cooking. Regardless, you should be capable of stepping into that role as much or as little as needed. However, just your staples of ramen, grilled cheese, and scrambled eggs will not do. Instead, try to learn at least five of your wife's favorite dishes so that you have enough variety to give her options and can cover almost a week's worth of dinners. While her comfort is paramount, so you should make the dishes she likes in the way she wants to eat them, be mindful of the nutritional needs of her and the baby. If the dishes are already healthy, then great! I think for most of us, what makes comfort food comforting is their lack of nutrition. In those cases, make sure to add side dishes and extra additions to help balance it out.

A lot of cultures show love and support through food. Even all of the world's great religions have important anecdotes involving food and eating together with loved ones. How many times did Christ dine with, feed, and perform culinary miracles for his friends and family? Even our own religious practice in memory of Christ revolves around food and remembering his last Pass Over meal. How many times have you already bonded with your wife and felt her love and care for you through her cooking? Even if she is not a great cook, you can feel her effort. Likewise, use this opportunity to return the favor and set a good example for your own children whom you can both eat and cook with down the road. I still try to cook for my wife once a week with my son and nephew. It all starts with sincerely trying to help the people we love the most.

J. E. Bassette

If baby sleeps, then you sleep
(and other questionable advice)

As a new parent you will often be told to "sleep when the baby sleeps." The idea is that you never know when they will go down for a nap, so you need to take advantage and work off some of your sleep debt. Sounds good in theory, but just as often as you hear this advice you will be told the rebuttal: "If I sleep whenever the baby does, when will I get any work done?" This can feel extra unhelpful during the baby's earliest days when they will sleep, like, 18 hours a day. So, who is right here?

It is best to not take the advice at face value and to instead think about the experience that led them to that advice. Some babies sleep through the night, but most do not. Those that do sleep well at night will not want to go down for naps in the afternoon as often. In both cases, your sleep schedule, your house work schedule, or both will be interrupted. In order to survive those first couple of months both of you will need to be flexible. We were very lucky in the fact that our son did routinely sleep at night (from 8pm to about 6am with only one or two feedings between), allowing us to get most of our sleep at night. However, many couples do not have this luxury and after getting only a few hours of sleep still try to go about their day working like normal while the baby naps. Sure, you may get your work done, but without naps yourself, that sleep debt will add up quickly. You need to be able to learn to nap, if you cannot already, and be willing to pick and choose when and how to do your house work opportunistically. Just sticking to your old schedules will not work and will lead to complete burn out. You will need to be flexible. Sleep (or work, or play, or nap, or plan, or whatever) when the baby sleeps.

She will be extra paranoid, so meet her halfway

We have already talked a lot in this book about neuroticism and how it is natural (even important) for women to worry more than their husbands. It helps keep children safe and alerts men to dangers they are ignoring in much the same way men help keep their wives grounded and not going overboard. Well, do you think adding a very tiny, soft, fragile human being to the mix is going to make her more or less neurotic? You will see your wife become a level of paranoid like you have never seen before. She will wake up suddenly in the middle of the night to check on the baby's breathing. She will turn the sleeping infant every few minutes, checking the color of their cheeks as they do so. She will check, recheck, and then check a third time when gauging the baby's temperature. She will put her hand into and out of the bath water a dozen times before calling you over to check once again that it is not too hot or too cold. Every single cough, sneeze, or unexpected spit up will be matched with a phone call to the doctor or trip to their office.

Some of this will drive you up the wall, but try to remember it from her perspective. The paranoid mothers were the ones whose kids were able to survive. We are the living offspring of crazy worried moms. If it worked for her grandmother, and her mother, then it should work for her too. She is only learning from the best. However, you are supposed to be her rock, to help prevent her from going overboard. How are you supposed to help here? You are never going to convince her that these efforts are in vain, nor would you want to. In the one-thousand-to-one odds of this being an actual problem, you would want her to catch it and save the baby's life. Therefore, your best course of action is to divide the mental load and just ask "Everything's OK, right?" whenever she does triple check everything. This will force her to acknowledge, out loud, that things are, in fact, OK and show you care at the same time. Volunteer to do the next check, although she will likely double check anyway. Do not worry, it gets easier with baby number two.

Work out a wake-up rotation

A baby waking up in the middle of the night can be a bit of a pain. They are often very loud and fussy with little regard for your sleep schedule. But before you get too angry at the newborn infant, keep in mind that the baby that wakes up in complete darkness likely thinks it has been abandoned or lost when the family fled a raid or tiger attack. A baby all alone will die 100% of the time. They must have someone to help them. The sudden fear of being alone and the cry for help that accompanies it, likely would have been the only way the child was able to survive in such a situation. That being said, not all cries are the same. Sometimes they wake up because they are hungry. Since you cannot help with that one, it should be fine for mom to get the baby that time. How about when the baby needs changing? What about when they just had a bad dream?

Making your wife get the baby every time is not super fair. She needs rest too and likely had to get them every time they cried while you were at work. However, you do have to get up and go to work and cannot feed them, so it does not make sense for you to get up every time. What you two need is a system for deciding who gets up and when. It does not matter how you come up with it or the exact details, just that before both of you go to bed, each side knows whose responsibility it is to get up when the baby starts crying for help. Perhaps it is based on feeding time, with mom getting up for those cries and you covering any that happen between them. Any plan is fine as long as both of you agree to it. Also, be flexible based on something like one of you getting sick, having something going on the next day, or the child's personality (my son did not like men to hold him, not even me, until he was a little older). Make a plan together and be a team.

Maybe have the baby within arms' reach

In Asia, virtually every baby sleeps with mom. While in the west it is common for the newborn to be swaddled and placed in a little baby bed or crib, this is almost unheard of over here. This likely stems from the rash of Sudden Infant Death Syndrome that hit the US and Canada years back. It's hard to say what caused it (hence the "sudden" in its name), but this was a way of clearing the name of parents who were accused of smothering or purposely killing their baby. The idea was that sleeping with your newborn is dangerous because you may accidentally roll over on them, drop them from the bed, cover their nose and mouth with your blanket, etc. By having the child in their own separate bed, this should reduce those incidents. It likely had more to do with parental substance abuse, but the awareness campaigns around the issue still sticks in many new parents' minds.

The issue is, I have no idea if this is true. Again, almost all parents sleep with their newborns in Asia and kids are being born and not dying all the time. I literally have no clue about the probability of any of this and research on it seems contradictory based on who's doing the research. From personal experience, I am going to give you two reasons I like the Asian system and then a compromise that I think will work for most families. First, sleeping with the baby is nice because when mom wakes up suddenly and has a paranoia fit and immediately checks the baby's breathing or temperature, she does not have to get up, making it much more likely she can get back to sleep. Second, when the baby needs to feed, mom can just roll halfway over and feed, which also helps with getting her more rest in the long run.

I think a good compromise is to have a little crib or baby bed directly next to mom within her reach and not in another room. This should cut down on those pesky "I cannot see mommy" cries, help with mom's late-night checks, and make feeding easier. Make sure the barriers on the bed or crib are both breathable for safety and transparent enough to see mom for maximum effectiveness.

What to do about your baby weight

While you may think that the issue of weight gain during pregnancy will be mostly an issue for your wife, you will be surprised how much you put on during those last five months or so. She's eating, so you are eating with her. She is less active, so you are spending more stationary time with her. She is stressed, so you are too, etc., etc., etc. I put on most of my extra pounds post army just from eating too much and not running on my bad knee. However, I reached a peak around the time my son was born. My mother-in-law reminded me that I needed to live as long as possible to help take care of my new family and even grandchildren one day. She encouraged me to lose weight and take my health more seriously. I talked about this in one of my Ph.D. classes at the time and a colleague from Germany said how rude it was for my mother-in-law to "fat shame" and that I should love my body as it was. The reality was that my mother-in-law cared about me and my future. My colleague just wanted to sound "kind" even if it killed me. After all, my death wouldn't affect her in any way. I knew I needed to get in shape.

For both myself and my wife it was about cutting out extra calories (especially from drinks) and exercising for an hour a day. That's it. With just consistent small progress, more calories going out than in, we eventually got back to our wedding weights. Part of this process is psychological, so replacing one habit with another is useful. Drink a lot of sugary energy drinks? Substitute black coffee. Too much soda? Diet soft drinks or ice tea could help. Always snacking? Make it something with virtually no calories and a lot of vitamins like fruits and vegetables. The fact that they don't taste as good will actually help you eat less: win-win! Make sure you trust the scale, not your eyes. You lie to yourself in the mirror every day, but the numbers will be frank with you. Finally, praise your wife in her successes to motivate her to keep going. Tell her she looks great and be specific, as your eyes will be honest about her great body long before hers will.

Hey, Sport. It's Me, Your Dad.

Have a family motto/creed

My family did not have something unique to just us when I was growing up. I knew that our name, Bassette, was the French spelling of a common English name that came from old Norse (it is actually where we get the name for the dogs from, as it means "short" or "close to the ground"). I knew our mom was German, but those ancestors came over when the concept of the country of Germany was still very new. We had no specific lineage to call from, but we did not need it. We were American. Our family creed was the National Anthem, our motto was the one written on our currency, and our family pride was in the red, white, and blue of the flag. Given how many times we had to move, including to other countries, this was not a bad set up. However, as my family expanded with my own wife, son, and nephew entering the equation (all of whom were very Korean), I had to expand what our family was to be something a little bigger.

Our family motto is "Even bad days have happy points." It is not very elegant (it does sound more poetic in its original Korean), but it was born from what I wanted my family to represent. I only got to where I am today because of faith and optimism. I am very much a realist most of the time, but only could make decisions and move forward into success because of "looking on the bright side." I did not have this mentality in high school, and I feel that the teenage version of me was the person I most wanted to distance myself from. He never looked on the bright side. Even on good days, he was looking for unhappy points. He was a loser and wanted to keep losing to justify his pessimism. I was not him anymore. I do not want my son or my nephew to be like that guy. Our family is not about that kind of life. In this house, we are always thankful, looking forward, and making that move towards success with faith and optimism. Find what you want your family to be about and make a motto of it. Say it every night. Live it every day.

Be rough and tumble

A lot of time, money, and political will has been spent on trying to pretend that children do not need both a mother and father. Any problem with children who are missing one or the other is always blamed on poverty or some social problem. The fact of the matter is, for most of human history poverty was the super majority and social problems were the every day norm. The kids still turned out OK. Poor folks in a bad situation who have a loving mom and dad will almost always out perform their richer, but more broken, counterparts. Literally every long-term study has shown this. People deny it, because they want to be seen as progressive or empathetic, as though saying that kids need both parents would be belittling the work of single parents. Quite the contrary. All the hard work that they do, and still have issues with their kids, is testament that we are designed to work as teams and someone needs to help them. A teammate, and not the government. The latter always screws it up.

So, what role does a dad play in this dynamic? Mom provides love, nurturing, care, and food. She is obviously important by any metric. What about dad? You as a father are vital in ways that can be summed up in the clinical term for how fathers interact with their children differently from mothers: "Rough and tumble play." Rough, because mom will always be more careful than she needs to be and someone has to let the kids try something a tiny bit dangerous to test themselves. Mom will always cut the sandwich for you. Dad will show you how to do it and then make you try. Mom will keep you on the shallow end of the pool, but dad will lead you out to the deeper end to test your swimming lessons. What mom is doing makes sense, she is keeping the kids alive. But dad is providing kids with boundaries (he is setting up the limits of the test), challenges to improve themselves (supervised individualism), and an example of how to do it and be successful. Mom and dad work together to make their kids the best version of themselves. So, be a little rough and tumble. Your kids need it, and mom cannot do it alone.

Read to them, and around them

If you are not much of a reader, you need to start now. A fascinating series of studies confirmed that children who see mom and dad reading, read with them, and even just grow up around books in general tend to have more success in school and in their immediate jobs afterwards. Just the act of reading alone exercises the brain in ways TV and games cannot. Not that those are bad, my hobby is video games after all, but I still read every single day and do so with my son as well. Some of this is just practical, as humans have brains that are very suited for communication, but have to practice and build up those skills over time. Starting young and doing it with dad not only means getting an early start, but you begin to associate reading with the "big, strong, successful man" who is raising them.

When I was a child, my father would read to us when we went to bed. When he got too busy at work, he recorded himself reading the books so that we could still have him read to us even when he was off at the office until late. Among these books were The Chronicles of Narnia by C. S. Lewis, whose writings would become a cornerstone of my own writing hobby and the intellectual tradition that ultimately led me to my work as a professor. In fact, I became so interested in reading that my dad would complain about 12-year-old me staying inside reading on sunny days instead of playing outside. Dad, you literally are the reason I liked books in the first place.

Regardless, if you are reading this you already have the intellectual grounds to pass these ideas on to your own child as well. When Fredrick Douglass earned enough money to buy himself out of slavery, he spent the next several years of his life teaching himself how to read. It was his love of the practice that created the foundations for his work as an abolitionist, statesman, and icon for not just black Americans, but everyone who sees value in a good self-education. Be that inspiration for your child.

Evenly divvy up bad cop and good cop roles

I think a lot of young parents go into the "good cop, bad cop" conversation assuming that they can just do it based on personality. My older brother, for instance, is a bit of a push over when it comes to his daughters. Fine, mom can just be the bad cop then. However, there are two issues that can arrive from this arrangement. The first is that whoever has to be the bad cop will also become the "fun police" of the family. If mom has to always say "no," and dad gets to always say "yes," there become incentives for the children to only ask and hang out with the "fun" one. That's not fair to that parent nor to the kids who may be missing out on good memories with both mom and dad.

The second problem with this set up is that you and your wife may just care more about some things over others. Maybe you care a lot about your children making commitments and following through with their promises. Well, when a soccer game comes up that your child volunteers for coincides with a trip to the beach, you will want to make them go to the game like they promised. But what if the game conflicts with homework that is due the next morning? Do you care more about promises or school work?

In reality, you and your wife are likely to be "bad cops" on some issues and more "good cops" on others. Use this dynamic to your advantage. My wife is the "school and homework bad cop," and I am the "be respectful to your elders and polite when talking to people bad cop." She cares about spending time outside the house, and I care about self-improvement. She cares about eating healthy food, and I care about not drinking too much sugar. By figuring out what we focus on more as a parent and as an individual, together you can make a battle plan for both good and bad cop responsibilities.

Work your hobbies around their schedules

I think a lot of men worry about losing all of their hobbies whenever the baby is born. It is true that you will have less free time and cannot stick to your original schedules, but that often gets exaggerated into the absurd. If your selfish instinct is to avoid children because they take up your hobby time, then think about how creative "past you" was at carving out time for activities. When your responsibility increased in high school, did you quit all of your hobbies, or did you just adapt to doing them in different ways or at new times? Same with getting your first job or getting married. You likely had to make major adjustments, but that was not the same as losing all time for yourself or your pass times, right?

In my case, my hobbies were reading and video games. Reading became something I could do while I was doing something else. I used audio books to read while I was working out, going to work, or even just on the toilet. I also created opportunities to force my hobby into my schedule, such as starting book clubs with my family and friends from high school. This allowed me to keep doing my hobby in a way that did not feel like I was taking away time from my son or not spending time with my family.

For games, I learned to play earlier in the morning or later at night. I also bought a nice pair of headphones to "silently" play while my son was sleeping on my chest or strapped to me in his baby carrier. As he got older, I started finding games that we could play together and spend more time doing both hobbies and dad time together. I was even able to do this with the audio books by reading them with my nephew while we were working out together. In both of these cases, responsibilities mean changing how you approach your hobbies and free time, not that you will never have them. Love soccer? Coach your kid's team. There are always ways to find time.

Make the rules predictable and consistent

In the Soviet Union, laws were meant to be unpredictable. Communist leaders are universally paranoid, as most are not particularly the brightest in their country so they always fear being out witted. Add in the fact that they back stabbed to get into power, and you have a recipe for someone always in fear of being usurped. How they dealt with it was through fear. Have the rules change all the time. Even language will change meaning based on how the party leader feels that day. This is literally where the concept of "politically correct" comes from, by the way. Keep the population in a constant state of confusion and fear, and they will not be able to overthrow you. Except, many did. A lack of consistency did create uncertainty and fear, but also resentment. Most could see that their leader was full of crap and both logically and intellectually lacking. No amount of propaganda would convince everyone all of the time.

The same is true for your household. Children, when they are very young, will just believe you when you say something because you are bigger and know more things. However, children will quickly catch on when you are arbitrarily changing rules, definitions, or deals. Children need to know that you have a logic and reason for doing the things you do, and if you break that trust, it is very hard to get back. The same is true if you do not enforce the rules you do have. Once they know that the rules are arbitrary and can be circumvented at the drop of a hat, they no longer have a reason to trust you. Make sure you understand what your rules are and the logic behind them before you make them your rules. Make sure the child understands at least the former when younger, but also the latter when they are older. When you do make exceptions, make sure to explain the logic behind it, and let them know under what circumstances these exemptions are allowed to apply. You are not a communist dictator; you are a monarch who needs to raise wise subjects.

Make everything a please, thank you, or sorry

Children are not naturally polite. My youngest nephew is a little snot who throws a fit if mom does not make his food exactly like he wants. Even when she does get it right, he is never one to say "thank you." He is the baby of the family, so mom is a little lite on him. I think the sparred rod is at risk of spoiling the child. Children have absolutely no context for how good they have it. Picky about food? 99% of children throughout history ate what they were given or they died. Mom giving you food three times a day is so taken for granted that they do not even think to say "please," or be grateful for the meal. They are just kids, however. How could they be expected to know that context? Do you wish they were starving in order to build up that perspective first? Heavens, no.

So, what do you do? Build up the polite and thankful habits first, and they will understand the context in due time. Force a "thank you," "please," and "sorry" from them at a very young age, even if they are too young to understand the reasons why. Language for kids can be confusing, so they are guessing most things based solely off of context clues and your initial reactions to things. By reinforcing polite language young, they will already be in the habit of it when they enter regular society through school and church and will begin to receive the positive reactions from others for their politeness. "Oh, so this is what it is for," they will think as people respond politely and graciously in return. This is not the whole story, as politeness is about more than just other's approval, but it will be a good secondary motivator. Finally, once they are older and can see ungrateful and impolite kids, they will glimpse the mirror reality of what they could have been and will appreciate the influence you had on them as children. Your job is to set them up for future success, and polite grateful kids are often quick to find it.

Come to an agreement about disciplining your kids

The question about disciplining children can be a contentious one: how, how much, when, for what, why, etc. I think there tends to be three conflicting factors in your mind. First, you hated being disciplined as a child, so fear that doing the same kind of discipline would drive your children away. Here, think about what was useful and what was unhelpful about your parents' process. Did they discipline too harshly? Were they too quick to do it? Did they not tailor the punishment to the crime, treating small infractions the same as big ones? Figure out what went wrong and fix that, rather than avoid discipline all together.

The second issue is that you and the wife might disagree about physical punishments like spanking. There is a lot of social pressure to tailor your punishments not to the child or their infractions, but to the opinions of other adults. I think there were surely past cases of actual child abuse or parents who used spanking as their default punishment, rather than as a larger deterrent to bigger crimes. However, I know far too many kids who did have spanking parents that turned out great, to include myself. It is best to think of it as another case of moderation being key and making sure that disciplines fit both the nature and scale of their sin.

Finally, there is the fear that mom or dad will be pegged as the "executioner" of the family: The one that always has to be the disciplinarian. I think much like "god cop/bad cop," you and your wife need to see which punishments you are best suited to enforce and work together as a team. This team work is also crucial to avoid things like double jeopardy (if both of you punish them twice for the same infraction, trust will be eroded), and accidently having one parent not follow through with another's sentencing. Work together and be on the same page. Do not spare the rod, but figure out which rods to use when and then do it together as a team.

Never fight in front of the kid

I used to be a yeller when I was in the army. Part of it was being raised by a yeller and the other half was being in a very loud environment where most leaders tended to make their authority known very vocally. I may have gotten a lot better at it post my time in uniform, but at least once or twice I may have raised my voice too loud at my wife. It was very rare for me to actually yell at her, instead just yell at myself or my situation, but that fact did little to comfort her. When our son was born, we decided that all fighting must happen behind closed doors and between the two of us. Outside of the stress and concern it causes children to see their parents fight, there is the very real fear that one party may say something in anger that they do not mean and now it is stuck in their child's mind. Even just in a heated moment, if a son hears his father call his mother "a whore," will he ever forget that? What about if his mother refers to his father as "a worthless bum?" No kid needs to hear that. Do not accidently plant bad seeds like that into their little minds that will affect not only their relationship with you, but how they will act towards their future spouse.

On a related note, do not be making snide criticisms about each other in front of your kids. Incorporating them into passive aggressive quips is even worse. One time I had agreed to do a raid in a video game with my brothers and sister. It was a scheduled thing that my wife already knew about, but she proceeded to say to our son "Sorry, but you cannot play on the PlayStation right now. Your daddy loves games more than he loves you." She would say later that it was just a joke and she was not being passive aggressive, but the bad seed was planted in our son's mind nonetheless. Do not do that. There is never any reason to bad mouth mommy or daddy in front of the kids. Do not set that precedent for your family or your children's future ones.

Don't undervalue making your kid "normal"

Every parent wants their kid to be amazing. Every father sees their son shoot a ball and imagines that they are the next Michael Jordan. You see your daughter draw her first picture, and dollar signs appear in your eyes at the thought that you have a budding artistic genius on your hands. Every parent does it, and it is good to set a high standard for your children and encourage them to do their best. But be careful to not set them up for failure by creating an impossible goal that will make them feel like a failure when they do not achieve it. If you tell them that they will be the next Michael Jordan and then they are "only" a solid athlete who is healthy, physically strong, and mentally disciplined, they will feel like a failure when they are actually doing great. Make sure to be realistic, but still a little optimistic, about your children and their potential.

It is also important to keep in mind that, even with the best parents and years of hard work, most children cannot not end up in the top 10%. Mathematically speaking, most do not make it into the top 49%. Having a child that is at least doing better than average is something not every parent gets to say. In the same way that you would be overjoyed to have raised a 99th percentile Albert Einstein, but equally enthused that you did not raise a 1st percentile Jeffery Dommer. Having a great, hardworking, well adjusted, normal kid is something worth celebrating. As long as they are trying their best and reaching some of their true potential, then it is a life worth holding up as one of the good ones. And make sure to tell them that you are proud of them for reaching that potential, even if it is a little lower than your imagination the first time they caught a Frisbee at six years old.

Find something they love and learn to love it too

My mother could care less about Pokémon. She would have been perfectly happy to never have heard the name "Pikachu," "Jigglypuff," or "Mewtwo." Despite this, she always played along when we would quiz her on evolution chains, what new monsters were going to be added in the next game, or taking us to Wal-Mart to see which new figures were in stock. She even got a Meowth that spoke Japanese because it was an import that had not officially launched in the US yet, but she knew it was one of my favorite characters. It is important to note that we had no idea she thought all of this was kind of stupid. Never did she belittle our interest nor did she try to make us switch hobbies to something she liked more. She just found something that we liked, and she tolerated, and played along.

I am not athletic, nor a sports fan. I cannot even name ten baseball players not on our team. I did not even have a baseball team until my 30's and my nephew started to show interest. He had a group of friends at school who all loved baseball, so he wanted to go to games and have something to share with his friends too. I knew the stadium was hot, expensive, and four hours of my life, but I took him anyway. I helped him pick out a favorite team (the Doosan Bears), and bought him a personalized jersey. I bought a hat for myself and posted pictures of our game together. Years later and I still do not like sports very much. It is still expensive and four hours of my life. However, I have four hats and will always respond with an enthusiastic "Go Bears" with every score update from my nephew. I will actively be the one to arrange buying tickets with his mother and to make sure to go at least once a month. I may not be a sports fan, but I am a huge fan of my nephew. His love and enthusiasm is worth all the hot stadiums, pricy pizza, and four-hour games in the world. Find something your kids love and try to love it too. Make something they love into something that you share.

J. E. Bassette

Are you a warrior or a temple builder

There are a lot poignant and thought provoking episodes from scripture, but there is one that has always stood out to me personally. King David may be the single most important historical character to the pre-Christ biblical canon. You could make the augment for Moses, but I think David's arc from shepherd boy, to war hero, to fugitive, to king, to murderer, to sorrowful father is equal parts inspiring and heartbreaking. He was both the best and worst king Israel ever had, rolled up into one complicated, talented, flawed, human being. He embodied the very concept of Israel: "Struggling with God."

However, it was one of his final episodes that hit me the most as a young man thinking about his future career. David thought that he would be able to build the great temple in Jerusalem. Considering the fact that this would be called "Solomon's Temple," you may be able to guess that David was not able to build it. It would be more accurate to say he was not allowed to build it. David, who wrote the Psalms and was once called the "man after God's own heart," was told he could not be the one to erect God's holy tabernacle. Why? Because he had too much blood on his hands. Both blood that God commanded him to shed to defend Israel, but also the blood of innocents, like Bathsheba's husband. His dirty hands could not build God's holy temple. That responsibility fell to his son, Solomon.

You may be a warrior or a temple builder. It is unlikely you will be both. For your children, you have to think very seriously about the kind of man you are going to be, because your sons may have to take the other path. I chose the warrior path so that my children have the option to be builders. It looks like Seogyun wants to be a warrior too, which is fine. I will help him be the best he can be. For Jay, I want him to know we were warriors so that he could have the opportunity to be a builder, if he is suited for it. As a father, think about what kind of man you are and where that puts your own sons in the future.

Hey, Sport. It's Me, Your Dad.

Chapter 8: Why Did Your Mom Choose Me?

"(Even) In bad days, happy points can be found."

-Bassette family motto

"How can a young man keep his way pure? By guarding it according to Your word."

-Psalm 119:9

"He who finds a wife finds a good thing and attains favor from the Lord."

-Proverbs 18:22 (ESV)

"Everyone thinks forgiveness is a lovely idea until he has something to forgive."

-C.S. Lewis

"Enjoy life with the wife whom you love, all the days of your vain life that he has given you under the sun, because that is your portion in life and in your toil at which you toil under the sun."

-Ecclesiastes 9:9 ESV

Jamin Bassette: I was handsome, by her standards

I have never found myself physically attractive. I took all of my mother's German genes, so I have the face and hair of a WW2 propaganda flyer for the enemy. Not the greatest set of features, especially in Japan in the 1990s when anti-Americanism was high. Nor was it useful back in the states when the rise in "tall dark and handsome" with the influx of Latino features was taking off. My eyes were the only thing I really liked about myself, and even those were a dime a dozen in the US. Heck, four in my family alone. In 2000's Korea, however, they were a standout perk of my looks. As if by sheer coincidence, two more generic features of mine (thin, high nose bridge and double eye lids) were very fashionable to have. I may be a 6/10 on most days (half that when I put on weight), but I wound up in a country where I was at least an 8/10. Never underestimate the rule of "exotic is erotic:" just being different can be a big attraction point because genetic diversity is good for healthy babies.

You may actually care far more about your looks than she will. Try your best to avoid failing to cross sex mind read. Physical appearance is very important to men and most of the things we find attractive correlate with healthy babies. Women, by contrast, find things attractive that we may not, because the survival of the babies after birth is even more important to their concerns. Take for instance scars. Can you think of a really attractive scar on a woman? Maybe a neat or interesting one, but an "attractive scar" may seem like an odd thing to the average male. My wife really likes the giant L-shaped scar her brother has. The reason being that it is from his liver surgery where he donated some to save their father who was dying of liver cancer. The scar tells her that he cares about family. A lot. He's a great father. Do your best with the looks that you got and find a girl who sees you as handsome in your own way. Scars and all.

I talked positively about my family a lot

When my wife and I were dating, my Korean was not very good. Better than her English, but communication was really difficult. Little did I know, this would ultimately work in my favor. Since my vocabulary was very limited, we were forced to talk about the few things I knew the words for in Korean. Most of our conversations revolved around my family, like my dad who played guitar, my sister who played the piano, and my brother who liked singing. Yes, family and music were some of the few topics I knew well enough to have basic dialog about. The knock-on effect was that she had the impression that I really liked my family (I do), that I admire their talents (I do), and I have very positive things to say about people in general (I did not have the vocabulary to talk intelligently about bad things, to be honest). She felt that I was a family focused guy who was positive and spoke well of others and their many talents. This made a great first impression on the young woman.

When you go on a date, remember that what you choose to talk about, and how you talk about it, will clue her into what kind of person you are and the things you value. If you choose to talk about the kinds of people you hate, even if they are the same people she hates, the impression of you will be fairly negative because your thoughts when meeting someone new should be in a happier place than that. Besides, would you want a second date with a girl that just complained about things she dislikes the whole date? If she is like that on date one, what will she be like after dating for a year? Start off on a good foot by talking about things you like, people you admire, and what makes you excited for the future. This will likely make a much better first impression and set the tone for the kinds of conversations you two will likely have in the future.

I was responsible and diligent

Many of the big five personality traits (Conscientiousness, neuroticism, extroversion, openness, and agreeableness) are slightly more common in one sex over the other on average. Conscientiousness, however, is something that men and women both can score fairly strong in and is seen as a universally positive temperament to have. Someone who works hard and takes pride in their tasks being done well is the kind of person you can see yourself making a family and a future with. Helping this impression was the fact that I was already a Staff NCO, and NCO of the year winner, at this point in my career. Whenever we talked about work, I often mentioned soldiers I was helping, many of whom were Korean conscripts, and what I hoped to accomplish with them. Having my real-life responsibility be something that I could demonstrate through my work was a nice bonus. It is one thing to claim to be a mature and dutiful person, but when my livelihood depended on it, the sentiment was much easier to believe.

It does not have to be your job, but find some way of expressing your diligence and willingness to take on responsibility. Maybe through a hobby that you have, a club that you are a part of, or volunteer work that you participate in. All of these are avenues to share not only your interests and passions, but also to demonstrate that you are the kind of man who takes his roles and actions seriously. This aura of dependability is vital to any long-term relationship and can be even more important than something like your current salary. Think about it: a guy who has a lot of money now, but no discipline and diligence will lose it all eventually. Conversely, a guy with only a little money, but a great work ethic and a plan for the future will almost certainly come into money someday, right? Show her that you are that second guy, and you will attract the right kind of girl you can build a future with.

J. E. Bassette

I showed initiative when her father was in the hospital

When my wife and I had our 100-day dating anniversary (it's kind of a big deal in Korea), we went to a medium sized restaurant and exchanged gifts. I gave her a notebook containing all our text messages with notes showing that I used them to study and learn Korean (she still has the notebook). She gave me a navy-blue hoodie which is very faded now, but never thrown out. It was a pretty nice date, but what makes this even all the more memorable (in a bad way) was the late-night message I got afterwards: her father was in the hospital. He had liver cancer and it looked like things were going to get worse before they could find a donor. I did not know where the hospital was, but I knew where her work place was. In my semi-delusional state, I assumed that she would go to work the next morning and, since I had that day off from guard duty, I would surprise her at work with flowers and a card. Needless to say, she did not go to work the next morning and was currently sleeping at the hospital after staying up most of the night with her dad. However, her co-workers took the flowers and my note with the promise of passing them along.

What this event did was a couple of important things. Firstly, it gave an anecdote for her co-workers to cite when saying something positive about me. Having people in her life that thought and spoke positively about me really helped solidify our relationship. Also, it showed that all of my talk about family and its importance was not just talk. My actions indicated that I truly valued them and extended that to her family as well. Finally, it demonstrated that I could take action and be proactive without being asked. I was actively finding solutions to a problem, even if they were not the best solutions: I was still trying. The effort spoke volumes for my character at an important junction in our relationship. Be a thoughtful and proactive person if you want to make a lasting impression.

I kept promises, like meeting her family

My wife and I dated for four years before we were married. I would not recommend waiting as long as we did, but there were special circumstances. The first was that, after dating for a year, I went back to the US. I was applying for Special Operations by switching over from Infantrymen (11B) to Civil Affairs (38B) and had about a year's worth of training to do between airborne school and Advanced Individual Training at the JFK Special Warfare Center at Ft. Bragg. I knew the distance between us was going to be tough, but I had seen hundreds of fellow soldiers do it, even with Korean girls in particular, so I was confident. My wife, not so much. About four months into it, she actually tried breaking things off, worried that there was very little chance of me coming back to Korea for work and she had no real way of moving to the US at the time. I convinced her to give it one more shot and promised to visit her in June to meet her parents and discuss options together.

That June I really did use up two weeks of my leave and came to visit her. I was already injured with the wound that would force me to leave the army, but I knew that these discussions would be secondary to meeting her folks and convincing all of them that I was a half-way decent guy who was trying to make the relationship work. My mission seemed to have been successful, as the issue of breaking up never came up again. This was another example to my wife that my actions matched my words. I was not just someone who said nice things, but someone who spent time, money, and effort to fulfill what those words represented. I was someone who kept my promises and a man who could both wait through the long-distance relationship and, maybe, be worth the wait myself.

J. E. Bassette

Her family already liked me

This directly links to the previous story, but long before her parents knew me, I was already in high standing with the Jung family. I first met her brother on a double date early into our relationship. He was serving out his military conscription, so we had a lot to bond over in terms of mutual interests and work talk. This started things out on the right foot, even if he later admitted that he was slightly disappointed with my appearance. When he heard that his sister was dating an American soldier, he imagined an athletic black man whom he could play sports with. I came up short in all of those imaginary criteria, but he still found me to be a decent guy.

Next was her older sister, who I actually stayed with briefly so that I would not need to pay for a hotel. The sisters had lived together their entire lives, so they held each other's opinions in very high regard. We did not have much in common, she worked in a lab and I in the field (quite literally), but we found common ground in liking the movie The Gladiator and our tastes in Korean food (especially the strawberry and chocolate ice cream "Pig Bars"). She could see that I really did love her sister and was even trying to learn the language and culture in order to better fit into the family.

Finally, I met her middle sister, who was already married when I first met her. While we initially had the least in common and not a lot of opportunities to spend any time together, we ended up having one of the better friendships in the family. She has even lived with us for the past decade. In each case, I was able to make connections with the people important in her life and they were able to put in the good word for me before I even had to impress her parents. Have as many of her people in your corner as possible before you have to make the big impression. There is safety in numbers, as they say.

I had a look-on-the-bright-side kind of heart

On one of the last dates we ever had before I returned to the US during that summer visiting her family, my future wife and I discussed financial options for our potential future. We knew that my injury was serious enough that I was likely to leave the army soon, but we had to deal with the realities of me having no job and being a graduate student for a couple of years. If I wanted a career in Korea as an immigrant, I really needed that degree. But how would we be able to support ourselves? I told her it was not a problem and that I had actually saved up almost 45,000 dollars during my time in the military. She almost laughed as she told me that the down payment for her current apartment with her sisters was over triple that.

Undeterred, I told her that this was just the start and that I could live in a very small apartment for the two years of school in order to save up even more. I eventually saved up almost 80,000 (insane, considering it was part time and mercenary tutoring/writing jobs), but even that was not enough. I told her not to worry, as I finished up my classes a semester early to focus on my dissertation and got a full-time job. We still do not have our own apartment to this day, but the house fund continues to grow larger every year, despite any setbacks that may occur.

What my wife appreciates about me, more so than my pretty blue eyes, my fancy degrees, or the money I slowly fill into our bank account, is that I seldom focus on a setback. Even during the pandemic when our paycheck was cut by more than half, I immediately thought of a plan and began to execute it. Even our family motto reflected my hope to always look on the bright side. Not just with my words, mind you, but also through my actions. When things are not at their best, your hands will say more than your mouth.

J. E. Bassette

Jeff, Your Granddad: List of 10 Qualities and Her Gideon Fleece

In March of 1979, 100 days before graduating from the U.S. Military Academy at West Point, NY, I began to correspond with your grandmother, commiserating about the current challenges in our lives. We continued to "court" at her twin sister's wedding in June, and my future father-in-law took pity on me and invited me to stay at the house for an additional two weeks after the wedding. We took our budding relationship out onto the dock overlooking Tampa Bay in St. Petersburg, FL. Sharing what was on our hearts, our expectations for the future, what we were looking for in a life-partner, our goals in life and family, and about our faith. We talked well into the night, while holding hands. That first evening on the dock lasted until her Mom flicked the lights on and off to get our attention; it was 2am.

I discovered Jan had a list of qualities she wanted in a husband – 10 in fact! First of all, and the real deal breaker, was he had to be Christian. The other nine were evidence of the "fruits of the Spirit" (Galatians 5:22-23). She even had a couple of "bonus points" - handsome and rich. I wasn't rich! Somehow, she found what she was looking for from our letters and our talks on the dock, and that I "possessed" all those qualities. But the confirmation for her was the "Gideon fleece" - the first kiss had to result in fireworks! The second evening began much as the previous - conversation out on the dock of Tampa Bay. We finally exhausted what was on our hearts, still holding hands, and then I leaned in to kiss her. There it was – fireworks or heat lightning (I'm still not sure which) – and we exclaimed to each other, "Did you see that?" That's when she shared her "fleece" with me. I then suggested that the wedding should have been a double wedding. She didn't object; instead urged me to talk to her father about marrying her. As we reflected on how we got together, we realized that God's hand and calling was evident in the process and the Spirit was guiding our every thought, word, and way, making easy the choice to choose each other. So glad she said, "Yes!" It's been a great adventure and a wild ride! I can't imagine journeying this life without her!

Something About a Man in Uniform, An Officer and Gentleman

One of the reasons your grandmother was even on my radar, and I on hers, was the summer of 1976, when my roommate (and future brother-in-law) invited me to his home in St. Pete. I first met your grandmother one afternoon and marveled at how much she looked "exactly" like her beautiful, twin sister. Unfortunately, she was sitting on the knee of her boyfriend! But I still got her attention that Sunday at church. Her dad, a minister, asked us two cadets to bring our dress white uniforms and participate in worship during the July 4th celebration. I certainly made an impression on her: "There's just something about a man in uniform!" Maybe that's when she first started "evaluating" how well I fit her list of 10 qualities for a husband. According to her, I already scored a "bonus point!"

She spoke that phrase every time I "dressed" up in my army blues or dress greens for a military function. I employed the etiquette lessons learned at the Academy whenever I was in uniform, but I needed a lot of practice, especially with women. I am the oldest of six boys and a sister. We weren't especially "genteel" with one another. But your grandmother helped train and reinforce the finer aspects of forming me into a gentleman: opening doors, extending my arm to escort her, adjusting her chair when dining, standing when she entered the room or excused herself to the powder room, and other such gestures to honor the woman who agreed to spend a life-time together with me. I'm a better man for it!

Provider with Potential

Since I was recently commissioned as a Second Lieutenant in the U.S. Army, there was financial stability "guaranteed" for five years, required as my initial obligation for attending West Point. Then there were expected promotions with increased pay, free base housing, medical coverage, and your grandma could have two cats (definitely a must have). Although we had to move every three years as part of Army life, so I did take her out of Florida, it ended up a true blessing for her – she deeply disliked the hot and humid weather.

Another benefit of Army life was it accommodated her desire to school our children at home. Since the 10th grade, she was determined to do so, and with an Elementary Education degree, she was more than qualified, and she had a heart to teach our kids more than just academics. With the constant moving, and 30 days of leave each year, home schooling gave her the flexibility to schedule around these "interruptions."

Family Man

Many of our conversations while courting revolved around family matters: what was it like growing up with five brothers and a sister, what was life like on the farm, how involved were we in church life, how did we celebrate holidays, where did we go on vacations? We realized that we had much in common: mostly good memories of family life, annoying siblings, parents committed to their marriage and children, active faith life and participation in congregational ministries, plenty of chores without an allowance, worked summer jobs for some personal income, vacations mostly visiting and staying with relatives, and a strong desire to have a big family of our own.

We weren't too specific about how many kids - boys or girls, but we enjoyed the family series, "Eight is Enough." That should give you a clue that we were trusting the Lord to fill our quiver, and He would let us know when our family was complete.

Growing Faith

Since your grandma is the daughter of a Presbyterian minister and I grew up Catholic, I knew I had to get well acquainted with the Bible. She is well versed and has strong convictions. She expected me to be the spiritual leader, so I needed to step into that role and grow as a student of the Scriptures. Those eleven months of engagement, prior to our wedding, I began the habit of daily Bible reading and finished the Bible prior to the wedding. This practice was just another aspect of my growing faith journey, which began at the Academy and continued during my first year in the Army.

When I asked her father to court and marry your grandmother, he had some reservations about the compatibility of our faith backgrounds. I assured him we had already discussed those differences and had come to some agreements and were working on resolving others – like where we would attend worship in the military. Anyway, after the "interview", he discerned that we had in fact worked out some issues, had a plan to worship together, and gave his blessing. The only stipulation was to wait a year before getting married. But your grandmother convinced him that May is a wonderful month to be wed. He did recommend that I read Shakespeare's "The Taming of the Shrew." I didn't until much later in life; instead trusting that God would help me work it out!

Family Liked Me
(Nan, Father/Mother, Suzette, Aunt Lin)

Yes, having the family members advocate for me helped confirm with your grandmother that I was, in fact, a good match! Starting with her twin sister who met me at the Academy during my freshman year, her fiancé introduced us – I was his roommate at the time. Don't know how much of an impression, but it must have been favorable. As alluded to above, I met her father and others that following summer and we hit it off. I wasn't in consideration as a potential husband at the time, but first impressions are important. I did help him out as a visual aid for the July 4th special worship service. Yes, the dress whites are "dazzling!" Even her youngest sister – a mere teen – at least thought I was good looking (bonus point)!

During the courtship and engagement periods, I had her dad's approval and blessing. Mother was a hold out (wait and see) until we "tied the knot!" Then I walked on water! Go figure! The rest of her family trusted their sister's good judgment, so there weren't any concerns or "push back" from them. In fact, her favorite aunt concocted a plan to get her niece and I together after her twin's wedding. By trickery (and I was a willing "victim"), she insisted I return the maid-of-honor's (your grandma's) flowers to her home the next day. That set up the father's invitation to spend the next couple of weeks at his home! That's a God-moment! So glad the family was on board with the likes of me!

Trevor Johnson: I was someone she wanted to get to know

My wife and I had a similar feeling the first time we saw each other. We had different footing and backgrounds the day we met. I was the "newcomer" to the area and she had grown up her whole life in Bedford county, Pennsylvania. Moving was nothing new for me as I had moved many times as a kid. So that day I first saw my wife, I was more than used to walking into a room of new people. It was a picnic on a summer day. I barely knew or had just met the hosts of the party. I was walking into their side yard and saw a group of younger people playing volleyball. One team felt a bit weaker and beat up and the other team had a group of guys and one lone woman in the center. She had bright red hair and was barking orders at all of her teammates with more aggression than I had anticipated out of such a beautiful woman. I could tell she was older than me by a few years and her command of her team felt a little intimidating. However, this thought rolled through my head more than once that day... "I want to get to know that girl." I didn't do that right away though; I didn't even speak with her that day.

Interestingly, Cara had almost the same exact thought that day many years ago. She wondered, "Who is that and how do I interact with him?" I would have never thought or assumed she had any interest in me at all. Over time we chatted and interacted together and the entire time I assumed that she was completely out of reach. She was older than me and seemed to get along with other boys really well. I found her attractive and interesting, but I never thought she would have any interest in me. A few years' age difference feels like a lot when you're young, but it becomes meaningless as time passes.

We both trusted her brother's judgment

Cara was a dog groomer in her youth and I clumsily brought my family dog to her to be groomed so I could interact with her some more. I'm fairly certain our dog had never been groomed and was petrified by the whole situation.

Cara has told me how she remembers a specific leather jacket and a certain hat I used to wear. The jacket was probably half beat to death and smelled of the restaurant I worked at. The hat was equally destroyed and unappealing. For her though, she remembered them and liked them because I was wearing them. Sometimes it isn't about having the perfect clothes or look.

After a couple years of friendship, Cara did something incredibly brave; she assigned her oldest brother the task of getting me to ask her out.

Jared is Cara's oldest brother and he invited me to get dinner with him. Between mouthfuls of hamburger, he very clumsily made it clear that if I wanted to date his sister he would be fine with that. One can imagine I was confused and suspicious. Was Jared just being weird? Was he sent by his sister to do this? Was this a prank? I wasted little time regardless of the reason and I very quickly asked Cara out. I couldn't believe that someone I wanted to be with might feel the same. Someone older and out of my league was interested in me. She later told me that she set her sights on me almost from day one and had decided that we would end up together. I was oblivious to her plan until she sent her brother to get the ball rolling. We began dating shortly thereafter.

I was brave when it mattered most

When I asked Cara how she knew she wanted to be with me forever she said "There wasn't one moment or particular thing that made me know you were the one for me. I just knew that I didn't want you to not be in my life and around me every day." She said it was my humor, intelligence, open and honest thoughts, and care and concern for everyone in my life that drew her to me. High praise I suppose. I hope I'm still fooling her.

In the end I had zero intention of making a move on the woman who would be my wife. Really, I was passive and was her friend first and only when presented with the opportunity took the chance of asking her out. I had to fight past the feelings of insecurity and inadequacy. This was a beautiful woman who was smart and intelligent and was already running a small business. I was a busboy and I felt like a busboy. That small brave act I took by asking her out changed my life completely and made my life complete and whole. How did I luck into that little bit of bravery? I'm not sure, but I'm so glad I took the leap. So, be brave. Ask the girl out who you're dreaming of being with. Find a way to be OK if she says no and muster up the courage to try again. It just might be a brave moment that changes your life.

Trevvor Clark: Similarly Different - Two homeschoolers at a large, public, state university

Don't discount the way you look - but it's not everything!

One thing that my wife, Stephanie, noticed right off the bat was how l looked: different enough from the general crowd of fellow incoming freshmen to be notable. At the time, I was competing in multiple athletic pursuits - soccer, track, and tennis were my spring sports - and working a couple physical jobs - property maintenance and unloading shipping trucks - so I appeared tanned and fit, and that communicated my physical capabilities and gave a hint of what I spent my time and effort doing.

Women will seek out a man they think can provide for and protect them, and physical appearance can provide clues to what capabilities a man might possess. You might be very athletic, or more inclined to pursue bookish, quiet activities, but in either case it's well advised to diligently grow your capacity to be physically strong and capable. A man's primary domain rests in work to provide a living for himself and his family, and modern work comes in many forms: physical, mental, technical, certified, skilled, selling, purchasing, managing, etc. Even if your day to day work is not physically arduous, as a man you'll be expected to shoulder the load in other areas at home or in your community. Deliberate practice builds strong character and strong musculature, and that practice and discipline early in life will serve you well later on.

J. E. Bassette

Embrace life and new circumstances with excitement - but act as though you've been there before!

At 18 years old, in a brand new place, surrounded by brand new people, there were numerous pressures on me to take it easy, relax, have fun, and come along with "everyone else." I'm thankful to have been homeschooled by my parents, to have grown up with an unusually capable and independent group of young men (including Dr. Bassette, Mr. Johnson, and Mr. Heinle) as peers and friends, and to have had chances to grow in my own independence through jobs and dual-enrollment in college courses in my last two years of high school.

These formative experiences inoculated me in a way to the allures of "freedom and fun" (from the world's perspective) available to me on the campus of a large, public university, hundreds of miles from home, because it wasn't my first rodeo: I had already kept up with my own study schedule, interviewed for and worked several jobs, balanced academic and athletic efforts on my own, etc. So, as I walked into this brand new place full of brand new people, I was excited for the new challenges the circumstances would bring; the newness didn't go to my head, and I was ready to continue living and growing! Stephanie saw that I was okay being "uncool" and eager to tackle new experiences at college, rather than getting sucked into this or that "cool" group to do their preferred activities, and that stood out to her as an attractive attribute as well.

Speaking of new challenges - do hard things!

Paul writes to the Corinthian church in his second letter to, "Be watchful, stand firm in the faith, act like men, be strong (2 Cor. 16:13)." A mark of manhood is embracing challenge and difficulty. This can be demonstrated through physical training and strength, as touched on previously, but is by no means limited to that realm. This brief, punchy verse from the apostle Paul delivers simple (not easy) truth for men to pursue, especially as it relates to a man's role toward his wife, family, and community.

As a college freshman, there were few demands on me to be watchful, faithful, manly, and strong - and definitely few environmental encouragements for me to desire to act in such a way! However, diligence in memorizing scripture, dedication to meeting with other young men to read and discuss the thoughts and writings of older, wiser men, and practice in working hard at jobs and in sports during middle school and high school all laid a foundation that I could build from and grow into capability for increased challenges. The world doesn't want you to have a foundation in Godly, productive pursuits, because that likely puts you on a path to be a producer rather than a consumer, and what the world wants is more consumers. Diligent practice in doing hard things, and making something of yourself for the benefit of others sets you on a trajectory to be a producer.

See the bright side of life - have joy!

After I recently asked Stephanie why she married me "way back when" and she'd thought a bit, she mentioned my smile and the joy I demonstrated around her and others. Perhaps it was my work experience in a restaurant and coffee shop: places where being purposefully friendly encouraged rapport with customers and made the experience for both parties more pleasant. Maybe it was being a member of different sports teams and the various groups that put me into where I needed to work together toward a common goal of a game, or a race, or a match.

Whatever it was, I did - and continue to - enjoy smiling and noticing or acknowledging other people: customers in my store, cashiers at stores I visit, waiters or baristas at eateries, the older guy in the plumbing section at the hardware store, etc. If a person is interacting with me, I make an effort to make eye contact with them, give them a smile, and if they have a name tag, I try to catch their name and address them by it, even with just a parting, "thank you, Deanna," as I take my bags and receipt from a purchase. Don't underestimate the power of a friendly smile and addressing someone by name - this used to be a much more common aspect of one's daily life, but as more and more tasks and transactions move contactless and digital, those opportunities to engage with a real, live person are becoming more rare. All the more reason to make the most of them!

Finally, a note on similarities and differences - some are crucial, some are unimportant!

When Stephanie and I met, as happens when one meets a new person, conscious and unconscious assessments began to happen: is this person like me? Do I want to expend time and energy getting to know them? What do they want from me? Etc. We quickly struck on many similarities: we were both brought up in Christian homes, raised in church, graduated as homeschoolers, were avid readers, had both enrolled at the same university due to similar scholarships, and ultimately (after graduation, you know) wanted to marry someone and raise a family. However, she was academic through and through, a gifted musician, and raised (almost) as an only child with a fairly isolated home life. I was academic enough, but more athletic than bookish, the oldest of four and raised around many stereotypical "big homeschool families" that made up my and my family's community.

Many of those differences and similarities still remain after years of friendship and marriage, and that's good! But if there had been early differences of faith, family, or future ideals - Christian versus non-Christian, wanting a family versus not wanting kids, seeking marriage versus seeking professional goals, etc. - then a lasting marriage probably would not have been in the mix. Some differences bring variety and interest into a relationship, but other differences are going to be non-starters, so take time to discern between the two!

Seth Heinle: Worlds Apart.

I will attempt to keep this brief, although I am not known for telling long stories short. I met Adina Daniela Constantin ("Dani" as her family called her at the time) in the summer of 2002 when I was fifteen years old (Dani was 16 at the time). We both volunteered at a retreat center for Christian Military families called White Sulphur Springs (WSS) in Manns Choice, Pennsylvania. At that time, I lived less than a mile away, just up the road. Dani lived approximately 5,000 miles away in Bucharest, Romania. Her father was a Chaplin in the Romanian Army who had visited WSS in 2000 for a conference. That summer we worked together for three weeks in support roles for the facility and got to know each other, along with the other members of our group.

Respectful & Obedient toward my Parents:

At one point during that time, my mother came by the facility while I was sitting in a group on the front porch. Dani recounts the interaction as I was very respectful and obedient toward her. Answering questions with "yes, ma'am," "no, ma'am," and politely introducing her to my group. She was impressed by the respect with which I spoke of my parents, and the way I worked to honor them over the years that followed. My parents instilled in me an appreciation for their God-given authority and wisdom, as well as an understanding that I was a representation of their legacy and our family name, and even at 15 I sought to honor them in my interactions with our community.

Seek God's Will:

The next year, in 2003, we once again found ourselves working together on the support staff for WSS. This afforded us more opportunity to get to know one another and build on the friendship we had begun the year before. Dani says that this was the time she truly fell in love with me, for multiple reasons. This was a complicated time in my life, at 16 I was struggling to understand my path in life and was openly discussing my struggles. Dani said; **"You showed an honest desire to do God's will in your life, to know Him, serve Him, and be in His will."**

Hardworking:

Much of the volunteer work that we were doing was very physical. We split wood, cleared trails, mowed lawns, shoveled gravel, repaired roads, carried luggage, and worked on whatever project was on our list to support the facility. Dani recounted that in spite of the work, which many of my counterparts complained about, I simply worked hard and kept a positive attitude. As we continued to get to know one another, Dani would continue to learn about my life of hard work on a farm. A life full of chores, housework, and construction projects. By 16 I had developed an understanding that work was part of our creation, that God put Adam in the Garden to work before the fall of man, and that work was an innate part of our purpose in glorifying God.

"You were non-judgmental, safe, and understanding of what I was going through. You weren't scared of being uncomfortable in my pain. You were there for me, I could count on you in good times and bad."

We parted ways that summer but remained in contact via email. Dani's father was undergoing treatment for leukemia at the time and had been for several years. As a young 18-year-old, dealing with her father's failing health was beyond difficult and many friends did not stick with her in this time of need. Many found it difficult to support her and hear her struggles when they didn't know how to help. Dani's father passed away on June 5th, 2004 and one week later she was back in Pennsylvania at WSS to work for the summer. I could see at that time that my dear friend was hurting, trying to grieve, and struggling to make sense of the loss of her father. I could also see that she was not getting the support she needed anywhere else. I would patiently wait for her almost daily to check in and see how she was doing, to sit with her in sadness, and try to lift her spirits when possible.

Kind & Gentle:

As we continued to get to know one another, Dani noted that I displayed kindness, generosity, and a caring nature to those around me. One specific example was when my youngest sister, probably 4 or 5 years old at this point, fell and I rushed to help her. Dani said I displayed a loving and caring attitude as I helped comfort little Emma in her pain.

Dani and I continued to correspond through email, remaining close friends until March of 2006 when we decided to enter into a romantic relationship. We were married in December of 2007.

About the Authors

<u>Dr. Bassette</u> lives in Seoul, the Republic of Korea, with his wife Mihye, son Jay, sister-in-law Eunhye, and nephew Seogyun. He currently serves as a Korean Government Official and Global Studies Professor. He is the proud dad of one son, and an equally proud uncle of one live-in nephew.

<u>Pr. Bassette</u> lives in Hollsopple, PA, USA, with his wife Jan and son Josiah. He currently serves as a supply pastor for three Lutheran congregations. He is the proud dad of six sons and one daughter.

<u>Trevor Johnson (TJ)</u> is a general manager of a chain of hardware and automotive stores in central PA. His talents include playing music in local venues, painting abstract art, and pop art. He also enjoys gardening and small engine repair, but his true passions are not having to leave his home or go to many annoying social gatherings.

<u>Trevvor Clark</u> is husband to one, father to six (four sons, two daughters), tinkerer on numerous things from lawnmowers to washing machines, reader of books, maker of excellent iron skillet cornbread, and continually seeking to lead and provide for his family with the work set before him.

<u>Seth Heinle</u> lives in Carlisle, PA with his wife (Dani) and son (Luke, 13). He is a former U.S. Marine, currently working in the Cabinet Manufacturing industry as a Continuous Improvement Manager. Seth enjoys woodworking, playing music, building guitars, drawing, and movies. But above all, he enjoys life with his loving family.

Recommended Reading for all Young Men

"The Moral Compass," by Dr. William J. Bennett, Simon and Schuster Publishing, 1996. –A collection of short stories, myths, tales, and legends from around the world with the theme of showing moral guidance and clarity on what makes a good man.

"The 5 Love Languages," by Dr. Gary Chapman, Northfield Publishing, 1992. –A look at how different people express love, and how to both show that to the women in your life, and how to let them know your own emotional needs in a mature way.

"A Conflict of Visions," by Dr. Thomas Sowell, William Morrow & Co. Publishing, 1987. –An honest look at the psychological and philosophical differences between students of western thought, and how to better understand political disagreements.

"Mere Christianity," by C. S. Lewis, Harper Publishing, 1952. –The single best one-volume look at humans as a spiritual creature and how the theology of Christianity plays into that world view.

"Sir Gawain and the Green Knight," Translation by J.R.R. Tolkien, William Morrow Publishing, 1975. –A collection of Middle English Poems that inspired Tolkien as a young man and his translations that were published after his death in the hope of inspiring others.

"Every Man's Battle," by Stephen Arterburn and Fred Stoeker, WaterBrook Publishing, 2000. –A frank, honest, open, and empathetic look at male sexuality and the need to work against your worst impulses in order to be a better husband, father, and man.

"Wild Swans," by Jung Chang, Simon & Schuster Publishing, 1991. –The tragic true story of three generations of Chinese women that looks at the brutal impact of war, Communism, and bad government on regular everyday people in a pro-woman, not anti-man, lens.

Hey, Sport. It's Me, Your Dad.

"12 Rules for Life," by Dr. Jordan B. Peterson, Random House Publishing, 2018. –Along with its sequel, Beyond Order (2021), this book looks at the psychological, metaphysical, and emotional problems hurting the young men who are struggling the most and how to overcome them by being the best version of you, one day at a time.

"The Guns of August," by Barbara W. Tuchman, Presidio Press Publishing, 1962. –A look at the First World War that shows the dangers of certainty, the damages of unaccountability, and the destruction caused by a lack of integrity by those in power and the toll it takes on the very young and very brave men in society.

"Ender's Game," by Orson Scott Card, Tor Books, 1985. A sci-fi representation of the good, and bad, that can come from joining a "gang," from the perspective of a teenaged boy who needed and benefited from the challenge and guidance, but was also mislead to a grave end.

For the Serious Advanced Readers:

"Leviathan," by Thomas Hobbes, 1651. —A brutally honest look at the role of government, power, and violence in the lives of the very flawed humans who create them and what part religion plays in intentional affairs in a realist and non-idealist framework.

"A Critique of Pure Reason." By Immanuel Kant, 1781. A look at the limitations of the human mind and the necessity for humans to be mindful of our hearts and our heads to make sense of the world.

"The Prince," by Niccolo Machiavelli, 1532. An unflinching examination of the costs to be successful in politics, and the moral double standards rulers often live, or die, by.

"Meditations," by Marcus Aurelius, ~170. Originally the diary and personal thoughts of the famous Stoic Roman Emperor, it contains frank and honest advice about what is and isn't within your power to change and how to accept your own limitations while striving for excellence.

"The Analects," by Kong Qiu (Confucius), ~498BC. The oldest of the recommended readings, its insight into the human condition transcends both culture and time to still show man's fallibility and the need to always be self-improving.

Hey, Sport. It's Me, Your Dad.

Works Cited

Chapter Zero:

Everyone has an opinion - Fitzsimons, G. J. & Lehmann, D. R. (2004). *Reactance to Recommendations: When Unsolicited Advice Yields Contrary Responses.* Marketing Science, 23 (1), 82-94

Chapter One:

Men will have more family than friends - Petrova, K., Nevarez, M. D., Waldinger, R. J., & Schulz, M. S. (2024). *Emotional support across adulthood: A 60-year study of men's social networks.* Psychology and Aging, 39(8), 933-945

Schools are designed by women for girls - De Bellis, M. D., Keshavan, M. S., Beers, S. R., Hall, J., Frustaci, K., Masalehdan, A., ... Boring, A. M. (2001). Sex differences in brain maturation during childhood and adolescence. *Cerebral Cortex, 11*(6), 552-557

Be careful of scammers - Čopková, R. (2020). *The dark triad in helping professions – Comparison of teachers and pedagogy students.* Journal Women's Entrepreneurship and Education, 1(1-2), 125-141

Your teachers are not gods - Lott, J., & Kenny, L. W. (2013). *State teacher union strength and student achievement. Economics of Education Review*, 35, 93-103

Be humble, as you know almost nothing - Kruger, J., & Dunning, D. (1999). *Unskilled and unaware of it: How difficulties in recognizing one's own incompetence lead to inflated self-assessments. Journal of Personality and Social Psychology, 77*(6), 1121-1134

Getting angry is easy, but helps no one - Thomassin, K., & Seddon, J. A. (2019). *Implicit attitudes about gender and emotion are associated with mothers' but not fathers' emotion socialization.* Canadian Journal of Behavioural Science / Revue canadienne des sciences du comportement, *51*(4), 254–260

School bullying, sadly, comes from nature - Alguacil, M., Escamilla, P., Aguado, S., Bonet, A., & Pérez, C. (2021). *School bullying occurs mostly among students of the same gender,* UV & Catholic University of Valencia

Sacrificing for the future - Tol, R. S. J. (2020). *The economic impact of climate in the long run* (Working Paper No. WPS-11-2020). Department of Economics, University of Sussex Business School

Work on your body and your mind - Ruiz-Ariza, A., Suárez-Manzano, S., López-Serrano, S., & Martínez-López, E. J. (2021). *Physical activity as means of cultivating intelligence in a school context.* Revista de Pedagogía, 79(278): 161–177

Every man has a religion, whether he realizes it or not - Li, Y. I., Woodberry, R., Liu, H., & Guo, G. (2020). *Why are women more religious than men? Do risk preferences and genetic risk predispositions explain the gender gap?* Journal for the Scientific Study of Religion, 59(2), 289–310

Chapter Two:

Puberty hits boys later than girls, and in spurts - Brix, N., Ernst, A., Lauridsen, L. L. B., Parner, E., Støvring, H., Olsen, J., & Ramlau-Hansen, C. H. (2019). *Timing of puberty in boys and girls: A population-based study.* Paediatric and Perinatal Epidemiology, 33(1), 70–78

Puberty affecting sleep/ Morning wood and wet dreams/ Puberty affecting how you smell / Puberty affecting your hair, voice, and looks/ Puberty affecting schoolwork - Todnem, S. (2019). *Growing Up Great!: The Ultimate Puberty Book for Boys.* Rockridge Press.

Do girls even like beards? - DatePsychology. (2022, September 12). *Women don't find Gigachad attractive.* DatePsychology. Retrieved from https://datepsychology.com/women-dont-find-gigachad-attractive/

Puberty affecting where you look at girls - Strahler, J., Kruse, O., Wehrum-Osinsky, S., Klucken, T., & Stark, R. (2018). *Neural correlates of gender differences in distractibility by sexual stimuli.* NeuroImage, 176, 499-509

You will never be more self-conscious than right now - Lisak, D., & Miller, P. M. (2002). *Repeat rape and multiple offending among undetected rapists.* Violence & Victims, 17(1), 73-84

Hating your body is understandable, but a little misguided - Van den Akker, A. L., Briley, D. A., Grotzinger, A. D., Tackett, J. L., Tucker-Drob, E. M., & Harden, K. P. (2021). *Adolescent Big Five personality and pubertal development: Pubertal hormone concentrations and self-reported pubertal status.* Developmental Psychology, 57(1), 60–72

You are not cool, but neither is anyone else - Gouda-Vossos, A., Nakagawa, S., Dixson, B. J. W., & Brooks, R. C. (2018). *Mate choice copying in humans: A systematic review and meta-analysis.* Adaptive Human Behavior and Physiology, 4(4), 364-386

Intrusive thoughts - Kralj, A., Payne, A., Holzhauer-Conti, O., Young, J., & Meiser-Stedman, R. (2024). *Intrusive thoughts and memories in adolescents with major depressive disorder or post-traumatic stress disorder.* British Journal of Clinical Psychology, *63*(4), 543-557

The utility of guilt and shame - Miller, A. E. J., MacDougall, J. D., Tarnopolsky, M. A., & Sale, D. G. (1993). *Gender differences in strength and muscle fiber characteristics.* European Journal of Applied Physiology and Occupational Physiology, 66(3), 254–262

No one looks out for the boys - Krys, K., Capaldi, C., van Tilburg, W., Lipp, O. V., Bond, M. H., Vauclair, C.-M., Manickam, L. S. S., Dominguez-Espinosa, A., Torres, T., Lun, V. M.-C., Teyssier, J., Miles, L. K., Hansen, K., Park, J., Wagner, W., Yu, A. A., Xing, C., Wise, R., Sun, C.-R.,... Salem, R. (2018). *Catching up with wonderful women: The women-are-wonderful effect is smaller in more gender egalitarian societies.* International Journal of Psychology, 53(3), 187-194

Short vs long term mating strategy – Holtzman, N. S. (2013). *Above and beyond short-term mating, long-term mating is associated with distinct personality correlates.* Evolutionary Psychology, 11(4)

Butterflies and porn addiction - Kral, K. (2016). *Implications of insect responses to supernormal visual releasing stimuli in intersexual communication and flower-visiting behaviour: A review.* European Journal of Entomology, 113, 429–437

Testosterone dropping as you marry - Gettler, L. T., McDade, T. W., Feranil, A. B., & Kuzawa, C. W. (2011). *Longitudinal evidence that fatherhood decreases testosterone in human males.* Proceedings of the National Academy of Sciences of the United States of America, *108*(39), 16194–16199

Chapter Three:

Learn to do things for yourself - DeCasper, A. J., & Spence, M. J. (1986). *Prenatal maternal speech influences newborns' perception of speech sounds.* Infant Behavior & Development, 9(2), 133–150

Get a college education even if you do not go to university – Reeves, R. V., & Secker, W. (2024, March 29). *Degrees of difference: Male college enrollment and completion.* American Institute for Boys and Men. Retrieved from https://aibm.org/research/male-college-enrollment-and-completion/

Defining yourself by your job - Frazee, K. M. & Shepler, D. K. (2022). *Interpersonal Needs and Suicidality of Discharged Army Veterans.* Journal of Veterans Studies, *8*(3), 13-24

Hey, Sport. It's Me, Your Dad.

Reject passivity, seek responsibility - Pollack, W. S. (2005). *Male Adolescent Rites of Passage: Positive Visions of Multiple Developmental Pathways.* Adolescent Psychiatry, 29(1), 5-12

The price of inaction is always highest - Stevens, M. (Host). (2017, December 6). *The Greater Good* [Television series episode]. In Mind Field (Season 2, Episode 1). YouTube Premium

Delayed gratification - Watts, T. W., Duncan, G. J., & Quan, H. (2018). *Revisiting the Marshmallow Test: A Conceptual Replication Investigating Links Between Early Delay of Gratification and Later Outcomes.* Psychological Science

Happiness is a motivator, not a goal / After winning, we like to start over (the hedonistic treadmill) - Mathias et al. 2024. *Running on the Hedonic Treadmill: A Dynamical Model of Happiness Based on an Approach–Avoidance Framework.* Journal of Happiness Studies, 25, Article 58

Boredom compels you to action - Bench, S. W., & Lench, H. C. (2019). Boredom as a seeking state: Boredom prompts the pursuit of novel (even negative) experiences. *Emotion, 19*(2), 242–254

But you really need a job - Lee, J., Allen, J., Lim, H., & Ryu, W. (2024). *How employment status affects adult men's depression over time: a comparative study of educational attainment.* Journal of Men's Health, 20(5), 112-118

The bar is so low right now for dateable people, you will stand out by being merely competent - Almås, I., Kotsadam, A., Moen, E. R., & Røed, K. (2019). *The Economics of Hypergamy.* IZA Discussion Papers 12185, Institute of Labor Economics

Assume every problem is something you can start to fix - Arsini, Y., Ahman, & Rusmana, N. (2023). *The Role of Locus of Control and Resilience in Student Academic Achievement. International Journal of Learning, Teaching and Educational Research*, 22(5), 49-6

Chapter Four:

Choose your experts wisely - Kisin, K. & Foster, F. (Hosts). (2023, September 20). *Have We Lost Trust in Science?* [Audio podcast episode]. In TRIGGERnometry

People exaggerate for fear or power - Schroder, A. (2023). *Scientific Theories and Their Psychological Corollaries: The Ecological Crisis as a Case Study in the Need for Synthesis.* Seeds of Science

Men want to feel power and respect - Seidler, Z. E., Dawes, A. J., Rice, S. M., Oliffe, J. L., & Dhillon, H. M. (2016). *The role of masculinity in men's*

J. E. Bassette

help-seeking for depression: A systematic review. Clinical Psychology Review, 62,
1-15

Imposter syndrome as a leader - Hunter-Johnson, Y. (2025). *Empowering Veterans in Career Transition: The Development of a Model for Overcoming Imposter Syndrome in the Civilian Workforce.* New Horizons in Adult Education and Human Resource Development, 37(2), 74-85

All young men end up in the army or gangs - Ewing, M. E., Gano-Overway, L., Branta, C., & Seefeldt, V. (2002). *The role of sports in youth development.* New Directions for Youth Development, 2002(95), 45-58

Beware of fad diets, money making scams, or trendy policies - Butler, C., & Vis, B. (2022). *Heuristics and policy responsiveness: A research agenda.* European Political Science, 22(2), 202-227

<u>**Chapter Five:**</u>

The drive to reproduce before death - Andreev, E. M., & Kingkade, W. W. (2015). *Average age at death in infancy and infant mortality level: Reconsidering the Coale-Demeny formulas at current levels of low mortality. Demographic Research, 33*(13), 363-390

Historically, most men were reproductive failures - Favre, M., & Sornette, D. (2012). *Strong gender differences in reproductive success variance, and the times to the most recent common ancestors. Journal of Theoretical Biology, 297,* 42–54

The one man/one woman compromise - Schnitzer, P. G., Ewigman, B. G., Kruse, R. L., & Adam, P. (2005). *Unrelated adults in the home and risk of fatal child maltreatment. Pediatrics, 116*(1)

Women's priorities are different, they must be pickier - Waynforth, D. (2007). *Mate choice in humans: a review of human sexual selection and its relevance for relationship formation. Evolutionary Psychology, 5*(4), 260-284

Women look for potential in their mates - Baize, G., & Tossell, C. (2021). *Women's mate-value and mate selection: The influence of mate value on selectivity in dating and pair bonding.* Personality and Individual Differences, 173

Women need someone they can talk too - Joshi, P. D., Wakslak, C., Huang, L., & Appel, G. (2020). *Gender differences in communicative abstraction and their organisational implications.* Rutgers Business Review, 5(2), 86-98

On a date, talk about your dreams and plans - Sakallı-Uğurlu, N. (2003). *How do romantic relationship satisfaction, gender stereotypes, and gender relate to future time orientation in romantic relationships? Journal of Psychology, 137*(3), 294-303

Different girls like different muscles - Durkee, P. K., Polo, P., Muñoz-Reyes, J. A., Rodríguez-Ruiz, C., Losada-Pérez, M., Fernández-Martínez, A. B., Turiégano, E., Buss, D. M., & Pita, M. (2019). *Men's Bodily Attractiveness: Muscles as Fitness Indicators.* Evolutionary Psychology, 17, 1-10

Why men like T&A: A biological perspective - Singh, D. (1993). *Adaptive significance of female physical attractiveness: Role of waist-to-hip ratio. Journal of Personality and Social Psychology, 65*(2), 293-307

Sex as a motivator for self-improvement - Smith, E. A., & Flinn, M. V. (2002). *Wealth transmission and inequality among hunter-gatherers.* Current Anthropology, 43

Women are the default, men are the exception(s) - Zajitschek, S. R. K., Zajitschek, F., Bonduriansky, R., Brooks, R. C., Cornwell, W., Falster, D. S., Lagisz, M., Mason, J., Senior, A. M., Noble, D. W. A., & Nakagawa, S. (2020). Sexual dimorphism in trait variability and its eco-evolutionary and statistical implications. *eLife, 9,* e63170

Chapter 6:

Men make more money after marriage - Korenman, S., & Neumark, D. (1991). *Does marriage really make men more productive? Journal of Human Resources,* 26(2), 282-307

No, half of marriages do not end in divorce - Peck, D. L. (1993). *The Fifty Percent Divorce Rate: Deconstructing a Myth.* Journal of Social Service Research.

Infant mortality and the blessing of the modern age - Bhatia, A., et al. (2019). *Learning From History About Reducing Infant Mortality.* (Policy & historical review).

Women need to worry more than men - Schmitt, D. P., Realo, A., Voracek, M., & Allik, J. (2008). *Why can't a man be more like a woman? Sex differences in Big Five personality traits across 55 cultures.* Journal of Personality and Social Psychology, 94(1), 168–182

Men need loyal women - Buss, D. M. (2002). Human mate guarding. *Neuroendocrinology Letters, 23* (Suppl. 4), 23-29

Menstrual cycle and women's emotions - Poromaa, I. S., & Gingnell, M. (2014). *Menstrual cycle influence on cognitive function and emotion.* Handbook of Clinical Neurology / Neuroscience review

Why women cheat versus men - Tagler, M. J., & Jeffers, H. M. (2013). Sex differences in attitudes toward partner infidelity. *Evolutionary Psychology, 11*(4), 821-832

Women need self-less men - Barlev, M., Arai, S., Tooby, J., & Cosmides, L. (2025). *Willingness to protect from violence, independent of strength, guides partner choice. Evolution and Human Behavior*, 46(6)

Chapter Seven:

You need kids, but you'll love wife more - Groër, M. W., Manion, M., Szekeres, C., & El-Badri, N. S. (2011). *Fetal microchimerism and women's health: A new paradigm.* Biological Research for Nursing, 13(4), 346-350

Everyone has an opinion, and they all have their reasons - Ju, C., Wu, R., Zhang, B., You, X., & Luo, Y. (2020). *Parenting style, coping efficacy, and risk-taking behavior in Chinese young adults.* Journal of Pacific Rim Psychology

Maybe have the baby within arms' reach - Makarious, L., Teng, A., & Oei, J. L. (2022). *"SIDS is associated with prenatal drug use: A meta-analysis and systematic review of 4,238,685 infants."* Archives of Disease in Childhood: Fetal & Neonatal Edition, 107(6), 617-623

Be rough and tumble - Freeman, E. E., & Robinson, E. L. (2022). *The relationship between father–child rough-and-tumble play and children's working memory.* Children, *9(7), 962*

Read to them, and around them - Moreno, M. A., Furtner, F., & Rivara, F. (2013). *Reading to children.* JAMA Pediatrics, *167(12)*, 1213-1214

www.ingramcontent.com/pod-product-compliance
Lightning Source LLC
Chambersburg PA
CBHW071952040426
42447CB00009B/1310